D1186655

LEEDS BE

Leeds Metropolitan University

17 0098026 6

THE NEW BRITISH LIBRARY

THE NEW BRITISH LIBRARY

Alan Day

Compiler *Walford's Guide to Reference Material*

LIBRARY ASSOCIATION PUBLISHING
LONDON

© Library Association Publishing Ltd 1994

Published by
Library Association Publishing Ltd
7 Ridgmount Street
London WC1E 7AE

Except as otherwise permitted under the Copyright Designs and Patents Act 1988 this publication may only be reproduced, stored or transmitted in any form or by any means, with the prior permission of the publisher, or, in the case of reprographic reproduction, in accordance with the terms of a licence issued by The Copyright Licensing Agency. Enquiries concerning reproduction outside those terms should be sent to Library Association Publishing Ltd, 7 Ridgmount Street, London WC1E 7AE.

First published 1994

British Library Cataloguing in Publication Data

A catalogue entry for this book is available from the British Library

ISBN 1-85604-070-4

LEEDS METROPOLITAN
UNIVERSITY LIBRARY

1700980266

BILS

158847   1.11.94

027.541

2 NOV 1994 £28.00

Typeset in 10/12pt Times from author's disk by Library Association Publishing Ltd
Printed and made in Great Britain by Bookcraft (Bath) Ltd

One of the strangest things about the lengthy saga of the new British Library at St Pancras is not its cost, its delays, its mechanical troubles or its status as an all-purpose Aunt Sally, but the fact that it has *happened* . . .

(Hugh Pearman, 'Brought to book', *Sunday Times*, 7 November 1993, Section 9, p28.)

CONTENTS

Preface   ix
Abbreviations   xi

Part I   General
1   St Pancras   3
2   Policy documents   40
3   Administrative structure   66

Part II   London
4   Humanities and Social Sciences   71
5   Special Collections   114
6   Collections and Preservation   134
7   Public services   143
8   Research and Development Department   145
9   Science Reference and Information Service   160

Part III Boston Spa
10   Document Supply Centre   181
11   National Bibliographic Service   210
12   Acquisitions Processing and Cataloguing and
      Computing and Telecommunications   234

Bibliographical and Historical Envoi   236
Index   243

PREFACE

The author has always considered the succinct advice to quit while you are ahead to be very sound. However, his previous book, *The British Library: a guide to its structure, publications, collections and services* (1988) was well enough received and one or two reviewers recommended it should be updated from time to time. One remarked that the British Library was perpetually on the move and was never still long enough to be pinned down. This the author knew to his cost: no sooner had his book appeared than the Library unleashed a torrent of reports, initiatives, policy documents and the like, with undiminished energy and gusto. The dilemma was whether to prepare a revised and updated edition or to embark upon a completely new although similar book. In the end it seemed preferable, and infinitely more interesting, to plump for the latter. So, shorn of the historical material which legitimately found its way into the earlier book, *The New British Library* attempts to chronicle the Library's fortunes during the difficult and prolonged period leading up to the relocation of its London-based collections at St Pancras, although this event by no means monopolizes its pages. The opportunity is taken to examine all the Library's major events, initiatives, and publications over the past five years.

A book of this nature could never have been completed without the generous assistance of numerous British Library staff who answered the author's no doubt tedious enquiries and requests for information with unfailing courtesy and patience. In addition to the unknown voices at the end of telephones in Bloomsbury, Holborn, and Boston Spa, who promised – and always delivered – essential research material, the author is especially indebted to Dr Bart Smith, Press Officer at 96 Euston Road, for his unstinting encouragement and for providing much useful ephemeral literature; his colleague, Ken Shirreffs, who devoted the best part of an afternoon to conduct the author on a personal tour of the St Pancras building; to Polli Appleyard, Press and Public Relations Officer at Boston Spa, who ransacked files of various newsletters to fill gaps in the author's collection; to Ann Rotherham, of the Medical Information Service, who sent valuable information which cleared some confusion on the author's part; to Andy Gregory, of the National Sound Archive, for elucidating some puzzling features of the National Discography at very short notice; to Stephen Lister, of the Newspaper Library at Colindale, for fielding some unexpected questions at equally short notice; to Valerie Hutchinson, Administrator of The Friends of the British Library, who went to some trouble to furnish the author with a complete file of the *Newsletter*; and to Dave Ferris, Head of BLISS, who often went far beyond the normal bounds of library provision to help the book along.

In Manchester, a former colleague, Shelagh Fisher, Senior Lecturer in the Department of Library and Information Studies at the Manchester Metropolitan University, acted as surrogate snapper-up of British Library ephemera at conferences and exhibitions which the author was unable to attend. A particular debt is owed to Eva Cadwalader and her colleagues in the University Library interlibrary loans department. A personal word of thanks is also owed to the editors of *Library Review* and *Information Management Report* for allowing the use of material first printed in their journals, and also to Library Association Publishing Ltd for once again relaxing their normal citation and capitalization practices.

Alan Day

ABBREVIATIONS

AACR2	*Anglo-American Cataloguing Rules,* 2nd edition
ABRS	Automated Book Request System
AP&C	Acquisitions Processing and Cataloguing
ARTTel	Automated Request Transmission by Telephone
BCM	*British Catalogue of Music*
BIC	Book Industry Communications
BIS	Business Information Service
BLAISE	British Library Automated Information Service
BLC	*British Library General Catalogue of Printed Books/ British Library Catalogue*
BLISS	British Library Information Sciences Service
BLNL	British Library Newspaper Library
BNB	*British National Bibliography*
BNBMARC	British National Bibliography Machine-Readable Catalogue
CABLIS	*Current Awareness Bulletin for Library and Information Staff*
CBM	Centre for Bibliographic Management (University of Bath)
CIP	Cataloguing-in-Publication
CLA	Copyright Licensing Agency
COMPASS	Computer-Aided Subject System
CPM	*Catalogue of Printed Music*
CRIB	*Current Research in Britain*
DDC	Dewey Decimal Classification
DNH	Department of National Heritage
DSC	Document Supply Centre
DTI	Department of Trade and Industry
ESTC	*Eighteenth Century Short-Title Catalogue*

GES	Gift Exchange System
H&SS	Humanities and Social Sciences (Collection)
HSS	Humanities and Social Sciences (catalogue)
HELPIS	Higher Education Learning Programmes Information Service
IFLA	International Federation of Library Associations
ISBN	International Standard Book Number
ISSN	International Standard Serial Number
ISTC	*Incunable Short Title Catalogue*
IT	Information Technology
JANET	Joint Academic Network
KIST	*Keyword Index To Serial Titles*
LIS	Library and Information Science
LISU	Library and Information Statistics Unit
LITC	Library Information Technology Centre
MARC	Machine-Readable Catalogue
MCPS	Mechanical Copyright Protection Society
NACSIS	National Center for Science Information Systems
NAO	National Audit Office
NBS	National Bibliographic Service
NHMF	National Heritage Memorial Fund
NPO	National Preservation Office
NSA	National Sound Archive
OAL	Office of Arts and Libraries
OC	Oriental Collections
OCLC	Ohio College of Librarianship Catalogue
OIOC	Oriental and India Office Collections
OP&SS	Official Publications and Social Sciences (Service)
OPAC	Online Public Access Catalogue
PIN	Patents Information Network
POMPI	*Popular Music Periodicals Index*
PRO	Public Record Office
PSA	Property Services Agency
R&D	Research and Development Department
RAS	Reader Admission System
RPM	Register of Preservation Microforms
RRG	Regular Readers' Group
SIGLE	System for Information on Grey Literature in Europe
SRIS	Science Reference and Information Service
STIS	Science and Technology Information Service
THES	*Times Higher Educational Supplement*

TLS	*Times Literary Supplement*
UKMARC	United Kingdom Machine-Readable Catalogue
UKOLN	United Kingdom Office for Library and Information Networking

PART I
GENERAL

1

ST PANCRAS

NATIONAL AUDIT OFFICE
A rumour to the effect that the first public duty of King William V would
be to officially open the new British Library at St Pancras fizzed round
library staff in the winter of 1991/2 and swiftly gained wide credibility. It
is said that the only doubters were those who expected Britain to be a
republic by then. At the time, of course, prospects of the new library
opening to the public on schedule in the summer of 1993 were dim, and
daily growing dimmer.

As long ago as August 1975, British Library had accepted the site on
the understanding that 'the detailed design of the new building based on
studies already made by the architect would proceed without delay and
that construction would start in 1979 if economic conditions at that time
permit' ('The New Site', *Second Annual Report 1974–75*, pp.5–6). But
the first stage of the construction was not approved by the government
until 1980 and construction work on site did not begin until 1982. Since
then delays, government indecision, opposition from organized and highly
vocal groups of readers wanting to retain the Reading Room at Bloomsbury, and perpetual uncertainties have continually dogged the entire project.

For many years a new building had been considered a *sine qua non*
for the efficient and effective use of the dispersed London-based reference collections. Millions of books had to be outhoused at Woolwich, ten
miles distant from the Bloomsbury reading room, causing intolerable
delays in book delivery to readers. With new stock being accessioned at
a rate of just under two miles of shelving a year a bad situation was
rapidly becoming unbearable. Storage conditions were generally unsatis-
factory, lacking a controlled atmosphere and environment. In the science
reading rooms at Holborn there was a desperate need for the different
subject and patent collections to be united on the same site. The quality

of service was inexorably deteriorating. The St Pancras project was seen by British Library as the panacea for all its ills: readers, staff, and the growing collections were all to be united in a purpose-built, environmentally sound building complex which would serve the Library's purposes for an indefinite period.

The go-ahead for phase 1 of the project was announced by Shirley Williams, Secretary of State for Education, on 7 March 1978; a decision on whether to proceed with phase 2 would be made in 1982. The total cost at 1977 prices would be £164 million. All the national reference collections in the humanities and sciences would be housed under one roof; eight general and a number of specialist reading rooms would banish the cramped conditions prevailing at Holborn and Bloomsbury; public facilities would include exhibition areas, a book shop, and a restaurant; closed-access storage areas would be below ground level, and books would be swiftly delivered to the reading rooms by a mechanized delivery system. When completed the new building would house 3,500 readers and 25 million books. An illustrated feature, 'A library to lead the world' (*Library Association Record*, **80** (4), April 1978:179–83), gave details of the site, the accommodation, and a large-scale street map of the area to show the considerable impact the new library would have on its environs.

Despite determined opposition from the Campaign to Save the Reading Room, a group of scholars and writers concerned to preserve the traditional services in the Round Reading Room at Bloomsbury, work continued on site but quickly ran £25 million over budget. Early signs of parliamentary disquiet surfaced in David Hughes' 'Cash probe into super library', *The Sunday Times*, **8481**, 22 February 1987:4. Significantly, it was the newspaper's political correspondent who reported that Mark Fisher, Labour spokesman on the arts and libraries, appalled by the Library's escalating costs, had referred the matter to the National Audit Office (NAO).

Fears that the St Pancras building would never be completed were expressed a year later in Robert Hewison's 'Library's unfinished chapters', *The Sunday Times*, **8537**, 20 March 1988:A5. Richard Luce, Minister for the Arts, was reported to have decided to call a halt because the project had taken far too long and was swallowing too much public money. 'I had to ask myself if this scheme was going to run and run into the next century and who in this generation was going to benefit.' British Library's Chief Executive told the press that 'as of today it's the end of the scheme and for the foreseeable future'. However, a letter from the

Minister in the next issue confirmed that all was not lost: 'Following a review of the Library's current requirements I have commissioned a feasibility study for the rest of the building so that the key requirements of the library are met at the minimum additional cost. We want the best value for the library user and taxpayer' (*The Sunday Times*, **8538**, 27 March 1988:B10).

The feasibility study's brief was to rationalize the building's main functions, from an existing three-phased plan into a redesigned phase 1, and, at the beginning of November, the government announced a final £90 million (setting a limit of £400 million on the full cost of the building) for a trimmed-down Library to be completed by 1996 – not by 2002 as planned. As if this were not severe enough, the Treasury decided that the extra money should accommodate VAT charges, costing the Library in the region of £10 million. 'As a result the central point, or key objective ... of the whole project stands to be compromised – the wish to bring all the various strands of the British Library's collections together in one place' (John Davison, 'The mysterious case of Luce's shrinking library', *The Sunday Times*, **8570**, 6 November 1988:C8).

British Library's initial reaction to the new scheme was one of guarded welcome. It was delighted that the government was to complete the building on a fast-track basis but disappointed that the Treasury had sliced 10% off its grant. Delight and disappointment soon changed to dismay once the Library had done its sums. To retrieve what it could from the financial morass, it was forced to contemplate the removal of some London-based departments to its Boston Spa site in West Yorkshire. A spokesman told *The Observer*: 'A bombshell hit us when we realised that not everybody could fit into the St Pancras building. Bearing in mind the Government's regional policy, we hope we may get a dispensation and have money spent from selling one of our buildings in London on a new building at Boston Spa' (Catherine Pepinster, 'Building cutback to split British Library', *The Observer*, 26 February 1989:3).

When *Gateway to Knowledge*, the British Library's second strategic plan, was published, Robert Hewison reported that:

> despite the £400 million-plus that will have been invested by the time the second and final stage of the building is over in 1996 ... the government has been steadily withdrawing its financial support for its daily operations. The government's grant-in-aid, currently £53 million, is not enough to keep up with the inflationary costs of materials, nor the salary increases the government negotiates ... Even without the costs of preparing to move into the most modern, automated and

computerised building in the world, the British Library would be suffering attrition from inflation. But it needs at least an extra £30 million to install computer hardware, and cover the costs of moving the books on to the shelves.

He described the St Pancras building as: 'the bibliographic equivalent of the M25. Its vast underground bookstores will be full to overflowing from the start, and there will still be a need to keep some books elsewhere – the very problem the new building was supposed to help overcome' ('A bad case of overbooking', *The Sunday Times*, **8592**, 16 April 1989:C7). Hewison's M25 analogy was later used by several other newspapers and was even referred to in *Selection for Survival*.

Meanwhile the NAO had been examining the arrangements for the design and construction of the St Pancras building, in particular the performance of the three organizations principally responsible for the project: the Office of Arts and Libraries (OAL) (the commissioning department of the government); the Property Services Agency (PSA) (PSA Services from April 1990), and the British Library. Its report, *New Building for the British Library* (HMSO, October 1990, 24pp.), addressed three main issues:

(a) how the project developed;
(b) whether the design and construction of the new building had been managed efficiently, economically, and effectively; and
(c) whether the British Library's requirements would be satisfied by the building under construction.

On the development of the project, the report found that because the plan was for a phased construction there was never a firm commitment by Ministers to complete the project or, indeed, any of its stages. Further, the outline design proposals of 1977 did not provide the basis for detailed cost estimates or construction timetables. Although staged approval allowed changes in operational requirements to be absorbed, the consequences were that the construction period was extended, improved reader services and the transfer of books to a controlled environment were delayed, and the release of the Library's accommodation in London was postponed. Theoretical reviews and comparable costing exercises in 1973 and 1980 for locating the Library elsewhere had been of limited value because no suitable alternative sites could be identified. During the course of these reviews British Library had given no specific attention to providing storage in cheaper locations for infrequently used material. Pressure on public spending in 1979 had been the cause of the project's first stage being split into two sub-stages to allow work to proceed while funding for the second sub-stage was reconsidered. Although making financial sense, the division of the project was impractical in construction and planning terms and, crucially, offered no yardstick for measuring costs.

After mounting concern in 1986 about the effectiveness of the project's management had persuaded Ministers to commission a review, it was found that OAL had little authority over its implementation, PSA had not provided adequate management information, and that the system used for measuring price movements was unsuitable. Moreover, the Steering Committee, chaired by PSA – which included senior management representatives from British Library, OAL, the Treasury, and the consultant architects, and which was intended to meet twice a year to review progress and to take decisions on major issues – had not in fact been convened since January 1983. To remedy similar weaknesses, identified by a PSA-commissioned independent audit in 1987, OAL had assumed the chairmanship of the Committee and had appointed an experienced project director.

NAO's conclusion was that 'the successful management of a major construction project requires . . . a clear definition of the project's requirements and of the roles and responsibilities of the parties concerned, specialist staff resources experienced in project sponsorship and management, and regular and reliable management information. *But until 1987 the management of the New British Library Project did not fully meet these requirements.*' Although the new building would meet the Library's key requirements, as formulated in 1987, these were on a less ambitious scale than it had originally planned. The mismatch was most obvious in the extremely modest increase in the number of reader seats, from a combined 1,103 in the humanities and science reading rooms in Bloomsbury and Holborn, to just 1,176 at St Pancras. Storage facilities had also been dramatically cut back; instead of British Library storage needs being accommodated on site until the year 2030, the trimmed-down building would only provide storage until the end of the century and this included the retention of Science Reference and Information's Micawber Street store. St Pancras would in fact be operationally full (i.e. 85% full to allow room for book movement) by the time the new building was completed in 1996.

A keyed diagram of the original 1977 proposals for a phased construction, showing the designated locations for library departments and administrative areas, and with an appendix tabulating British Library's existing London estate building by building – detailing their function, floor area, storage capacity, rent and rates payable, and target vacation dates – was included in the NAO report. None of this information is easily accessible from other sources.

Press reaction to the NAO report was caustic. Although the performance of all three organizations responsible for the design, construction, and management of the project was investigated, the extent of British Library's culpability for the delays, poor programme management, and excessive spending tended to be magnified out of all proportion in the headlines. 'Building of library run badly for 12 years' (*The Independent*, **1264**, 31 October 1990:3); 'British Library called to account' (*Sunday Correspondent*, **51**, 2 September 1990:7); and, more ominously, 'MPs to scrutinise British Library' (*Bookseller*, **4929**, 9 November 1990) were typical examples. Yet the division of responsibilities outlined in the NAO report assigned to the British Library only the task of producing a detailed project brief. It was OAL's responsibility to appraise and approve the brief and to provide the required funding, and PSA's to manage the project within the agreed cost limits.

At no point was there any criticism of British Library's original brief and it is hard to see how blame can be laid at the Library's door for ministerial indecision, for OAL's lack of authority over the project's implementation, or for the inadequate management information furnished by PSA. Neither the poor accounting system adopted, nor the failure of the Steering Committee to meet for three years, can be attributed to the Library. There *is* a comment that the Library gave no specific consideration to providing storage in cheaper locations for infrequently used material in the 1973 and 1980 cost reviews but, as the Library informed the NAO, this was because the main objective of the new building was to bring readers and books closer together. It saw no good reason to assist in the burial of the original plan. The headlines made no mention of OAL or PSA; it was the British Library that took all the flak that was flying.

'Savage Attack on British Library', *Architects Journal*, **192** (18) 31 October 1990:3, summed up the whole sorry mess better than most:

> While the NAO avoids blaming individuals, what does emerge in its report is a catalogue of short-term decision making, inadequate cost monitoring and management structures, and project revisions which all add up to what the NAO sees as a recipe for how not to build a major new national institution. Not until 1987, more than a decade into the project, did a clear definition of the project's requirements and of the roles of the key players emerge.

HOUSE OF COMMONS COMMITTEE OF PUBLIC ACCOUNTS

The House of Commons Committee of Public Accounts, whose task it is to examine the accounts showing the appropriation of the sums granted by Parliament to meet the public expenditure, discussed the NAO report on 19 December 1990. Called to give evidence were the Second Permanent Secretary, Department of the Environment; the Chief Executive, PSA Services; and the Chief Executive, British Library Board. Its Minutes of Evidence and Summary of Conclusions and Recommendations were printed verbatim in *Committee of Public Accounts Eighteenth Report A New Building for The British Library* (HMSO, 1991, xiv, 21pp.).

Judging by the number and severity of the questions addressed to the British Library representative, MPs were intent on eviscerating the other two. Specific questions from the chair relating to the revised storage accommodation, the number of British Library rented buildings still in use after 1996, and to environmental control in the new building elicited information rather than excuses. The Chief Executive readily agreed with a committee member that the staging of the construction was a political decision by Ministers, not by any one of the three organizations responsible for the project. He had no great difficulty either in replying to points regarding the prior consultation of professional bodies who would presumably use the new building more once it was completed than they currently used the Library's dispersed reading rooms. He admitted that patent agents had expressed concern at different times about the amount of material on open access.

In an exchange about the pressure on readers' seats in the new Library, the Chief Executive somewhat incautiously remarked that in order to reduce the pressure it would be 'quite likely that we shall have to resort to devices like giving daily passes, rather [than] more extended passes' (Minute 1522). His questioner pointed out what an inauspicious start this was: access was being restricted even before the new library was opened. Apart from this very minor contretemps, he was able to field the questions and comments directed at him with unruffled composure.

The Committee's conclusions and recommendations followed very much along the same lines as the NAO report its members had in front of them. On the question of reader accommodation, the Committee expressed surprise that the number of seats was to increase by less than 7%, whereas the original plan provided for the number to be trebled; and that British Library had not considered it necessary to update its forecast of the new building's likely usage since 1976. The most stringent comment was reserved for OAL which, despite having commissioned and funded the new building, did not regard itself as responsible for keeping control of the project. The failure of the Steering Committee to meet for three and a half years was condemned as indefensible. Michael Latham, one of the MPs on the Committee, subsequently went into print blaming the government, and particularly the Treasury, for dithering and wasteful indecision: 'The net result is a building far below what was originally intended in size and suitability.' Seven years had elapsed after the architects were commissioned to design a new building on the Bloomsbury site before stage 1A had gained ministerial approval, during which period no decisions to build anything at all had been taken. Even by 1985, 14 years on, the project design was only three-quarters completed. ('Brought to book, library saga is classic tale of woe', *Building*, 8 November 1991:29).

Before the Select Committee's report was published, the Chief Executive, Kenneth Cooper, on the eve of his retirement, attacked in forthright terms the cuts in the Library's grant-in-aid of £4.5 million for the 1991–2 financial year. Despite government talk of the computer age, it had failed to understand the new library's information technology needs:

> There seems to be a lack of real concern by our Government. Do we want to spend £450 million on a new building delivering a second-rate service without enough terminals, with a rapidly diminishing number of journals and probably with insufficient staff . . .? We need £3.5 million towards the £8.5 million programme to develop new systems for St Pancras with a new integrated cataloguing database and access to it through public terminals.

He declaimed, in no uncertain terms, that 'by the time we get to St Pancras the library will be depressed and disfigured . . . we planned for 250 terminals in 1993; now it will have to be 150, and queuing for every terminal' (David Lister, 'British Library second rate', *Independent*, **1387**, 27 March 1991:2).

Cooper explained why British Library was publicizing its 1991–2 funding on Channel 4 News the same day:

> As a matter of responsibility we thought we should let the world know before they started asking what we are doing. We shall seek to manage the situation positively, our deep concern is that if we don't

recover from these cuts and are not given a margin of extra resources we shall be in rather serious trouble when we open up operations in the new building.

The cuts would bite hardest in a freeze on recruitment to some 150 posts, saving £1.8 million, but having disastrous knock-on effects on library services. Catalogue backlogs would pile up, information sources would be reduced, and photographic services might be severely affected. And, following a cutback in the acquisition of scientific journals in 1990, it was feared that further acquisition cuts would seriously damage the Library's holdings.

And then real trouble arrived. In May came the first intimations of further setbacks which eventually resulted in an indefinite postponement of the transfer of the London collections, due to start in the summer of 1991, and the opening of phase 1 of the new library in 1993. When a prototype range of Bruynzeel mechanical mobile shelving was tested in the King Edward basement at Bloomsbury, so that staff might gain experience of its use, it became apparent that books were 'creeping' on the shelves in a way that might cause a long-term problem. Further tests at St Pancras over a three-month period uncovered more serious problems with the driving mechanisms, which jammed the shelves and rendered them inoperable. If that were not enough, the paintwork on the shelves and uprights was not of the high quality expected. Engineers from Bruynzeel Storage Systems inspected 500 faulty cogs in August at which time a British Library spokesman declared that 'the library's planned initial move in 1993 has not been affected by the new little difficulties' (Geordie Greig, 'Jinxed library calls in the Dutch to open shelves', *The Sunday Times*, **8713**, 18 August 1991:5).

By this time the Library's frustration at the never-ending delays was close to brimming over. Tired of being everybody's whipping boy for the faults and deficiencies of other departments, it demanded that it should be more closely involved in the project management. Dr Brian Lang, the new Chief Executive, told *The Times*, 'the British Library's influence could have been stronger and its vision is that much more difficult to achieve as a result. What we are trying to do now is retain as much of that dream as possible' (Simon Tait, 'Library demands priority', *The Times*, **64124**, 13 September 1991:2). Two months later the Library confirmed that:

The British Library is rescheduling the largest bookmove in history to accommodate problems . . . with the basement shelving in the new library building at St Pancras . . . Originally scheduled for summer 1991, the book moves will now begin during 1992. The exact date will be announced when the library has been satisfied that the shelves will house the national collections safely and securely over the lifetime of the building.

A press release in December warned that:

the original programme allowed 8 months between the handover and the opening of the Rare Books reading room in February 1993. This would give the Library the opportunity to install the computer-based catalogue, train staff, and to become familiar with the new building. A delay of two months would curtail this important period and could prejudice the scheduled date for the reading room's opening.

The Chief Executive admitted that the delays were both worrying and frustrating:

But it would be wrong to hold to provisional opening dates and jeopardise the need to have the service infrastructure firmly in place.

Worse was to follow. Inspections of the above-ceiling voids in the basements revealed some problems relating to the ductwork and, more seriously, with components of the air-conditioning system. Considerable delays in St Pancras opening were now inevitable; the 'new little difficulties' had grown immeasurably.

Talk now was of the end of 1994 for the Queen's official opening. A *Sunday Times* report disclosed that Bruynzeel had agreed to replace much of the 200 miles of shelving because it was showing signs of rust (Ian Birrell and Caroline Rees, 'New chapter delays in sad saga of British Library', *The Sunday Times*, **8760**, 12 July 1992:1.9). In November the Chief Executive told the press at the launching of the Library's *Nineteenth Annual Report 1991-92* that the Government could not give an opening date for the new building; it would not even tie itself to a year. He made it clear that he considered it a mistake that the Library had not been involved in managing the building of its own premises. 'Tempers have risen, phones have been red hot, and tables had been thumped. One can handle delay when it is finite. What is much more pernicious is the uncertainty' (David Lister, 'New British Library hit by delay in opening', *The Independent*, **1888**, 4 November 1992:4).

What was clear from the *Annual Report* was that the Library had been forced to impose a damaging series of economy measures to finance essential preparations for the move to St Pancras in the absence of specific government funding:

> Because there has not been adequate support for automation and St Pancras planning, funds have had to be diverted from core activities. Grants for external research have been restricted, and the collections have been adversely affected by reduced preservation budgets. But the Library's acquisition spending has been hurt most. Over the past six years this has dropped by some 35% in real terms. Book purchases for the European language humanities collections have been severely curtailed, and gaps in the science collections are growing following the suspension of two hundred scientific serials in 1990–91.

This was not all: 'major economy measures were necessary in 1991–92 to fund relocation. It was decided that acquisitions could not be reduced further and cuts were implemented elsewhere, including a 6% reduction in the salary budget. This led to the loss of more than fifty posts, with consequent negative effects on operational efficiency and revenue-earning capacity in some areas.' The result was that 'the recession and delays to St Pancras have seriously disrupted the Library's financial plans. The Library's operational activities cannot be bled any further, and help and advice from the Government during this complex transitional period is desperately needed.' There was one bright spot in this litany of despair: 'a welcome £250,000 funding boost means that in 1992–93 the fall in the Library's acquisitions fund will at last be halted'.

Two days later the gloom deepened. Then, it was reported:

> the second phase of the new British Library, due to be completed in 1996, is almost certain to be mothballed after the autumn public spending round. According to sources within the Department of National Heritage the development . . . will be completed only when more money becomes available. For the time being, and to the delight of regular readers, the round room in Bloomsbury will be kept on (Joanna Coles, 'Cash squeeze brings new British Library delay', *The Guardian*, 6 November 1992:3).

The 'top person's' newspaper thundered that 'the monstrous new British Library will remain unopened for the foreseeable future. It was once a £170 million pet project beloved by the most powerful in the land; it is now left unloved and virtually on the shelf after expenditure of £450 million' ('Production spending', *The Times*, **64484**, 7 November 1992:19). This possibly marked the nadir of the British Library's fortunes. When the details of the Department of National Heritage's (DNH) budget became known it appeared that the Library had been reprieved from this doomsday scenario. A DNH spokesman denied that mothballing had ever been contemplated.

A close investigation of the project's history appears in Deyan Sudjic's 'Just a little overdue', *The Guardian*, 9 December 1992:2: 2, which points out that in 30 years the architect had designed six different buildings on three different sites. Apportioning the blame for the interminable delays to successive governments reviewing the project every two years instead of just getting on with it, with catastrophic frequent and radical design alterations, Sudjic goes on to applaud Colin Wilson's 'commendably level-headed refusal to succumb to the persecution complex that so many architects develop in the face of criticism. If Wilson is to be believed', he concluded, 'by the early years of the next century, the library's brick will have mellowed, moss will have started growing in the mortar joints. The space in front of the library . . . will be alive with stalls and picnickers. The exhibition space and restaurant inside will be bustling, and all the fuss will have been for nothing.' On the other hand, 'if the rude mechanicals can't sort out the problems in the boiler room, the aircraft carrier on the Euston Road will haunt the future as a ghastly warning of the shortcomings of the British way of doing things'.

OPPONENTS

From the outset the St Pancras project has been plagued by *ad hoc* groups of readers who, for various reasons, objected to the eventual evacuation of the famous British Museum Reading Room. In the summer of 1990 an unofficial, self-selected committee of the great and the good, a collateral if not a direct linear descendant of The Campaign to Save the Reading Room of ten years earlier, presented a private report to the Arts Minister which was subsequently published in *The Times Literary Supplement (TLS)*. Acknowledging that the move to St Pancras 'will have the advantages of providing spacious modern library facilities, ending a landlord and tenant relationship between two major national institutions', the report nevertheless regretted a 'considerable loss of amenity and of historical connection'. To assuage their grief the committee members put forward alternative solutions. One was that the British Library should retain the Reading Room, ferrying books to and from St Pancras, and spending £1.5 million on duplicating essential reference works at both sites. 'Readers could to a considerable extent be allowed to make their own choice between speed and surroundings. If their primary concern is the former they could go to one of the St Pancras rooms. If the latter they could give the additional notice required in the Round Reading-Room.' ('The future of the Round Reading-Room', *TLS*, 3 August 1990:822). Or, alternatively, if the library vacated the Reading Room, the British Museum should accommodate its own Department of Prints and Drawings or other large London-based collections there.

Perhaps fearing even at this late stage that their move to St Pancras might be thwarted, British Library took the unusual step of issuing an argumentative press release on 2 August 1990, *Library Confirms Leaving Round Reading Room in 1996*, pouring cold water on the first suggestion, regarded as a non-starter four times over. It would be impractical to redesign the building and any savings from such an exercise would be highly questionable, the benefits to readers resulting from concentrating all the central London collections would be lost, it would be very expensive to run a twin-site operation, and it would make no conservation sense.

Less easily seen off was the Regular Readers' Group (RRG) formed by a number of researchers, writers, and academics, who felt that their views were being ignored by the Library mandarins. Early in March 1990 RRG addressed a letter to the Chairman of the British Library Board, signed by 75 readers, expressing a threefold unease about the move to St Pancras. RRG was concerned not only about the physical disruption but about the long-drawn-out three-year period the move would last, during which whole sections of books would be unavailable at various times. Above all it was disturbed by reports that, because of a lack of storage space, British Library would in future cease to be the repository of every printed book and journal in the English language (if the national library had ever harboured such an ambition, it had long since been discarded). Subsequently, the abandoning of the guardbook catalogue 'in favour of a technological system with all its pitfalls of breakdowns and terminal queues' was added to RRG's list of woes.

An inconclusive meeting of five of its members and a phalanx of British Library heavyweights was held in July. Brian Lake, of Jarndyce Antiquarian Booksellers, RRG's Honorary Secretary, reported: 'The picture that emerged from the management was a confused one. Yes, they want dialogue, but unfortunately decisions have largely been made.' On the question of the future of the Round Reading Room, it was made clear that the Library would regard it a sad and sorry day if it were to continue in long-term use. Similarly the guardbook catalogue was regarded as obsolete and would not be retained: 'It appeared that there was very little

direction coming from the Directors, except to muddle through to a conclusion' ('The future of the British Library', *Rare Books Newsletter*, **37/8**,
November 1990:18–19). A more turbulent meeting in November ended
with an accusation that, in evacuating the Reading Room, British Library
was about to commit 'an act of vandalism on a truly barbaric scale'
(David Lister, 'Library accused of cultural vandalism', *The Independent*,
1277, 15 November 90:5). Sustained by the NAO report, and by the Chief
Executive's outspoken and forthright comments on the government's
funding of the St Pancras computer system, RRG persisted in its determined fight to retain the Reading Room. At the end of July the following
year it took direct action, circulating a bright orange leaflet in the Reading
Room itself:

Save the Round Reading Room for BL Readers before It Is Too Late

The British Library Regular Readers' Group has sent a Report to the
Minister of Art and Libraries, Timothy Renton, about the future of the
British Library. It details our grave concern on numerous counts: min-
imal increase in seating, the continuing need for considerable out-
housing, wrong priorities for books urgently in need of conservation
and serious problems with technical installations. The report also
offers a practical, pragmatic and cost-effective plan which entails
retaining the Bloomsbury reading rooms.

The Report, which has been widely circulated to prominent people
known to be seriously concerned about the future of the Library, is
available at £5 from the Regular Readers' Group, 46 Great Russell
Street, WC1, diagonally (r) opposite the main gates of the British
Museum.

Please help support our cause – by writing to the press, the Minister
and adding to the hundreds of signatures (at the above address) of
those who share our aims – and save the Bloomsbury reading rooms
for British Library readers before it is too late.

The aim of the report *Is the British Library Falling Down?* was to draw
attention to RRG's serious concerns about the move to St Pancras, and to
request the Minister's intervention and the commissioning of an independent report. Specifically, the main area of concern was the numerous
changes to the original brief: 'it is difficult to escape the conclusion that
reduced provision from that originally promised will leave the sum total
of half a new library, and the complete loss of the old one'. The serious
problems with technical installations mentioned in the orange leaflet cov-

ered all aspects of the new technological systems at St Pancras: the computer terminals for readers to locate and order books (the numbers were to be reduced and readers would consequently have to queue for access); the mobile high bookstacks to maximize storage space (inherent design faults had been known for at least 20 years); and the computer controlled mechanical book handling system, crucial for operations in the new building, was completely untried and there was no back-up system. The computerized catalogue had introduced its own errors whilst the old guardbook catalogue was to be relegated to an outhouse. Lack of consultation, reduced opening hours for sections of the Library, and low staff morale and downgrading were also noted in a list of grievances. The report urged a swift review of all aspects of the move in the light of the budgetary restrictions imposed; full funding for completion of the new Library rather than selling off of the remainder of the site; an early commitment to the retention of the Bloomsbury facilities until St Pancras was completed; and that the Round Reading Room, the finest space for learning in Europe, should be kept in use.

Simultaneously an offensive was launched in the *TLS*. Felicity Baker's 'Incompetence at the British Library? The Regular Readers' Group's Case', *TLS*, **4609**, 2 August 1991:12, reported events to a wider audience and posed some disconcerting questions. What sense does it make to stop the funds for the new Library when only one stage is complete? Why have a new library at all if there are to be only 73 more seats for readers, and the new storage space for books has no room for expansion? If there is to remain only half a library, why refuse to retain the reading rooms in Bloomsbury? 'No credible justification has reached our ears for the "philosophy" of the clean sweep, the total severance of the new from the old. This is no philosophy at all. It is the repudiation of any idea (old or new) of what libraries are for, in favour of a book-balancing jargon (the only books that count).' There was more: the argument that books could only be conserved in St Pancras' 'ideal environment' could not realistically be sustained. Three of the four Bloomsbury stacks offered near-perfect conditions for storage whilst 'the human book-delivery system in operation there seems gentler than the High-Tech Mobile Book Stacks at St Pancras, which will "whip, vibrate and jolt" the books'. An emotive and nostalgic plea for the retention of the Guardbook Catalogue followed. If, as British Library insisted, it was obsolete and unnecessary, 'why are so many readers still to be seen using it today, when Bloomsbury has computers? With its heavy card pages and the millions of tiny rectangles of printed paper glued on to them over the years, and the corrections carefully hand-written on many of the entries, that old catalogue is a concrete embodiment of historical continuity.' High technology, moreover, frequently fails.

Baker's diatribe inevitably attracted notice. Vincent Brome pointed out it was the government, not British Library, that had cut its funding, so crippling its full realization:

> The library is in serious financial difficulty and the RRG proposes increasing this by expending another (non-existent) £2 million on maintaining three separate venues – St Pancras, the Round Reading Room and the North Library. The result would be to treble staff and security requirements, distribute readers between three venues and risk the high probability of half-empty reading rooms ('The Round Reading Room', *TLS*, **4610**, 9 August 1991:15).

Undeterred, Baker declined to leave it at that, claiming that: 'Our memorandum is widely acknowledged, both within the Library precincts and without, as having a high degree of accuracy, not just about government underfunding, but, mainly, about alarming effects of management decisions' (*TLS*, **4612**, 23 August 1991:15).

A follow-up report, *Bloomsbury and St Pancras. A future for the British Library*, was despatched to the Prime Minister in November 1991. At times RRG's exuberant zeal parted from reality. It argued, reasonably enough, that retaining all the British Library reference collections in close proximity at Bloomsbury and St Pancras would obviate the need to send low-value material to Yorkshire. But to confuse the Library's stated intention to store *low-value* material at Boston Spa with *low-use* books of high research value which would continue to be held in London displayed a disturbing lack of expertise. On the question of reader demand RRG was on firmer ground: the 14% increase in reader numbers for the May–August 1991 period compared to 1990 sat uneasily with the Library's decision to lower to 18 the age limit for a reader's ticket. This unleashed the possibility of heavy undergraduate use. (Perhaps the Library reckoned that undergraduate library use in May, June, July, and August invariably plummets.) RRG's condemnation of St Pancras's mobile shelving – 'it is inconceivable that such a shelving system could be ordered in the first place without approval from British Library' – no doubt brought unaccustomed blushes to senior management cheeks.

RRG reminded the Prime Minister that the British Museum building – including the Reading Room and the King's Library – was a Grade 1 listed building and as such required listed building consent for any changes to its fabric. Only now was the British Museum consulting English Heritage and Camden Council yet, at RRG's invitation, two representatives of those bodies had already inspected these premises and had expressed the opinion that, because they had been designed round the books, consent for the books' removal might be withheld. It is surely beyond belief that a hitch of this sort should hold up a £450 million project at such a late stage. The irony is, of course, that it was a hefty Camden spanner in the works that had led to St Pancras in the first place.

Operating on a shoestring, with no real chance of persuading either British Library or the government to make fundamental changes in policies or planning, RRG was undoubtedly successful in keeping the Reading Room issue alive. Suddenly the Group achieved credibility. In a long article in *The Independent* Simon Garfield speculated that the British Library's critics were growing louder; each day their influence increased. They included leading figures in the literary establishment and many influential scholars and peers: 'They believe that the new British Library – the proposed jewel in our cultural and educational crown and the biggest civil construction this century – is at best a shattered dream, and at worst a complete disaster' ('And so, dear reader, the fairytale ends', *The Independent*, **1522**, 31 August 1991:25). And, as late as 18 October 1991, the Arts Minister told RRG's co-founder Etienne Lymbery that he had no objection in principle to retaining the Reading Room provided the Library had no objection. Of course, the Minister was well aware that the Library would never agree but, even so, it was a chink of light through a previously uncompromisingly closed door. The strongest expression of public support came in an *Evening Standard* editorial, 'Centre of learning', on 5 November 1992:

> The British Library must certainly be completed . . . But now we must reconsider the case for retaining the glorious Round Reading Room in the British Museum for its present use . . . Those who argue for its retention can no longer be dismissed as eccentrics. Peter Brooke must see the new British Library project to fruition, but he must listen again to the Library's Regular Readers Group and their 'compromise' proposals to keep the Reading Room.

In their Bloomsbury fortress the beleaguered senior management team was no doubt relieved to discern a few gleams of approval shining through the murk of discontent and delay. One of the earliest, and certainly one of the most literate and polished valedictory articles was Hugh Casson's 'Last orders, please', *The Guardian*, 20 December 1990:21, described as 'a personal plea for calm as the British Library prepares for its move'. In autobiographical and nostalgic vein, Casson captures the true atmosphere of the Reading Room but has the good sense to know that 'the Library has grown out of the British Museum'. As a distinguished architect, he is particularly appreciative of Panizzi's iron building, not least of the speed at which it was conceived, approved, and erected. But still the collections grew, as the number of London outhouses can testify, until at length a move to a new building became imperative. 'This move has come in for some vociferous protest, with fogies old and young huffing and puffing apoplectically about the cultural vandalism involved in losing the domed Round Reading Room. To hear some of them talk you would get the impression that there were plans to demolish Panizzi's dome.'

A sympathetic approach is also evident in 'The British Library reborn', *Times Higher Education Supplement*, **958**, 15 March 1991:40. It is already plain, the anonymous correspondent writes, that the new library 'is a building in which it will be possible to be comfortable – not intellectually lazy, of course, but at effective ease in terms of the routines of modern academic life . . . Perhaps the vernacular undemonstrative architecture of the new British Library fits the new mood better than its eloquent critics, past and future, suppose.' At first sight Michael Jenner's 'A fond farewell to the Reading Room', *Bookseller*, **4474**, 20 September 1991:782–3, is just another panegyric of the Reading Room and North Library:

> square, dignified, dark and mainly quiet but for the electronic chatter of personal computers transcribing in one corner. There are long, broad tables with stately chairs, lamps casting pools of light and large wooden bookrests . . . For a select minority the loss of the North Library with its otherworldly atmosphere of comfortable decorum . . . will be more grievous than that of the more illustrious Reading Room.

But rampant nostalgia is securely on hold. Jenner is conscious that British Library has a bright future as well as a glorious past. He looks forward to what the new building at St Pancras will offer: 'A sneak preview has lifted my spirits . . . it is a building designed from the inside out: functional planning has dictated the external shape.' He was more than amazed 'by the opulence of the intended fixtures and fittings. A solid and rich atmosphere should predominate in the stone from Purbeck and Portland, travertino, handmade bricks, brass railings and for the furniture, American white oak and green leather. Not a square inch of concrete will be visible.'

Philip Howard also assessed the new building not as an aesthetic architectural design but as a functional cultural national asset:

> So far, public discussion has been mainly about the external architecture and the cost . . . Sentimental fogeys, like the Prince of Wales, have niggled about the bold post-modernist look . . . populist Rottweilers complain that £450 million is too much and will never be recovered by market forces . . . Our descendants will be amazed that we could ever pretend to believe such garbage.

Both these groups, he contends, miss the point. 'The overriding duty of the British Library is not to provide a bookish theme park for the masses, or to make a profit, or to compete with the Gothic spires of St Pancras station and hotel.' Rather, 'it is to store the books, and preserve them from decay, and make them available as quickly as possible to readers'. In contrast, the majestic British Museum buildings were now quite inadequate for the storage and care of books. 'Our new British Library building, sited next to what will become the hub of Britain's national and international transport system, will not only be a major attraction for scholars from all over the world, but will establish London's role as the cultural centre of Europe.' ('Miles of aisles for bibliophiles', *Times Saturday Review*, 6 July 1991:12). It was a far-sighted and generous salute.

Apart from correspondence in the quality newspapers, British Library has never publicly responded to its critics. The nearest it came to offering a rationale for St Pancras was Michael Smethurst's *The British Library in the 1990s* (Cambridge, Provincial Booksellers Fairs Association, 1990, 31pp.), the text of the first Alice Brett Memorial Lecture, published in a limited edition of 500 copies. As clear and concise an explanation of the Library's current stance on its function as a national library confronting the twenty-first century as could reasonably be expected, and a balanced justification for a modern building, the text concludes with a verbatim report of a question-and-answer session at the end of the lecture. Concerns expressed by his bookseller audience ranged over the effect of a possible Channel tunnel terminal at King's Cross, the cutbacks in conservation and acquisition, what the Round Reading Room would be used for when the British Library departed, the consequences of a reduced Library at St Pancras and the undesirability of selling off land at the northern end, why the Oriental Collections were moving to the India Office Library, the procedure for public admission to St Pancras, the difficulties of using online public access catalogues (OPACs) terminals, and what would happen if the automated systems broke down.

To all these questions Smethurst was able to respond authoritatively, reasonably, and with some conviction. For once British Library may have missed a trick in not publishing something of similar length aimed at a popular audience. Correspondence in the newspapers, paragraphs in the *Annual Report*, articles in the library and information professional press were not enough to ward off sometimes ill-informed criticism. An attempt was made in *The British Library Past Present Future* (1989, 64pp., 32cm x 24cm). Sponsored by Chadwyck-Healey, written by specialist British Library staff, and edited by Robin Alston, this sumptuously illustrated corporate brochure was designed to convey the richness and diversity of the Library's collections. It effectively reviews the range of services offered to the Library's varied clientele but, magnificent production though it undoubtedly is, nowhere does it really get to grips with why St Pancras is necessary or reassure readers with chapter and verse that services will improve there. The future is fobbed off with 11 lines of text and three photographs: an oil rig at sea, Big Ben and the House of Commons, and the Senate House tower of the University of London, whose combined significance or inspiration, if any, must be subliminal.

CONSTRUCTION

Construction work began on stage 1AA of the British Library building at St Pancras in April 1982. Managing the design and construction was the responsibility of PSA's Directorate of Civil Accommodation. Until its sale in 1992 to Tarmac Construction Ltd 'for a negative consideration' of £49.75 million, PSA was an agency within the Department of the Environment. A team of consultants to assist on the project was appointed: Ove Arup & Partners (structural engineers); the Steenson Varming Mulcahy Partnership (mechanical and electrical engineering); and Davis Langdon and Everest (quantity surveyors). Laing Management Contractors was appointed as the construction manager on site. André Beaumont's 'Another Chapter', *Building Design*, 770, 17 January 1986:16–18, discusses the site's characteristics and notes that only rarely does a site as large (nine acres) as the former Somers Town marshalling yards emerge so near the centre of London: 'It is even rarer for the site to be blessed by having little necessity to address its neighbours. On two sides the level of building is insignificant and not historic. It has two real neighbours: one is St Pancras station, the other Euston Road itself.'

Principal architect of the new building was Colin St John Wilson, Professor of Architecture in the University of Cambridge, who had been involved in the design of the proposed new British Museum Library in Bloomsbury in 1962. When local authority pressure to conserve Bloomsbury's reputed traditional atmosphere forced British Library to look elsewhere, he was the obvious choice to design the St Pancras library. In its final form Wilson's brief contained 8,500 computerized pieces of information specifying environmental conditions, equipment, and spatial parameters for every library department: closed- and open-access rooms; storage on site in controlled environmental conditions with provision for growth; workshops and studios for conservation, binding, photography, and reprography; exhibition galleries and workshop; offices; and amenities for readers, staff, and the general public. The Library's structure is of reinforced concrete with columns on a 7.8-metre grid supporting concrete floors. External finishes and materials are red brick, slate roofs, and brick and stone paving. Bronze-colour metal trims the column facings and roof plant housings. These materials were selected with weathering in mind and to relate to St Pancras station.

Wilson contributed a magisterial overview of the design aspects of the new library in a paper, 'The New Building For The British Library', to the 1987 IFLA Conference in Brighton, printed as pre-conference paper, no. 16, BUIL/INP/POBL–INF, Division of Management and Technology, Section of Library Building and Equipment. He distinguished three major factors influencing the design: the planning requirements of the nine acre, wedge-shaped site; the operational brief; and the need to build in discrete phases of occupation to permit a controlled move of vast quantities of books, along with the piecemeal funding that such a massive project was likely to attract. An eastern range designed to house the open-access Science Reference and Information Service (SRIS) collections, and a western range to hold the collections from Bloomsbury – manuscripts, printed books, music, maps, *etc.* – linked by a central section are the main features. Access to the reading rooms, the exhibition galleries, the auditorium, and seminar rooms is gained from the entrance hall in the central section which faces on to an approach forecourt – a traditional courtyard surrounded by walls, railings, and trees behind an entrance portico from Euston Road.

Huge pylons accommodate primary services such as ducting, escape stairs, wet services, and vertical book delivery systems, ensuring the self-sufficiency of the staged construction phases. Book storage is in the largest and deepest basements to be found in non-military London. A mechanical conveyor loop connecting the north and south basements is located on the top basement level so that a network of horizontal and vertical runs facilitates book deliveries to control points in the reading rooms, staff offices, the conservation laboratory, and photographic studios. Natural light streams into the reading rooms through the roof and the tall clerestory windows. In an interview with Kathy Stansfield, printed as 'Designing a National Monument', *Construction*, **67**, November 1988:12–15, Wilson claimed: 'British Library will have been in and out of fashion ten times before I've finished. You have to build to a concept and stand by it. This is a 1975–76 design, and, I claim, very much in advance of its time. But it still has to stand, whenever it's conceived.'

Martin Spring's 'Reading in Depth', *Building*, **253** (3), 15 January 1988:48, 50, 52–5, examines the structural engineering problems, the protracted construction period, PSA's financial control, the structural surveys of neighbouring buildings, Arup's top-down methods of constructing the basements, and work currently under way on the superstructure. But the most exhaustive interim survey of work in progress is the special British Library issue of PSA's journal, *Construction*, **67**, November 1988, which carried six illustrated articles in addition to the Wilson–Stansfield interview. 'Project Management' (pp.21–3) outlines the specific responsibilities of key personnel on site, the direction of the project, the relationship with PSA, the pricing and tendering process, and the safety aspect. PSA's current project manager temerariously remarks that projects like the British Library (were there any?) showed off the Agency's skills to advantage: 'multi-disciplinary project roles are probably better organised in PSA . . . project management is not a question of training but skills in management itself'. This remark could charitably be construed not so much as a hostage to fortune, more as a self-excavated grave fully commensurate with British Library basement depth. 'Digging Deep' (pp.25–7) explores the complexities of the five-level basement area for book storage, the intricacies of the top-down excavation method, secant pile walls, and the placing of 119 large diameter bore piles in steel casings to support the concrete floors. 'A Storehouse of Knowledge' (pp.28–30) looks at the Library's book storage requirements and provides a clear and succinct exposition of the computerized request, retrieval, and delivery system designed to cope with 25,000 separate book movements daily. 'Fire Protection' (pp.30–1) investigates the Library's sprinkler, smoke, and fire detection systems, and stresses that unproven technology has not been used. 'Drainage' (pp.38–9) explains why a sophisticated drainage system had to be contrived to effect a swift removal of surface water and to cope with the water level in the natural acquifer under London. 'Cladding' (pp.42–4) emphasizes the advantages of aluminium over other materials, and reviews the types and sizes of coping, and the Library's fascia, feature wall, and circular column cladding.

Quite the most succinct account of the vicissitudes suffered by the new building project, and of Colin Wilson's involvement from day one, first with the proposed buildings in Bloomsbury, then with the seven-phase incremental structure at St Pancras that was to gather all of the Library's buildings under one roof, the apogee of the Library's ambitions; to the 1986 completion phase which reduced the project to finishing off various stages by 1996 within a specified total cost, and selling off the unused part of the site – is Martin Pawley's 'Building a time bomb', *The Guardian*, 31 October 1989:35. His was an encouraging message:

> Far from being a Rip van Winkle project, the British Library is a modern time bomb, ticking away until its opening in 1993, when it will reveal architecture of a power and authority not seen in Britain since the heady days of Coventry Cathedral and the Royal Festival Hall. A butt of jokes and a target for government cost-cutters for years, the new British Library is destined to become a treasured institution.

By the following spring, when the building was at last taking a distinctive shape, other writers in the quality and professional press were being won over. Martin Spring's 'Epic volumes', *Building*, **255** (9), 2 March 1990:50–5, reports that 'topped out 19 months ago, the seven-storey concrete-framed superstructure is now nearly fully clothed in brick-work. With three years to go before the first phase opens to the public, the architectural design is rapidly assuming a finished form.' He added, 'fortunately it is a form that bears little relationship to the soulless artist's impressions that incurred the royal wrath'. (This refers to the Prince of Wales' remarks that the St Pancras building resembled 'an academy for secret policemen' and 'a dim collection of brick sheds groping for some symbolic significance'). And when plans for the second, 'completion' phase were unveiled they met with general if not unqualified approval. Mary Holman's 'British Library Complete At Last', *Architect's Journal*, **191** (23), 6 June 1990:14–15, which included an axonometric of the completed building, briefly recounted the history of the design, and the changes wrought by financial cutbacks in the long gestation period, but acknowledged that 'a coherent, legible building is gradually emerging'.

Despite being 'monumentally unfashionable when it opens for business', taking a long time to build, costing a lot, and having 'shrunk to the point where it won't even do the job it was planned to do in the first place', and carrying 'the usual weight of prejudice against any grandiose public-sector palace of culture', the new building was accorded a 'qualified thumbs-up' in Hugh Pearman's 'A 20-year story with a happy ending?', *The Sunday Times*, **8651**, 10 June 1990:5: 3. Pearman found the eastern building 'uncannily like an aircraft carrier, complete with bridge, funnel, portholes and launching ramp jutting right up to the main road'. On a less impressionistic level, he described the design as 'an attempt to create a large-scale elevation on a relatively small budget. Architectural tricks are employed to make a little accommodation stretch a long way visually – such as the central, semicircular feature on three levels which looks important but is nothing more than a staff canteen. It comes off, though it needs refining.' He also commends the architect's use of natural light in the main foyer and humanities reading room: 'a vital propaganda exercise for the British Library administration, who have to persuade deeply conservative readers to transfer from their historic home, the round reading room at the British Museum'.

Almost three years later, when the removal of the scaffolding revealed the full majesty of the new library, Marcus Binney's 'Booking for a new millenium', *The Times*, **64642**, 12 May 1993, was equivocal on its external aspects:

> The new library's largely blank walls are an almost abstract composition, building up to a clock tower, and especially impressive viewed from the west, where the science library has the look of a large cargo ship piled with containers and rising to a dramatic prow. But unfortunately those blank walls are also a little too evocative of numerous 1980s supermarkets and shopping centres. The piazza in front is unquestionably grand, as large as the public squares in many Italian towns. But again the red brick paving is too relentless.

He found the most striking exterior feature to be the colourful trim: British racing red for the bands of aluminium capping over the brickwork, and Fiat Amazon green for the louvres and windows of the science library. From certain angles, however, 'the asymmetry is so marked that the library seems almost half a building: like Battersea power station when it only had two chimneys'. But Binney's reservations fast disappeared when he entered the main doors:

> From the door the room fans out in every direction. The floor rises, the ceiling rises, the walls recede. Flights of steps invite, indeed com-

pel one towards the hidden source of light illuminating the balconies behind. Majestic when empty, it will spring alive with the bustle of a large throng . . . at the back the balconies are in fact bridges, symbolically linking the arts and humanities libraries . . . The science library is a brighter space with the flow and geometric precision of Frank Lloyd Wright.

He, too, commented that 'there will be improvements in convenience for even the most ardent supporter of the present domed Reading Room in the British Museum'. But, he asked, will the Library be worth £450 million? He concluded that 'the nation has the monument the politicians wanted, and undoubtedly there is a vast amount to be made of it'.

More eulogistic still, Peter Dormer's 'The things you've read are wrong', *The Independent*, **2065**, 2 June 1993:16, argued that the new library will be an outstanding building. In his view St John Wilson's team 'are creating a building – certainly on the inside – of beauty, civility, finesse and usefulness'. Final judgement on the exterior, he remarks, must await completion: 'however it is clear that Professor Wilson has avoided the dull, bureaucratic solution of creating a monolithic box. The buildings are not lumped together, but are stepped back and terraced. And the layout makes lively use of the asymmetrical shape created by the streets that bound the site.' Like Binney, Dormer is overwhelmed by the entrance hall – which he likens to a secular cathedral providing an atmosphere of great dignity and liveliness – and by the four great basements, each the depth of an eight-storey building, housing 186 miles of shelving. All in all 'the building makes a lie of the complaint that craftsmanship is dead: the quality of the work is extremely high'. Besides Frank Lloyd Wright, Dormer invokes the names of Alver Aalto, Le Corbusier, Leslie Martin, Sir Denys Lasdun, and Sir Norman Foster as influences on the architectural design which, he claims, 'has survived the cacophony of Brutalists, Internationalists, Hi-Technologists, Post-Modernists, Neo-Classicists – and Royalists'.

British Library has not been reticent to excite public and professional interest in its new building. In the summer of 1989 two brochures with the same title, and identical cover designs, were issued. The larger version of *Building The New British Library* (24pp., 29.5cm x 23cm) was aimed at 'opinion-formers', principally MPs and journalists. Beginning with an outline chronology of the building's planning, design, and construction, 1972–96, it emphasized the new library's storage capacity and conservation potential and promised that 'through newly computerised catalogues and an advanced automated book retrieval system, a comprehensive range of materials will be accessible to readers much more quickly and more efficiently'. Reminding the 'opinion-formers' that the building was described by the Royal Fine Art Commission as 'a brilliant solution to an extremely complex problem', it pointed out that the major factors influencing the design were:

> a complex operational and technical brief, prepared in considerable detail to take into account the needs of a very special library, the urban setting including the surrounding architecture, the excellent transport links, the substantial redevelopment of the King's Cross railway lands, and the fact that the sheer size and continuous growth of the collections required the design should be built and habitable in discrete stages (p.6).

Interior descriptions of the entrance hall, reading rooms, and of the automation and book delivery system leave no doubt that both readers and the public will be well served in impressive surroundings. Profiles of the British Library's Project Team, the architects, engineers, contractors, and surveyors, complete an eye-catching publication.

The British Library at St Pancras (1990, 20pp., 31.5cm x 25cm), gives more details of 'a unique national and international resource', with illustrated descriptions of the Humanities Reading Room, the King's Library, specialist reading areas, book storage and delivery, climate control and conservation, exhibitions and public spaces, and the Library's immediate neighbourhood. What distinguishes this particular brochure is its exceptional design and production: text, technical data, and artists' drawings, are all blended in complete aesthetic harmony. An artist's impression of the Library's south-west elevation is particularly fine. Extended reports on progress at St Pancras appeared in British Library's *Annual Report* from 1986–7 onwards.

An air of optimism suffused British Library in the summer of 1993, nurtured by reports that the shelving contractors were fast approaching completion of the remedial works programme, during which shelving was dismantled, cleaned, inspected, and graded into nine different categories according to the amount of remedial work judged to be necessary. Six categories were treated on site; shelves in the other three were promptly replaced. In all about 290,000 shelves were scrutinized to guarantee a long and trouble-free life. Moving the first books into the new building early in 1994 became a distinct possibility. But then, right on cue, a new problem surfaced which threatened to rival the great shelving disaster. Up to 80% of the plastic insulation of the heating and lighting power cables running throughout the building was feared to have been stripped off whilst being drawn through the metal trays carrying the cables, leaving exposed wires. An 'insider' informed one newspaper 'Every time anyone finds a bit of bare wiring, they have to examine the rest of the cable in that area . . . It's a big issue because it affects the timing and it is now holding everything else up. It's sheer chaos' (Susannah Herbert 'New British Library hit by blunders over wiring', *Daily Telegraph*, **43084**, 30 December 1993:2). As 1994 dawned, the King William V joke was beginning to look like a remarkably shrewd prediction.

Growing concern that the government intended to sell off the 'surplus' 4.5 acres of land to the rear of the St Pancras building once it was completed was voiced in Michael Saunders Watson's Foreword to the *Eighteenth Annual Report 1990–91*. A working party is looking at the Library's post-1996 space requirements and at the potential uses to which this land might be put. Although as yet no firm plans had been drawn up, 'it is clear', he remarked, 'that we must resist any premature disposal of this important piece of land before the Library's future needs have been fully worked out and proved'. Shortly after the *Annual Report* was published the Library submitted outline proposals to the DNH; a more detailed plan including cost-justifications was communicated in March 1993. Top of the Library's priority list is a Conservation Bindery and photographic processing accommodation. Future requirements include new premises for the National Sound Archive and an additional reading room. The 'mediatech' of which so much had been made (Chris Brockhurst, 'Multi-media plan for BL's spare land', *Library Association Record*, **94** (9), September 1992:561) remains a longer-term project. It is British Library's contention that if it is to further enhance its services, and operate at maximum effectiveness, all these facilities need to be located on the St Pancras site. The Library's architects have prepared designs for three phases of construction which the Library suggests could be funded by the National Lottery and private sponsorship in addition to government grant-in-aid.

FACILITIES

As the scheduled date for opening in 1993 drew nearer, British Library newsletters regularly printed columns on the new building and its facilities. Highly technical articles by Library staff and others infiltrated the professional press. These retain a strong interest although the dates they projected were of course soon hurled aside by the march of events. A masterly and authoritative account of how the British Library coped with the long history and the protracted time-scale of the construction project was contributed by Dr Ruth Coman, Director of the Occupation Project, in a paper presented to a joint meeting of the Aslib Biosciences Group and ALISSE at Reading University in September 1990, 'St Pancras: A focus for change at the British Library', printed in *Aslib Proceedings*, **43** (4), April 1991:143–51.

Dr Coman reminded her audience that over the entire period of the project senior staff had grappled with three crucial changes to the original objective: the nature and size of the organization to be accommodated in the new building (from the British Museum Library to the British Library's London collections incorporating the Patent Office Library and the India Office Library and Records); a change of site to one totally different in shape and size; and government authorization of only a trimmed-down building to be constructed within strict financial limits. What proved much more difficult to contend with was the necessary cultural change, 'a pervasive change of attitude and working philosophy within the organisation'.

After some initial errors in planning the transfer of services and operations to St Pancras, which started in earnest in 1986, 'an enormous quantity of detailed information had been amassed' in a two-year period, but 'the work . . . lacked clear direction and strategy, and there was an increasing sense of disillusion and anxiety amongst the people involved'. Realizing that possible disaster lay ahead, and that it did not possess the necessary in-house skills to avert it, British Library enlisted the aid of the British Institute of Management (BIM). Dr Bert Darnell, of BIM's Asset Management Group, who had direct personal experience of managing large-scale projects and of advising senior managers on project management, recommended that British Library should adopt formal project management techniques. Specifically, the Library needed to regard the occupation of the new building as two closely related projects. The first concerned the nature and provision of library operations and services during and after the move, whilst the second concerned the physical move itself, notably its time-scale and its budgetary constraints. Furthermore, British Library should learn the techniques of project management and manage the whole operation without bringing in expert project managers from outside.

In Darnell's view the lack of a clear command structure exacerbated the confusion surrounding the project. An entirely new approach to strategic thinking and the defining of individual staff responsibilities were urgently needed if staff commitment and expertise were not to be dissipated. British Library took immediate notice: a new project structure, with a Project Director for each of its two dimensions, was swiftly adopted. Coman continued:

> One fundamental point which had been ignored earlier was the upheaval which would result from the integration of units with a history of widely differing traditions. Rigid departmental autonomy and a multiplicity of varying procedures, the heritage of a multi-site development would have to be modified or disappear altogether. The whole organization at St Pancras would inevitably be very different from the sum of its parts. Moreover, this difference would need to be made explicit. It would require endorsement at the most senior level and everyone involved with the Projects would have to be totally clear about it before the detailed development of work could be undertaken.

A process involving eight discrete stages was created: three relating to the operational planning, three to the transfer of services to the new building, and two additional stages of integrating the operation units into a new organizational structure. In addition there was to be a post-occupation evaluation of both the building and its services to determine whether either needed modification.

In implementing these stages a finalized plan for the transfer to the new building was embodied in two forms: a computerized network containing nearly 7,000 activities each logically linked in sequence and each attached to a resource requirement; and a 'Project Execution' handbook for staff directly concerned in the transfer. This included a summary of the operational planning, a description of the strategy and main features of the Occupation Project Plan, an explanation of the management and support systems for the plan's implementation, and a description of the interface with the construction project.

Ilse Sternberg, Head of the Overseas English Collections at the British Library, provided an early résumé of the size of the task of moving stock, staff, and services, and of how library users might be affected by the move and afterwards, in 'Moving the British Library', *American Studies Library Newsletter*, **32**, December 1990:43–7. By the opening of phase 1 the bulk of the Library's London reference collections (some 200 kilometres of stock) would have been moved, 700 staff transferred, and 50 or so operational units would be in place. 'A robust low-risk strategy' was developed to ensure that the required moves from the existing reading rooms and outhouse stores would operate smoothly over an 18-month period. Separate plans were devised for moving the three major collections – the general humanities stock, the rare books, and the science, technology and business material – in that order. Generally the least used material would be moved first to minimize the need for recalling books once they arrived at St Pancras. Existing reading rooms would continue to function for the first 18-month period. Fax would be used for transmitting requests to St Pancras and a shuttle van service would deliver books to the reading rooms. On conservation grounds once rare books were transferred to the new Library they would have to be consulted there. During this initial period, maps, Western Manuscripts, and the Oriental and India Office Collections would remain where they were, only moving to St Pancras when phase 2 was completed in 1996. Readers were assured that, although blocks of books would be temporarily unavailable during the move, none should be out of circulation for more than ten working days.

Derek Greenwood, St Pancras Occupation Project, and John Shawyer, Humanities Book Moves Manager, Collections and Preservation, combined to provide a detailed description of planning the transfer of books and the development of an automated system to manage this operation in their 'Moving the British Library – the Book Control System', *Aslib Information*, **21** (1), January 1993:28–31. Factors complicating the move included the sheer magnitude of the collections – some eight million books, periodicals, patents, maps, and manuscripts; the number of dispersed outhouse storage units in many different buildings around London; and the enforced disruption of the sequence and ordering of the collections on the shelves owing to long-standing congestion in the stock areas. British Library recognized these complexities early and obtained advice from Ernst & Young, management consultants, who prepared the Book Move Control System (BMCS), an automated system to help in the detailed planning, monitoring, and control of the book removals.

BMCS stores details of the height, width, and depth of each bay of shelves in the St Pancras storage areas, with facilities for adjustment when required. The collections are divided into manageable sections of about 500 metres in length each so that they may be removed to shelving of the appropriate type at a known location at St Pancras. 'When there is a firm date for starting the book move, the BMCS can predict when collections will be moved, basing its predictions on the estimated length of sections of the collections, and the controlled move rate of 400 metre per day.' When known, this information will be relayed to readers via the Library's reader service points.

What can the taxpayer expect for £450 million of his or her money on arrival at St Pancras? A striking feature of the new library as compared with the reading rooms in Bloomsbury is the extensive provision of automated systems for readers and staff. The Reader Admission System (RAS) will hold data on about 200,000 current readers. New style credit-card size readers' passes in British Library corporate red and black have a machine-readable strip on the reverse allowing readers to operate the reader gates. A standard pass will allow entry to the main reference areas but a higher-level pass will be required by users consulting 'select' material: rare books, manuscripts, and printed music scores.

The primary method of obtaining books not on the open-access shelves in the reading rooms will be by consulting the Online Public Access Catalogue, OPAC 92, through 86 catalogue terminals in the reading rooms – that is, one terminal for every seven reader seats. By 1996, when phase 2 of the building is completed, it is expected that there will be 450 terminals on the system. Initially OPAC 92 will hold the retrospective and current catalogues of the Humanities and Social Sciences (H&SS), SRIS and Music Collections. Access is by author and title and it will also be possible to search the majority of files by publisher, date of publication, shelfmark, and subject. At a later date other major British Library catalogues of the cartographic collections, the Summary Manuscript Catalogues, the Newspaper Library Catalogue, and the Document Supply Catalogue will be added ('Catalogues at St Pancras', *London Services – Bloomsbury Newsletter*, **3**, Spring 1992:3). At the end of April 1993 it was announced that the British Library had secured its biggest ever private sponsorship deal. In return for £1 million-worth of computer systems, Digital Equipment Company would have one of the three exhibition galleries at St Pancras named after it for ten years after the building's official opening.

> Chosen by the Library itself, the computer technology will be integral to the automated user services . . . it will be the power behind the Online Public Access Catalogue and the Automated Book Retrieval System and will make the task of identifying, retrieving and delivering items both quicker and easier. It will ensure that books from the 12 million volume London collection will be delivered to users within 30 minutes of a request being made ('Thanks A Million Digital', *British Library News*, **178**, May 1993:1).

Using the OPAC terminals, readers will be able to call up the books they require through the Automated Book Request System (ABRS 92), which will hold information on the availability of the item requested so that the reader may be informed immediately whether it is missing, destroyed, already in use, or stored elsewhere. The transit of the books from the basement storage stacks to the reading rooms will be by means of The Mechanized Book Handling System (MBHS). Books to be moved will be placed in protective red plastic boxes each holding eight average-size books and moved along horizontal conveyor belts (1.6 kilometres in total) and up vertical elevators controlled by three computers in a single workstation. Boxes and destinations are identified by bar codes read by light pen and 42 sensors guide the boxes en route. The conveyor belts move 15 metres per minute, giving typical travel times of about 6 to 15 minutes from the basements to the reading room outlets, although total delivery time will be longer because of the time needed to retrieve books from the stacks and to process them in the reading rooms. Even so, it will at least halve the waiting period readers experienced at Bloomsbury.

First distributed in March 1993, *Moving the British Library Catalogues and Book Delivery at St Pancras*, an illustrated twice-folded leaflet brochure, emphasized the improved facilities of the online catalogues (British Library's reader surveys had amply demonstrated that lingering doubts and uncertainties among Reading Room habitués had by no means disappeared), the advantages of the new procedures for ordering books, and the relative speed of the ABRS. It was a brave, if not wholly convincing, effort to reassure not a few slightly dubious readers.

For their comfort inside the reading rooms readers will find aesthetically pleasing but functional furniture, desks, chairs, and individual carrels fashioned in solid American light oak to match the pale walls panelled in the same material. The desks will be noticeably larger than readers are accustomed to in Bloomsbury. Shallow partitions will separate facing desks, each partition carrying sockets for computer terminals and a light which will indicate when requested books are ready for collection. The science reading rooms will have a grey-green carpet with desk-top leather in a complementary green shade whilst the humanities areas will have a blue carpet and museum-blue leather for the desk tops. ('New Reading Room Furniture and Fittings', *London Services – Bloomsbury Newsletter*, 1, Summer 1991:3–4).

Disabled people will find improved facilities at St Pancras where the new building will fully comply with British Standard BS5810 *Code of Practice for Access for the Disabled* and with BS5588 part 8, *Means of Access for Disabled People*. There will be a wheelchair ramp from the forecourt to the main entrance doors; an automatic door at the front entrance; a wheelchair lift at the main loading bay for the use of disabled drivers using the car park; a ramp in the main entrance hall; and lifts and escalators connecting the lower ground, ground and upper ground floors. All reading rooms will accommodate at least one two-person soundproof carrel which may be used by the blind or partially sighted accompanied by an assistant. Toilet and washing facilities will be available on all above-ground floors. (From 'Provision For People With Disabilities At St Pancras', *London Services – Bloomsbury Newsletter,* **6**, Spring 1993:3).

When readers have taken their bearings and start using the open-access collections in the General Humanities Reading Room, and the Rare Books and Music Reading Room, some of them may notice that the books have been reclassified according to the Dewey Decimal Classif-ication (DDC) scheme. The history of this decision, going back to a 1972 working party which was asked 'to examine the various classification and indexing systems currently in use in the various component parts of the British Library and to consider the possibilities of rationalisation, tak-ing into account the need for standardisation nationally and internation-ally', is narrated in John Byford's 'The British Library, DDC and the new building', *Catalogue & Index,* **103–4**, Spring/Summer 1992:1, 3–5. When DDC was adopted for the small social sciences collection in the Official Publications Library, and for the Library Association Library (now British Library Information Sciences Service – BLISS) in 1974, it was noted that it would be possible for the enlarged humanities open-access collections to be arranged by Dewey in the new British Library buildings, although opinion was divided on the merits of DDC for the science collections.

In 1989 Russell Sweeney, Head of the Department of Library and Information Studies, Leeds Polytechnic, and British representative on the DDC Editorial Board, was asked to examine the use of DDC in the Humanities Reading Room at St Pancras. After preliminary meetings with staff responsible for planning the reading rooms there – which encompassed the existing arrangements at Bloomsbury and the perceived needs of users – he conducted a study in the reading rooms during the period August–October 1990, assessing the range of subjects covered, the amount of material on each subject on the shelves, and what the result would be if Dewey were to be applied. Sweeney's unpublished report, 'Classification of St Pancras open access material: a study under-taken for British Library' was submitted to the Library's Committee of Directors in December 1990 and endorsed at their April 1991 meeting when Dewey was accepted 'as a suitable system for the relevant open access collections in St Pancras'. Subject to satisfactory modifications Dewey would also be applied to the Special Collections when they arrived in 1996.

The public exhibition galleries are on two levels sharing a common ceiling at the same height, effectively creating three discrete areas. An upper low-ceiling Treasures Gallery (600 square metres) will display some 350 of the most valuable and irreplaceable items in the collections; a lower Way We Work Gallery (200 square metres), aimed at younger visitors, will explain what libraries are and the way they work. It will also present displays: the history of writing, the relationship between manuscripts and print, popular literature, children's books, and a reconstruction of one of the foundation libraries are all mentioned as possibilities. A large high-ceiling gallery (450 square metres) will mount a series of practical displays to include relevant 'museum' items such as printing presses, bookbinding material and equipment, early gramophones, science equipment, and computers. Further details of what is planned are to be found in Jane Carr's 'New exhibition facilities for British Library', *Rare Books Newsletter*, **35**, February 1990:27–9.

At the heart of these activities will be the Centre for the Book, first proposed in the Library's second strategic plan, *Gateway to Knowledge*, and publicly announced in a press release, *Centre For The Book*, 20 March 1990, 'to promote the significance of the book in all its forms, as a vital part of the cultural, commercial and scientific life of the country, past and present'. Funding would be sought to establish fellowships and lectures; readings by authors of their books would be arranged; and, as part of the Library's plans to establish the new building as the logical venue for book events and to encourage use of the meeting rooms and auditorium, space would be made available for exhibitions originating outside the Library. It was not the intention that the Centre should confine its activities to London: travelling exhibitions would venture into the regions, possibly in collaboration with other agencies. Mike Crump, the Centre's executive secretary, summed up:

> the Centre will assume a role of interpreting . . . not only the scholarship of the Library's curators, but also the National Library itself . . . it is also hoped that the Centre will give an impression of the diverse role of the national library from sound to science; from reference to inter-library loan; from rare books and manuscripts to Research and Development and compact discs, and will demonstrate the place of that library as a part of the nation's library services ('Centre for the Book', *Aslib Information*, **18** (78), July/August 1990:238–9).

Tim Rix, who retired as Chairman of the Longman Group in 1990, a past president of the Publishers Association and Chairman of the Centre's Advisory Committee, also explained why British Library was establishing the Centre. The Library was not identified in the eyes of the public at large, as opposed to the library and information community, as the focal point of the British book world. No other existing institution carried out 'the central role of promoting and monitoring the whole range of activity concerning books in our society'. Moreover, 'the proliferation of other information, education and entertainment media may mean the *rightful* and *effective* place of books in our culture and society needs to be asserted'. This was not to be seen as a sentimental or nostalgic reaction against the relentless advance of information technology (IT) which, in some circumstances, might be preferred because of its cost-effectiveness and ease of use, but as a concerted promotion of the book where it remained the most suitable or effective medium. There could be no more opportune time to set up the Centre for the Book than when it could be housed in an imposing new building which would attract large numbers of visitors. Rix also outlined a prospective agenda. Only limited British Library resources could be allocated to the Centre, so future activities to a large extent depended on what outside funding could be raised. In addition to lectures, seminars, and exhibitions, a publishing programme was planned including an annual report which might eventually be recognized as a report on the general situation of books in British society ('In the Cause of Books', *British Book News*, May 1991:306–7).

Crump's 'The Centre for the Book', *English Today*, **8** (2), April 1992:3–8, gives further details of its proposed publishing programme:

> Prior to the opening of the new library the Centre will develop a number of information leaflets and databases for the general public. It is hoped to launch a monthly listing of book events throughout the country which will be available as a database and which can also be published if funding can be secured. The Centre will also, in co-operation with the Library's Education Officer, prepare a number of leaflets that support the exhibition galleries and give further information and short bibliographies of further reading on such subjects as binding and marbled paper.

Progress reports on developments at Bloomsbury and St Pancras, and peeps behind the scenes, appear in *London Services – Bloomsbury Newsletter*, an occasional publication first issued in summer 1991. 'St Pancras – The Building, Moves, Automation, Works of Art', *British Library*

News, **159**, August/September 1990, gives details of the 1996 completion phase and prints a diagrammatic map showing 13 identified locations. A series of 9.5cm x 21cm folded leaflets, opening into broadsheets, was published under the general title of *Moving The British Library* to inform readers how each stage would affect their use of the collections, but subsequently had to be withdrawn to avoid confusion arising from the successive delays. An amended version of *Information For Readers And Users* (December 1992) unfolded on the reverse side to a superb annotated plan of the St Pancras building, indicating the position of the reading rooms and the exhibition galleries. *A Visit To The British Library At St Pancras* is concerned with the entrance hall, the education service, the bookshop, and the exhibitions. A 15-minute video, *Moving The British Library*, was shown regularly in a seminar room off the King's Library at Bloomsbury and in the St Pancras Information Room at SRIS in Southampton Buildings. Updating of the video proved difficult when the uncertainties over the completion and opening dates were revealed.

OTHER MOVES
If the long-impending move of British Library's London reference collections inevitably tends to monopolize public and professional attention, another move – hardly less significant to staff uprooting their homes and families from London and the south-east to settle in Yorkshire – was successfully accomplished. It was after the government cuts in the Library's budgets announced in November 1988 that the British Library Board determined to effect worthwhile economies by relocating many of its London-based activities, involving 300 staff posts, to its 60-acre site at Boston Spa. Planning the move included the formation of a Relocation Unit within Central Administration to put into effect a policy of meeting staff concerns where possible.

For all the careful preparation and planning the move north in December 1990 and January 1991 proceeded amidst 'a certain amount of chaos, confusion, dislocation and disorientation [which] had to be overcome before it could be said that we were all happily resettled. Causes of wailing and gnashing of teeth included computer and network problems, mud, foul weather and domestic upheavals which made the usual Christmas traumas feel trifling' ('Record Supply In The Broad Acres', *BLAISE Records News*, **5**, Summer 1991:1).

Further rationalization of its London estate was effected by the transfer of Oriental Collections (OC) to join India Office Library and Records in Orbit House, near Waterloo, south of the Thames. A new purpose-designed reading room provided more space and facilities than the two former reading rooms combined; two floors were converted to staff accommodation; and air conditioning was installed for OC's rare books and manuscripts. The physical move was seen as a pilot project to test the microcomputer-based system devised by Ernst & Young, British Library's book move consultants for the move to St Pancras. It proved especially useful in testing the feasibility of moving books at the target rate of 500 crates a day to planned locations. Full details of the move, including a timetable of major milestones along the way, August 1990–April 1991, may be found in 'Move Into Orbit House Completed', *OIOC Newsletter*, **46**, Spring/Summer 1991:1–2.

The full story of a relocation of a major part of the Map Library's sheet map collection in the early months of 1990 – involving the removal and resiting of some 300,000 maps in sequence, housed in 464 mild steel cabinets and weighing 130 tons, from two sites in Soho (the third floor of Novello House, originally built as a warehouse for the music publishers in 1906; and Sheraton House, then accommodating the British Library's Central Administration) to three garages at the British Library repository at Micawber Street in Islington – is graphically told in James Elliot's 'The Logistics Of Moving A Map Collection', *LIBER Bulletin*, **37**, 1990:103–10. In the light of the British Library's experiences and planning for St Pancras, his concluding words demonstrate a vital truth:

> thorough planning of a move of this scale is essential, and that any plans must be flexible, easily understood and, above all, simple to operate. It is equally important to communicate your requirements and expectations to all involved in the operation as it is essential that everyone is aware of their exact responsibilities and the exact sequence of events. Finally, both operational staff and contractors should have ready access to a single individual whose clear responsibility is the supervision of the move as a whole, and who is in a position to resolve any unexpected problems as they arise.

2

POLICY DOCUMENTS

AUTOMATION STRATEGY

Outlining the changes and advances British Library would need to embark upon to fulfil its users' broadening expectations in the exploitation of its vast collections, *Automation Strategy* (1988, 31pp.) was the first of a series of policy documents issued in quick succession. Accepting that the quality of the Library's planning, and its skill in using IT, would be 'the essential vehicle by which services are provided as well as being crucial to internal support mechanisms', its automation strategy was inextricably linked to developing its future services. Since the publication of *Advancing with Knowledge* in 1985, a threefold advance had been made to clarify responsibilities and to assist in the formulation of a coherent plan for determining objectives, priorities and resources. The Directorate for Computing and Telecommunications was now responsible for the operation and development of the Library's telecommunications and mainframe computer systems, and for ensuring the availability and training of specialized staff with the appropriate knowledge and skills to co-ordinate the automation aspects of all Library projects.

Secondly, two library-wide committees had been established: the Automation Library Committee, responsible for operation co-ordination; and the Automation Planning Committee, to monitor ongoing plans and developments and to ensure corporate or interdivisional initiatives in problem areas. Thirdly, local automation plans had been drawn up in each separate Library division or department.

By embracing IT on a complete library-wide basis, the British Library was forced to take note of potential problems caused by its unique circumstances. Fortunately, automation was not an *ab initio* project. Various systems had been adopted in the Library's bibliographic and cataloguing services; in its information services; in document supply; in networking programmes; and in its administrative, management inform-ation, and preservation support systems. Not so fortunately, the pattern of development had been uneven, not all the systems in use were compat-ible, and in some areas – notably the provision of OPACs – the Library was less advanced than it might have hoped.

British Library's future strategy for automation, designed to respond flexibly and rapidly to changing service demands, is outlined in detail. The main aim in reader services is to provide users in the Library's St Pancras and other buildings with OPAC terminals, linked at St Pancras with an automated book request information system, and allowing entry into the 12 most heavily used catalogues of the London-based collec-tions. This would depend on the conversion of the catalogues to machine-readable form; the development and application of appropriate data creation standards; and the development of the necessary automated systems so that readers might easily access the catalogues.

Because of the integration of catalogue access, information services, and document supply, there was at Boston Spa considerable potential for providing high-value, rapid-response services by exploiting developments such as the availability of full-text digitized video disc and CD-ROM stor-age, and improvements to fax and telecommunication networks. In Acquisitions and Cataloguing priority would be given to serials acquis-ition control and its data structure. Catalogue records would increasingly hold details of the item's preservation status, its availability in other media, and its precise location in the collections.

To finance the Library's automation plans, an increased level of resources would be called for, but in the event the wide-ranging strategy was effectively scuppered by the lack of additional government funding, even though such investment would eventually be recovered through sig-nificant savings in operating costs. A much reduced plan was initially funded from the Library's existing resources. A new automation strategy is expected to be published in 1994.

GATEWAY TO KNOWLEDGE

In September 1988 the *Bookseller* contrived to scoop the world by pub-lishing what was described as an edited report of a special meeting of the British Library Board held behind closed doors at Trinity College, Oxford, on 23–24 June ('British Library 2000', *Bookseller*, **994**, 9 September 1988:994–8). The so-called 'report' is in fact no more than unedited minutes; it cannot be contemplated for a moment that British Library would allow a document to reach the public eye whose second sentence reads: 'The library must avoid uncritical acceptance of the government ethos; nor must it allow Mrs Thatcher to be the Jorkins to our Spenlow.' Even in this leaked guise it must have caused acute embarrassment.

Notwithstanding its dubious status, the *Bookseller* report accurately foreshadows the content of *Gateway to Knowledge: The British Library Strategic Plan 1989–1994* (April 1989, 35pp.) published four years after its first strategic plan *Advancing with Knowledge*, which stated the Library's central aim, its functional objectives, and its key strategies. In this new document the Library nailed its colours firmly to the mast with a Declaration of Purpose:

> The British Library has to be a leader – for the cause of books and for the love of learning, for other libraries and for information services.
>
> The statutory basis of the British Library, the range and strength of its collections and services and its ultimate responsibility for preserving the written record of the British people enable and require it to pursue initiatives on behalf of libraries and their users.
>
> The new British Library building at St Pancras will be a declaration of the continuing importance to the cultural and economic well-being of our society of the printed word; of the spirit of humane and liberal inquiry which guided our predecessors; of the application of modern methods and media to the communication of information and ideas; of discovery, invention, scholarship and research.
>
> Our purpose is to advance knowledge;
>
>> to give ready access to our collections and to other significant collections and databases;
>>
>> to pursue and promote research about the collection, preservation, communication and exploitation of knowledge.
>
> To this end we must:
>
>> know our users' needs and make our collections and services widely known;
>>
>> build and preserve our collections, particularly of British material, and provide accurate and timely catalogue records;
>>
>> cultivate co-operation with others, in the public and private sectors, both in this country and abroad;

be enterprising and expert, alert to new opportunities, new ways and new technologies.

As a cultivated expression of the 'vision-thing' this could hardly be bettered.

The decision to publish a new plan was prompted by the fact that, whilst British Library's aims and objectives had remained essentially unchanged since 1985, circumstances had drastically altered. In planning the occupation of St Pancras the time had come 'to extend the Library's planning horizon from the date of first occupation to the end of the century, and to consider the pattern of services we shall offer during the 1990s' (para. 1.2.1, p.7). Secondly, the government had introduced a programme of three-year funding and a requirement for quinquennial spending plans and performance targets. *Advancing with Knowledge* had been drawn up in the expectation of level funding; *Gateway to Knowledge* in the context of government policy to reduce the real value of the annual grant-in-aid in the early 1990s – and, quite possibly, for a longer period still. Anticipated salary increases and continuing rises in book and serial prices would severely heighten the Library's budgeting difficulties.

British Library perceived the major theme of this second strategic plan to be 'the conviction that the Library exists to serve a community of users, and that it must be seen to be making a contribution to the wealth and to the cultural and educational well-being of that community'. Associated themes discerned were the notion of a service-oriented library crucially dependent on its staff's skills, energy, and commitment; co-operation with other institutions in the straightened circumstances currently prevailing to derive maximum value from national resources; and a working philosophy that revenue-earning activities should be managed and priced effectively to earn a profit without detriment to the Library's users.

Progress since *Advancing with Knowledge* appeared was reviewed. The planning assumptions underpinning the earlier document – namely, the growth in demand for information; the emphasis on tradeable information; and the advances in IT – were generally proved to have been correct. Much as expected, 'British Library's central position in the UK library network has been reinforced by the difficulties caused to other libraries by public sector financial constraints . . . The demand for services from the British Library . . . is therefore rising at a time when its own resources too are under constraint' (para. 2.1.2, p.9). Not least, the importance of a more formal approach to planning and appraisal was underlined by the government's philosophy of continual and long-term financial accountability. The progress review ends with a long series of 'action points' demonstrating the activities that mark the intervening period since *Advancing with Knowledge* was published. These are chronicled at length later in this book.

How British Library perceived its pattern of services in the year 2000 occupies the next section. From Boston Spa and St Pancras the Library would offer an integrated service based on a single collection and a number of national and international co-operative schemes. An improved service to scholars and researchers in the sciences and humanities, and to information specialists in business and industry; a growing range of value-added information services offering data analysis; and a swifter and more comprehensive external document supply service aided by new technology are all planned. Comprehensive access to knowledge rather than the comprehensive nature of the Library's own collections is the keynote strategy of the 1990s.

A diagram of three concentric rings illustrates the pattern of services to be in operation at the end of the decade. At the core is the delivery of books and documents from the Library's own collections; around this core is a ring of services offering guidance to the less experienced user, help with the catalogues, and referral to other libraries. On the outer circle are more specialized value-added or premium services, including bibliographies and reading lists; book- and subject-based enquiries; external database searches; and a loan, photocopy, or electronic document delivery service from other libraries. This pattern of service is regarded as an essential dividend on the huge investment the St Pancras library represents. Moreover, it would be obligatory for the information services to scholarship and invention in the United Kingdom to match those provided in competitor countries.

So much for the vision; what of the resources needed to translate it into reality? Two financial chapters examine British Library's strategy to overcome the probable fall in real terms of the annual grant-in-aid at a time when extra resources would need to be found in the run-up to St Pancras, notably for the new technology to be installed. The Library contended that 'the exceptional costs of planning and executing the move into St Pancras building should be met in full by the Government. They should be regarded as a relatively modest but essential part of the investment in the new project' (para. 9.3.2, p.33). Perhaps as a measure of desperation to ensure continued government support, the Library volunteered to find from its own resources, as part of its ongoing operations, the £13 million estimated to be the cost over a five-year period of an identified range of basic computer applications.

To accommodate this extra expenditure firm priorities would have to be identified, especially in the acquisitions and preservation budgets. Even as a short-term expedient this would crucially diminish the quality of the collections and almost certainly lead to a decline in public services. Some leeway would be gained from a financial and budgeting efficiency drive encompassing a rationalization of the use of the Library's buildings in London, a relocation of a number of activities from London to Boston Spa, and savings arising from the implementation of the Enright Review of Acquisitions and Retention Policies.

The irony of building a massive new library costing an astronomical sum whilst simultaneously cutting back acquisitions and services was not lost on the press. Robert Hewison unerringly put his finger on the crucial point: *Gateway to Knowledge* had only one reader in mind, the Prime Minister: 'Not only the last major public building project of the 20th century, it is also the biggest. And all the money for construction has come from Mrs Thatcher's Treasury.' He concluded: 'This, rather than the Channel Tunnel, will be Mrs Thatcher's monument . . . it will reflect the flaws in her policies as well as her achievements. As the library's strategic plan makes clear, what the government is giving with one hand, it is also undermining with the other' ('A bad case of overbooking', *The Sunday Times*, **8592**, 16 April 89:C7).

A further chapter surveys developments in the services provided for specific reader groups. Although committed to the provision of basic library services at no charge to the user, a review of pricing policy had defined three categories of service:

(a) services charged at less than full cost: those wholly supported by grant-in-aid (i.e. free of charge) and those partially supported by grant-in-aid;
(b) services priced to recover full costs; and
(c) services expected to generate a surplus.

High on the agenda was the question of introducing charges for admission to the reading rooms:

Taking into account the principle of free access; the likely influence of British Library policy on other libraries; the Minister's firm intention to maintain free access to the public libraries; the likely financial benefits and the administrative costs of imposing charges, the Board has concluded that the financial benefit to the Library would be insufficient to warrant breaching the tradition of free access (para. 5.4.1, p.18).

Ominously, the Board signalled its intention to review this issue in four or five years' time. It continued to exercise wide indignation.

Unease again surfaced early in 1992 when David Lister, Arts Correspondent of *The Independent* newspaper, quoted a British Library spokesman as saying, 'We are looking at the total charging and pricing policy and admission comes into it . . . the nub of the problem is: should you charge readers for the basic business of going into the reading room?' (*The Independent*, **1671**, 25 February 92:3). A firm 'No' was entered by Fiona Draper, Chairman of the British Library Trade Union Side, who very reasonably pointed out that 'the taxpayer has paid for the collections in the library and should not have to pay again for access to them' (*The Independent*, **1673**, 27 February 1992). This, of course, was not entirely accurate but the point was valid: according to its *Nineteenth Annual Report 1991–92*, British Library had swallowed up nearly £64 million from the taxpayers' purse in that year alone.

An opposing view was expressed by David Adamson, a regular user, who argued that an annual fee of £40 for an entry card, and smaller sums for daily and weekly tickets, 'would provide the library with some extra revenue but, more importantly, they would give readers a stronger moral right to protest against slowness, inefficiency, inadequate opening hours and other failings in the service' (*The Independent*, **1675**, 29 February 92:13). After its summer meeting the Board endorsed its policy of not charging for admission but stated its intention of discussing it again once the St Pancras building was opened. Readers with a touch of cynicism in their make-up have subsequently been reassured on the grounds that this event is likely to arrive this year . . . next year . . . sometime . . .

A constant thread woven throughout *Gateway to Knowledge* is an acknowledgement that the Library could no longer fulfil its traditional role in the national library system on its own resources. Put another way, its ambitions had long outstripped its means. References to sponsorship, joint funding, private sector involvement in the publishing programme, collaboration with other institutions in research projects, are all evidence of this harsh reality. Nowhere is this more obvious than in its plans for collection development and management:

> Our long-term strategy is to work with others to achieve comprehensive access to recorded knowledge. In the next five years we shall be obliged to spend less on adding to and caring for the collection, but we shall seek to make progress both in the better organisation and exploitation of our own resources, and in co-operative arrangements with other libraries. This means that we shall build on the strengths

we already have; and we shall make clear the areas where we shall expect others, better placed than ourselves, to carry the central collecting responsibility. (para. 6.1.1, p.24)

The torrent of copyright material received under the legal deposit regulations was to the forefront of the Library's attention. Its uncritical acceptance was a prime concern of the Enright Review of Acquisitions and Retention Policies whose report had not yet been published. At this stage British Library confined itself to a statement that it would be giving early consideration to its recommendations in consultation with others concerned.

Significant changes to traditional British Library practices were reported: all its collections were now treated as a single entity; duplicates in specific fields had been reduced, and certain other material, previously held for reference only, was now made available for loan when necessary. In the humanities the primary aim remained the development of the collection of English-language material. For foreign material most emphasis would be on high-quality research material published in Eastern and Western Europe and in the Orient. Further efforts would be made to apply a common stock principle to the scientific and business collections at the Document Supply Centre (DSC) and SRIS. Here, too, economies would need to be adroitly managed to avoid potential long-term damage to the national document supply operation or to the science reference collection.

In the field of catalogue record creation three key strategies were propounded to reorganize and restructure catalogue procedures in an effort to arrive at an effective balance between resources, workload, and users' requirements; to modify record content and format favourable to the British Library's largely automated interactive systems; and to develop the national bibliographic service in the light of changes in record design and the changing information environment. A centralized acquisitions, processing and record creation directorate for all UK copyright and overseas English-language material would be located at Boston Spa although a subsidiary unit would remain in London where language skills were available.

Staff development was given a sharper profile in this second strategic plan than in the first: the section devoted to it largely derives from an internal document, *Into The 1990s: Staff Development and Training in The British Library* (Central Training Unit, April 1989, 41pp.). The required scholarly, managerial, specialist, and entrepreneurial skills would be recruited and developed within the Library's overall philosophy of service provision to the research and information community and would be based on a structured liaison between line managers, trainers, and employees. British Library's previous *laissez-faire* approach to staff development and the lack of clear organizational targets had left it seriously short of essential skills.

British Library predicted that flexible working conditions might help in recruiting and retaining staff. Full discussion would be held with the trade union side: 'our goal will be to ensure that staff as well as the Library derive maximum benefit from any changes' (para. 7.8, p.29) but friction between management and staff, surfacing in the ensuing months, was to cause difficulties, leading eventually to a restriction of services and a shortening of opening hours in the Bloomsbury reading rooms.

If, as one commentator had remarked, the true purpose of *Advancing with Knowledge* had been to alert the government to the fact that economies would only go so far, and that if a truly effective service to science and industry were required then it had to be adequately resourced, its successor can only be interpreted as a forthright and well-argued reminder, less confident in tone, more anxious, more defensive. Hard choices would have to be made and, in one sense, *Gateway to Knowledge* is a determined, last-minute attempt to ensure that these choices would not be impossibly difficult.

SELECTION FOR SURVIVAL
In 1987, as part of its ongoing planning processes, the British Library invited Dr Brian Enright, Librarian of the University of Newcastle upon Tyne, to conduct an internal review of its acquisition and retention policies. The specific terms of reference were:

(1) to review the priorities which underlie existing policies on both the acquisition and the permanent retention of material in the collections of the British Library;
(2) to consider the case for, and the implications of, a revision of these priorities;
(3) to consider the case for and against imposing a ceiling on the growth of British Library stock devoted to lending (i.e. document supply), having regard both to the service and revenue of the British Library and to the cost-effectiveness of UK libraries generally; and
(4) to consider the development of 'common stock' (i.e. material serving both reference and lending functions) which any ceiling on the growth of lending stock might require.

The review team consisted of Enright and two British Library Project Officers, Lotte Hellinga and Beryl Leigh. Their report, *Selection For Survival: A Review of Acquisition and Retention Policies* (104pp.) was published in the autumn of 1989.

In effect the Enright review was questioning the fundamental objectives of the national library, traditionally accepted as the provision of historical and current research material encompassing, but not necessarily limited to, all academic disciplines and the bibliographic control and retention of the national current printed output acquired through legal deposit. These two disparate but related functions were potentially irreconcilable in times of financial constraint. The team defined its contribution as 'the identification of a series of massive mismatches between current acquisition and retention policies, accepted practices and expectations, and . . . the extent of the mismatch between national resource provision for the British Library and the claims made on it both by existing collections and by current acquisition and retention liabilities and obligations'. At this period in its history it would be 'prudent for the Library itself to identify and assess crucial problems rather than be subjected to the arbitrary imposition of unsuitable remedies from outside, with external or governmental agencies setting the agenda for reshaping the Library and its future'. Moreover, it seemed likely that 'additional resources necessary to maintain the collections and services will be more forthcoming, together with sustained public interest, if convincing evidence is available from within the organisation of cogent and realistic analysis of policy options and firm control of priorities for expenditure' (para. 1.3, p.3).

Priorities underlying existing acquisition and retention policies, and their current practice, reflected not only the Library's perception of its users' present and future needs but also long-standing public expectations that it would acquire all British and most overseas publications of research interest, that it would hold extensive manuscript collections, that business and industry's needs would be met, and that heritage items would be extensively held and frequently displayed.

Recent H&SS development plans indicated the broad strategies to be followed to fulfil its primary role as the major repository of national heritage material by acquiring appropriate items through legal deposit, donation, and purchase. Since 1988 H&SS had been active in promoting the Conspectus system, which 'enables libraries to record and compare quantified data on the strength of their collections and collecting practices in particular subjects. It serves both as an information file and as a basis for collaborative collection development' (Stephen Hangar, 'Collection development in the British Library', *Journal of Librarianship*, **19** (2), April 1987:89–107). H&SS retention policy centred round preservation, which in the past five years had switched away from expensive techniques to more emphasis on microfilming, boxing, furbishing, and deferred conservation, with greater selectivity in the more expensive processes of conservation and first binding. Because of its national archival responsibilities for legal deposit material H&SS had no formal policy on deselection or dispersal. Massive amounts of official publications acquired by exchange from 1950 to 1980 would not have satisfied current selection criteria but there was no methodology or existing process by which unwanted publications could be discarded.

At DSC acquisition policy was 'driven by the UK demand from research, higher educational and industrial organisations for recorded information, mostly in the form of printed material, printed throughout the world'. Accordingly DSC collections included an extensive set of research-level English-language books, conference proceedings, doctoral dissertations, official publications, and reports; an extensive collection of music scores; and a selective collection of foreign-language books and theses. No general retention policy had ever been formulated at DSC, which was totally geared to the acquisition and supply of a wide range of material to satisfy the major proportion (i.e. 85%) of user requests from its own resources. Duplicates were periodically weeded on an *ad hoc* basis dictated by space problems but DSC had no sophisticated case data to allow systematic disposal.

To meet the needs of scientific and technological research, and of business and industry, SRIS acquired literature on all branches of science and technology at postgraduate and technical innovation levels relevant to current research and development. In the field of business information, publications for the practitioner were acquired rather than those on business practice theory. Serials at the appropriate level were acquired as comprehensively as the budget allowed, regardless of language. Material more than 50 years old was not generally acquired although older material received through legal deposit was retained. Historical circumstances prevailing before the collections were incorporated into British Library had bequeathed a tradition of deselecting materials, but no large-scale deselection or transfer had occurred in recent years.

Retention strategy outlined in *Advancing with Knowledge* had been limited to a corporate plan involving 'selective and clear formulation of priorities coupled with the choice of the most cost-effective method'; to the development of co-operative programmes of microfilming; and to increasing the national awareness of the urgent need for preservation. Current pressures affecting policy included the diminishing acquisition and preservation budgets and accommodation limitations: 'On present projections made by H&SS and SRIS the space available in London at St Pancras and the outhouse store in Micawber Street would be full by the year 2002, i.e. within ten years of the first moves to the new site.' At Boston Spa the long-term prospect was no better with space for the expansion of monograph holdings until the year 2000 and for serial growth until 2008. It was imperative that the British Library made the most effective use of its storage space and that its retention policies were well argued and defensible.

Almost 20 formal recommendations, both general and specific, regarding acquisition and retention policies were listed. A more corporate approach was urged: 'a collection development statement should be drawn up; it should be made publicly available, should be reviewed on a regular basis, and enter into considerably more detail than the statements in Gateway to Knowledge'. Existing acquisition policy statements should be concentrated and the priorities for the various divisions included. Preservation priorities and policies for stock reassessment, relegation to reserve stores, common stock holding, and disposal should also be indicated. A guide to selection should be produced for internal use to heighten awareness of policies and practices in each department and a regular programme of case studies focusing on particular types of stock or specific subject areas should be introduced. A common stock policy should be pursued to reduce the acquisition of certain classes of current material to one copy to support all services in order to slow down the increase in overall storage space requirements.

DSC should review its intake of Russian science and technology monographs; review unselected intake through Booknet, and establish selection criteria; organize the systematic weeding of duplicated serials and monographs and, as the opportunity arose, of material which would not be acquired under current selection criteria; and introduce a scheme for reassessment of all newly acquired serials within an appropriate timescale. Retention policies should be developed taking into consideration categories of stock: where a copy for reference should be retained, categories where common stock would suffice, and categories of unique holdings where disposal might be considered. For SRIS the recommendations were that it should consider methods of reassessing non-current stock for retention, relegation to store, or disposal, and develop retention priorities.

Recommendations relating to H&SS were that it should consider methods of developing subject priorities, allocate curatorial staff with responsibility for preservation selection, develop retention priorities, urgently reassess the policy of retaining all of the unselected (often uncatalogued) collections of official publications outhoused at Woolwich, set a timetable for decisions to be made, and urgently reassess the policy of retaining on British Library premises material housed in a closed store scheduled to be vacated (this refers to collections such as Hong Kong colonial copyright material in Chinese which would not be added to stock).

In any normal library these recommended housekeeping practices would be regarded as part of the customary library routine and it might appear that the Library had been unusually remiss in not introducing them years earlier. But the British Library is not a normal library: each of its disparate constituent libraries had its own traditions, purposes, and practices. The sheer size and proportions of its activities; the fact that it had had a corporate existence of only 16 years when *Selection For Survival* was published; and the fact that for most of that time it had been hugely preoccupied with the shifting fortunes and progress of its new home – all these were powerful factors preventing and hindering a comprehensive acquisition and retention policy which, in any case, would require staff resources on a scale the British Library was in no position to allocate. In addition there is the Library's biggest acquisition headache of all – the annual torrent of books and serials incessantly flooding into the Copyright Receipt Office (CRO).

This most intractable of problems had surfaced in the spring of 1988 when it was announced that the Enright team had produced an interim report: 'A major concern is the huge volume of material arriving every day under the legal deposit arrangements . . . although there is no initial purchase cost the Library has to process, catalogue, store and preserve these items, which involves a considerable financial investment over the lifetime of any individual title.' In 1986 the daily number of titles received at the CRO was 200; by 1993 it was expected to rise to 300. 'The Review asks whether all the items currently deposited are appropriate for the national library's collection. A second point concerns the wisdom of all six deposit libraries acquiring and retaining such material at a time when there is such pressure on resources' ('Review Of Acquisition Policies: An Interim Report', *British Library News*, **136**, April 1988:1). The battlelines had been drawn.

Enright and his colleagues acknowledged CRO's practical difficulties:

it suffered from 'a long history of successive moves, of low staffing levels, of being a complex organisation dependent on other equally complex
institutions, and in its turn of direct influence on all divisions of the
British Library' (para. 5.3, p.39). Routine material that passed through its
hands was dealt with capably enough, but its overall efficiency was
impaired by the non-receipt of a considerable amount of material which
should have been deposited, necessitating up to 8,000 items a year having to be claimed, and, conversely, the receipt of a great number of titles
not required to be deposited – mainly reprints and second or subsequent
editions containing no substantially new material. Libraries receiving
materials deposited under the Copyright Act were not obliged to keep
them for ever: 'it has, however, been generally accepted that such materials are held indefinitely, and there is a widespread expectation that the
Library will continue to do so'. But, 'if this expectation is to be fulfilled,
copyright material must be subject to preservation programmes', and 'a
differentiation should be made between materials which the Act required
to be deposited, and materials which have been accepted without such
requirement' (para. 5.4.5, pp.41–4).

The review's recommendations concerning legal deposit acquisitions
and retentions were headed by an observation that 'the establishment of a
centralised British Library processing unit will cause a complete change
of course for CRO: the opportunity should be taken not only for reorganisation, but also for thinking through the principles behind the organisation'. (The CRO was renamed the Legal Deposit Office and based on
two locations – Colindale for newspapers and Boston Spa for all other
publications – with effect from January 1991.) Improved staff resourcing
was recommended to allow for an intensive operation claiming unde-
posited items from publishers, the selection and rejection of material
according to clear guidelines, and the disposal of duplicates and unwanted items. In recognition of the constant pressure on the British
Library's human and spatial resources, 'continuing contact should be
maintained with the other Copyright Libraries in order to work out a joint
strategy in the national interest, to pool resources in claiming and possibly to pool responsibilities for archiving and lending in particular areas'.

Although *Selection For Survival* was published in the late autumn of
1989, the press had sight of it when it was presented to the British
Library Board. Comment focused immediately on the possibility that the
Library would no longer automatically retain every book it received.
Martin Bailey's 'British Library to cut back book stock', *Observer*, 2
July 1989:3, dived straight in: 'The British Library is to stop collecting

every book published in this country, ending a practice which dates back more than three centuries.'

With the advantage of having a day or two more in which to study the document, *The Independent* devoted an editorial to it which showed evidence of detailed reading: 'the proposals have met with some indignation, but there is a suspicion that they form one prong of the British Library's campaign to enlist public support . . . to warn of possible cutbacks in the stock is one way of encouraging the public to denounce the Government for parsimony and want of cultivation'. It concluded: 'perhaps it really is the case that the boom in publications is making the idea of a copyright library unworkable. If so, we will have a literary culture which can no longer manage its own product.' But, it continued, 'if there is still a case for full representation – and the very technologies behind the proliferation can presumably store them too – then no one should argue about shelf space' ('Snarl-up at the library', *Independent*, **852**, 4 July 1989:16). Later in the week the *Daily Telegraph* talked of vans discharging their avalanches of cargo, 'over 2,000 a week, eight miles a year, or putting it another way, stacking up on end to a height of 42,000 ft', and asked, 'does the National Memory really need an annual book mountain higher than Everest?' (Ivor Rowan, 'Slimming down the volume of work', *Daily Telegraph*, **41691**, 8 July 1989:13).

The Times took a realistic long-term view, acknowledging that the British Library was facing difficult decisions on how to move away from its policy of maintaining a comprehensive collection of books published in Britain: 'With 62,000 volumes now being published in Britain every year (expected to reach 100,000 by the end of the century) as well as 300,000 newspapers, journals and pamphlets, the library is reeling beneath the load.' If this were not problem enough, 'the swift deterioration of modern paper confronts staff with a daunting task of maintenance. It is now said to cost an average of £50 to catalogue each work and £1 a year to keep it (almost literally) in good shape.' Although the Library's options remained open, the acquisitions and retentions report could lead to only one conclusion: 'the library must reduce the rate of increase'. Meeting the implications head on, *The Times'* remarkably well-informed leader writer continued:

> The tradition of retaining every dot and comma that is published in the country every year is not quite as old as is commonly supposed. Though laid down by law in 1662, it was not fully practised until the 19th century. In fact the intake is still not complete, if only because of the inefficiency of those responsible for submitting a free copyright copy'.

Alternative ways out of the impasse included the rejection of unaltered editions of books already on the shelves – 'there is a limit to the number of copies of *Black Beauty* which the library should bequeath to the nation's heirs'; sharing the burden with the other copyright libraries; and, most controversial of all, deciding not to retain certain material at all, a policy that would not be entirely dispute free: 'the needs of sociologists (every last work in imitation of Barbara Cartland) are different from the needs of critics (every last emendation of even the most obscure poet' ('A Question Of Bookkeeping', *The Times*, **63454**, 24 July 1989:17).

An authoritative commentary by one of the British Library review team, Lotte Hellinga's 'The British Library's Policies on Legal Deposit', pp.33–7 in *Gutenberg-Jahrbuchs 1991*, poses three questions currently preoccupying the copyright libraries:

(1) is it possible to arrive at a division of responsibilities on a national basis without infringing on the rights of each institution?
(2) is there a possibility of areas of specialisation for peripheral materials in particular institutions?
(3) would it be possible to establish policy priorities for the preservation of legal deposit material, if not for its acquisition?

Although it is too early to expect answers, Hellinga expresses satisfaction that the questions are at least being faced.

A balanced review article in *Alexandria. The Journal of National and International Library and Information Issues* perceived *Selection For Survival* as of threefold importance:

> as a model for the kind of enquiry that contributes to strategic planning; as a report on current policy, practice and problems of the British Library, providing an agenda for discussion, both within the library itself and in the wider arena which provides the funding and the users of the library; and as an epitome of the influence of tradition.

A peculiarly sombre note is struck: 'given the financial basis of the library, the national government will expect some action, and could well see this document as giving scope for further reductions in financial support' (Geoffrey Ford, 'Review of *Selection For Survival*', *Alexandria*, **3** (2), August 1991:121–5). Of course, only a government possessed of an ideologically narrow vision could see in this document cogent reasons for reducing the library's grant-in-aid, so perhaps this bizarre observation was not entirely beyond the bounds of reason.

Within the library and information profession the impact of *Selection*

For Survival was so pronounced that the National Acquisitions Group organized a two-day meeting at the Josiah Mason Hall, Birmingham, in November 1990, to consider its implications. Edited by Clare Jenkins and Mary Morley, the papers presented at this important seminar were published under the title of *Survival of the fittest? Collection management implications of the British Library Review of acquisition and retention policies* (Loughborough National Acquisitions Group, 1991, 107pp.). Michael Smethurst's 'RARP: an overview' was the keynote paper.

After considering the reaction to the review in the press, and amongst librarians of the copyright libraries – who feared that it would spark off a publishers' campaign to repeal the 1911 Copyright Act – this paper presented a grand survey of British Library's acquisition policies, exposed a number of myths surrounding them, and underlined the constraints within which they operated. Over 50 problem areas had been identified which had to be tackled if the Library were to move from mechanistic collection management to collection management based on meeting users' needs. Confirming that the review's recommendations were being taken seriously, 16 of those problem areas had been listed as urgent. The paper ended with the statement that the British Library:

> is not in the business of diminishing or weakening its own or the nation's valuable stock of materials: it is looking for more cost-effective solutions than the present haphazard arrangements for achieving a more effective library service . . . it is essentially in the business of seeking to ensure positive retention of that which is valuable, and full access to that material (p.14).

It was announced early in 1991 that British Library, after consultation with its partners in the newly formed Copyright Libraries Working Group on Legal Deposit, was preparing to ask Parliament to extend the categories of material exempt from the need for automatic deposit. Material in the following categories would henceforward be taken selectively or not at all: colouring and fill-in books; puzzle books; diaries; stationery; press releases; programmes of public events (without editorial matter); paper dress patterns; cut-out and press-out books; examination papers; toys; computer tapes or disks which are only incidental to the printed publication; and printed matter not intended for the public and of interest primarily to members, employees, shareholders, or customers.

In November 1990 DSC issued a four-page A4 leaflet, *Acquisitions Policy At The Document Supply Centre*, enabling its customers 'to identify the very broad range of material which is currently purchased'. This was followed in October 1992 by *The Collections Portfolio*, a series of illustrated A4 leaflets lodged in an attractive laminated folder, concerning the different types of material currently held at DSC – for example, serials, report literature, UK local government publications, indicating the breadth and scope of the collections. These are to be updated as the collections grow. Further evidence that the post-Enright British Library was beginning to take shape came in Brian Lang's 'The Future Of The British Library', *London Services – Bloomsbury Newsletter*, 5, Winter 1992:1–2, where it was confirmed that the British Library was adopting a corporate approach to collection management in order to make the best use of its resources and to improve services. By the year 2000, when 13.3 million items will be held in the London collections and seven million at Boston Spa, a single copy of an item will be used to support both document supply and reference functions whenever possible and practicable. The Library will have appropriate technology in place to allow accurate recording of use so that for the first time the collections will be able to be managed effectively and continuously.

FOR SCHOLARSHIP, RESEARCH AND INFORMATION

For scholarship, research and innovation. Strategic objectives for the year 2000 (May 1993, 39pp.) was described to the press by the Library's Chief Executive as 'a bold and imaginative look at the Library's services, responsibilities and relationship with the global library and information network'. In contrast to the reception of British Library's two previous strategic plans, press reaction was muted; perhaps the endless comment on the Library's continual trials and tribulations had sated editorial interest, although it has to be said that this latest document was longer on hopes and aspirations and shorter on expectations than its two predecessors. Specifically, 'financial uncertainties remain, particularly with respect to Government funding, and we may have to extend our timescales for reaching our goals'. By now this was an all too familiar and depressing refrain but one which had been forced on the Library not simply by its determination not to compromise on its main strategic objectives, but by prolonged government indecision and by its doling out the cash in dribs and drabs, making long-term planning a hazardous exercise fraught with disastrous confusion. 'If only the Government had just given us a sack of fivers and told us to get on with it', a member of staff murmured disconsolately, 'we could have done the job in half the time'.

Like *Advancing with Knowledge*, and *Gateway to Knowledge*, *For scholarship, research and innovation* was primarily concerned with extracting sufficient government resources to enable the Library to achieve its targets: 'if the Library is to provide the services which are expected of the national library, the necessary investment must be made to develop the collections and to keep abreast of technological advances in the delivery of those services. Moreover improvements in the net contribution from our priced services and the Library's cost- effectiveness will depend on this investment' ('Chief Executive's introduction', pp.5+7). The objectives the Library will 'work towards' in the period 1993–2000 are six in number:

(1) establishing a single library and operating a single collection, based on two main sites;
(2) restoring the acquisitions and preservation budgets;
(3) maximizing access to services through the full use of new technology on site and over electronic networks to other major library networks and users;
(4) ensuring the Library remains a world centre for the capture, storage and transmission of electronic documents;
(5) developing a programme of exhibitions to widen access to the collections; and
(6) acting as leader in the development of library systems and services.

'The British Library Statement Of Purpose' (p.9) bears roughly the same message as the 'Declaration of Purpose' printed in *Gateway to Knowledge*, but in less resonant, more mundane sort of tones, conscious of the buffeting it had experienced in the intervening period:

> The British Library, through its incomparable collections, is the world's leading national research library. We have expert staff and we give ready access to our collections in our reading rooms and by remote supply.

> Our function is to serve scholarship, research and enterprise. Our purpose is to promote the advance of knowledge through the communication of information and ideas.

> We celebrate and interpret our rich and varied collections to encourage the broadest possible awareness and accessibility of the nation's recorded heritage.

> To achieve this:
> we identify and respond to our users' needs for a national library service;

we build, catalogue and conserve the collections;
we provide entry to the world's knowledge base;
we provide leadership and initiate cooperative programmes for the
national and international research library community; and
we exploit our collections in enterprising ways to raise support for our
activities.

We are committed to maintaining our position of leadership by
embracing innovative, cost-effective and flexible methods of working.

This is not so much a clarion call, more an assurance that the Library is
doing its best in difficult circumstances.

The main text is divided into Service supply; Collections; Leadership,
partnership, and co-operation; Scholarship; Staff development; Information technology; Estates; and Finance sections. An annex outlines service
delivery targets and remote document supply and reading room services.
Ample 'we shalls' and 'we shall continues' pervade 'Service supply', but
buried within its prolixities, nuggets of hard fact and information can be
mined. There is a firm intention to invest in the Library's cataloguing
infrastructure, to complete the automation of cataloguing and processing
in order to improve access to the collections and to worldwide databases.
'This access may be controlled, and may be subject to charges, but it will
be comprehensively available' (para. 8, p.16). Plans to supply information
to remote users as fast as possible will 'depend critically on our ability to
negotiate rights with publishers to enable the electronic document storage
and transmission techniques to be exploited' (para. 17, p.17).

> The development of improved access to international networks and
> the simultaneous development of new carriers for information remove
> many of the obstacles traditionally associated with a library's ability
> to select and interpret information for its users . . . but if the Library is
> to be fully competitive in the volatile world market for such services it
> needs to seek partners from the private sector and from other organi-
> sations, both to share the capital risk and to ensure valid commercial
> assessments of the market opportunities. The Library will seek to
> develop new partnerships to improve its capability to create new
> priced services (para. 21, pp.17+19).

As for the St Pancras reading room with its extremely modest 6.5%
increase in the number of readers' seats, a note of acute realism is injected: 'with the opening of the new Library and the introduction of
improved services, any significant relaxation of criteria for admission is

likely to result in overcrowding. Admission to the reading rooms will therefore be based on need to use the collection' (para. 10, p.16).

Since the publication of *Selection For Survival* in 1989 its recommendation that 'continuing contact should be maintained with the other Copyright Libraries in order to work out a joint strategy in the national interest, to pool resources in claiming and possibly to pool responsibilities for archiving and lending in particular areas' (p.44) has hardened into:

> In cooperation with the UK copyright libraries, we shall seek to ensure comprehensive coverage, recording and preservation of UK and Irish publications in all subject fields. We shall also work with the public library authorities to improve the capture, retention and accessibility of local publications . . . The Library will be increasingly selective in its retention policies, through the development of cooperative retention schemes with the copyright libraries under which there will be a shared responsibility for the retention of popular low-use literature (para. 36, p.21).

As for the rest, it is a case of a series of 'we shall maintains' apart from a plan 'to establish the Library as a major world centre for the storage and transmission of digital texts required for research and scholarship. We shall seek to establish service-driven programmes for collection and preservation of digital material and digitisation of other material and shall invest in the necessary technical infrastructure' (para. 43, p.24).

A corporate approach to collection management devised to make the best use of a single copy for both reference and document supply depended on 'planned development programmes for network services and for the digitisation, storage and transmission of digital texts' (para. 45, p.24). 'A conceptual framework for managing the Library's collection, particularly in the location and preservation of stock, within broad date spans' provides three definitions of material: 'current stock to support the core services of reference and document supply, older material from all sources which supports the function of the Library as an international archive of research material, and "heritage" material' (para. 46, p.25). To strengthen the concept of British Library operating from two sites, a single unified finding list of the Library's mainstream printed books and serial stock will be created. Basic stock control records, location and availability information, and value-added enhancements to subsets of records to meet specialized service requirements, will all be incorporated. In what format the new finding list will appear is not vouchsafed.

A statement of intent to restore the value of the Library's preservation budget to an appropriate level by the year 2000, a list of priorities in spending it, and a reminder that the new building at St Pancras will protect the collections there against harmful environmental factors, occupy the preservation section. 'Leadership, Partnership and Cooperation' makes it clear that:

> the Library is unlikely to have sufficient resources, particularly for investment, to realise by its own efforts every potential development for new services during the decade. Indeed, in many instances it will be highly desirable that developments should be collaborative, since partnership offers a means of integrating the strengths of the Library with those of other organisations. The nature of such partnerships will span cooperative arrangements, joint ventures and contracting out. In particular, we see significant value in developing strategic alliances to gain technological investment and expertise to improve our services (para. 54, p.29).

In 'Staff Development' there are plans for a systematic staff training programme, with an increased budget, 'to develop an adaptable, well-motivated and well-trained staff, possessing a complex blend of knowledge and skills in managerial, technical, scholarly and specialist disciplines' (para. 60, p.30). Not much of significance appears in 'Information Technology' except for an announcement that a new IT strategy will be published in 1994.

Estate developments to 2005 will be restricted to major investments in new buildings at St Pancras, Colindale, and Boston Spa unless alternatives offering clear benefits or cost advantages are identified. Crucially:

> we shall continue to impress on Government the absolute necessity of retaining the land to the north of the St Pancras site. Further development, critical to the Library's future needs, will be prevented unless this land is retained. Its loss would severely impede the Library's ability to provide services and maintain its collections. We shall develop proposals for the judicious use of the land to meet the Library's needs beyond 1996 (para. 69, p.33).

But all these projects and major initiatives will demand substantial capital expenditure. New buildings; national and international networking; electronic document storage and transmission; to say nothing of restoring moneys lopped off the acquisition and preservation budgets to meet essential short-term programmes associated with the relocation to, and occupation of, St Pancras will need enhanced annual investment. Increased revenue from priced services and volume of sales, the reduction of costs through the application of new technology and the cessation of services failing to meet their direct cost recovery targets, increased sponsorship, and the opening up of new methods, cannot finance the programmes the Library has identified as being of vital importance to the efficient functioning of the national library. For that the Library will 'continue to depend on adequate financial support from Government to ensure both stable and continuing provision for our core programmes and investment necessary to maintain the central position of the Library in the network within which it operates' (para. 80, p.36). That is the message the British Library wants to ram home.

If *For scholarship, research and innovation* failed to attract attention in the national press, John Sutherland's 'How not to do it', *London Review of Books*, **15** (14), 22 July 1993:7 unmistakably heralded its arrival. Before going into detail he inveighed against the document's 'distressing standard of English' in which 'every key word gives off the stench of top-management leadership weekends and stale memorandum-speak', translating the Statement of Purpose's 'we [will] exploit our collections in enterprising ways to raise support for our activities' as 'we'll flog everything that is not nailed down'. Here he might have possibly attracted some sneaking sympathy to his first premise – British Libraryspeak is by no means universally approved – but, if so, it was immediately dissipated by his hasty, uninformed and over-the-top conclusion.

One by one Sutherland raised further bogeys: the British Library, as Panizzi redesigned it and we have known it, is doomed. What the Library has in store for the average reader in the year 2000 is:

> ulcerating levels of frustration and delay: if you want a foretaste of what the BL of the future will be like, imagine the bank of six British Library Online Catalogue terminals in the Round Reading Room: any time you want to use them, they will be occupied by other readers, racing to cram their search into the allotted seven minutes. At peak times there will be grumpy queues formed behind each user.

Students, 'that part of the tax-paying voting population that most needs it', will be barred from the Library. And when the Library proclaims 'we shall for the present continue to provide free access to the reading rooms. This policy will be kept under review', it is really declaring that 'charges are on the way, and we'll keep raising them until you stay away in large enough numbers to let us do our job'. By 2000 the continuing tendency will be towards remote document supply which Sutherland contends will be a tricky proposition because copyright holders will not allow the British Library to digitalize and distribute other people's property free of charge.

Pointing to the uncertain outcome of whatever negotiations the Library is conducting with the Publishers Association, Sutherland is in no doubt that whatever the outcome the end-user will not find it cheap. What is more, the absence of a legal deposit law for electronic documents – he dismisses the British Library's pathetic urging of the government to extend legal deposit to such publications – means that in future all that it can hope for is a small educational discount for this highly expensive form of publication. 'Having been extorted for some ten million volumes over the years publishers will look very coldly on the BL's begging bowl.' Consequently 'the one certain thing is that BL's electronic holdings in the year 2000 will be unworthy of "The World's Leading Resource for Scholarship, Research and Invention".'

Rightly emphasizing that resources were the big questionmark hanging over what he called 'this depressing document', Sutherland blamed the Library for 'moving so decisively to a high-tech environment . . . on an escalator to potential disaster' which, combined with the likelihood of the government refusing to release the surplus land to the north of the Library, meant that it was contemplating a not-too-distant nightmare, with no discernible convincing strategy.

> In short, the BL is committed to spending large amounts of new money on a number of fronts, and will get less from the Treasury than it has in the past. It needs more space and – barring some unlikely change of heart on the Government's part – it will lose such a large chunk of its new site as to render the whole point of moving invalid.

Only one remedy remained: 'What are now free services (e.g. the readers' ticket, access to stored material) will become "priced services". Where priced services (e.g. cheap Xeroxing) "fail to meet their direct cost recovery targets" they will be discontinued or raised to the highest level the market will bear.' That really set Bloomsbury's feline population among the Euston Road pigeons!

If the editor of the *London Review of Books* was confidently anticipating a swift rejoinder from British Library, thus providing up to a page of free copy, his confidence was not misplaced. A point-by-point rebuttal of Sutherland's polemic was forthcoming from Sir Anthony Kenny,

Chairman of the British Library Board. Three of Sutherland's criticisms were quickly dismissed: students will not be barred if they really need to use the Library 'but it is not reasonable to expect the national library to be the library of first resort for those pursuing first degrees'; despite Sutherland's assertions the Board had no intention of introducing admission charges; and the Library 'has not sold, and will not sell, any of its unique holdings'. Next Kenny corrects Sutherland's apparent misconception of the nature of the British Library: it is not identical to the pre-1972 British Museum Library; it is also heir to several other national institutions, notably the former Patent Office Library and the National Lending Library for Science and Technology. Scholars in the humanities, in science and technology, and business people all constitute the Library's clientele. As for the move towards online technology which Sutherland found so distasteful:

> It would be good to know to what extent readers in this country in the year 2000 will prefer to gain their information electronically rather than from books in hard copy. Unfortunately, no one knows: authors do not know, publishers do not know, booksellers do not know, and librarians do not know ('The British Library will survive', *London Review of Books*, **15** (16), 19 August 1993:4).

And when it comes to lambasting British Library's 'pathetic' urging of the government to extend legal deposit to electronic publications what else can the Library do than to urge the Government to change the law when the law needs changing? To sum up, Kenny's reply may lack Sutherland's orgy of hyperbole but it is based much more firmly on hard facts and reasonable conclusions.

If *For scholarship, research and innovation* charts the general direction in which the Library intends to proceed towards the millennium, it is left to its rolling five-year corporate plans to map out how the Library will move forward year by year. The current Corporate Plan, covering the period 1993/4–1997/8, produced by the Chief Executive's Office, was submitted to the DNH at the end of March 1993. It contains a statement of the Library's objectives for the period and an indication of the progress made in the previous year towards achieving them; an account of the planned deployment of resources based on revenue estimates and grant-in-aid planning figures; performance measures and targets, together with a review of the extent to which earlier targets have been achieved; a description of the consequences of the plan for the Library's operations and services; and the number of staff to be employed each year. Key targets during the period 1993–8 will be to complete preparations for the transition of services to St Pancras; address future needs for legal deposit of audiovisual, electronic, and other non-print materials; achieve real increases in the value of the acquisitions, preservation, and research budgets; continue progress in developing full active management of the entire British Library collection in line with the Review of Acquisitions and Retention Policies; improve the efficiency and effectiveness of acquisitions processing and cataloguing, in part by establishing shared cataloguing arrangements for 30% of UK copyright material; increase the margins on its key revenue-earning activities and raise total revenue to £36 million per annum by 1997–8; achieve maximum economy, efficiency, and value for money; pursue plans for meeting its strategic objectives for expanding remote document supply and exploiting digital storage and transmission; develop fully costed implementation plans for each of the programmes identified within *For scholarship, research and innovation*; and persuade the government to retain the land to the north of the St Pancras site for future use by British Library. If all these targets are achieved the Library will face the twenty-first century in good shape and confident mood.

3

Administrative Structure

Although the British Library Board was invested with the control and management of the Library under the terms of the 1972 British Library Act, in practice the responsibility for the day-to-day management of the Library rests with the Chief Executive. Board members are selected by the Secretary of State for National Heritage for their 'knowledge and experience of library or university affairs, finance, industry or administration'. Subcommittees of the Board advise on fundraising, the management of the Library's Trust Funds, the preparation of the new Corporate Plan, and the St Pancras project. This last subcommittee receives monthly reports on the St Pancras construction, operation, and automation projects so that it may assure the Board that the whole enterprise is in good shape and on schedule.

ADMINISTRATIVE CHANGES
Significant changes to British Library's administration were announced in January 1991 when the retirement of a number of senior staff, and the mass transfer of operations and services from London to Boston Spa – to the extent that staff numbers were now almost equally divided between the two sites – presented an opportune moment to put into effect substantial changes which the Board had long been contemplating. 'Running The Library Effectively', *Eighteenth Annual Report 1990–91*, pp.37–8 summarizes their import:

> A key target for 1990–91 was to start to put in place the organisational, administrative and financial structures appropriate to the British Library in the nineties, especially taking into account the major moves north and into St Pancras. Although the changes were a reflection of earlier strategic discussions, the effect was substantial . . . The Director Generals took a line management responsibility for ser-

vices either at Boston Spa or in London, while retaining certain corporate responsibilities for functions on a Library-wide basis. Departmental Directors had their roles clarified and strengthened. A number of directorates were restructured in the lead up to St Pancras and relocation and every Director was given more clearly defined budgetary responsibilities.

An internal administrative review, conducted by a senior civil servant seconded from Whitehall, working in collaboration with a Library Director, recommended root-and-branch changes. A whole tier of administration was largely expunged and the essential core of work was consolidated into a smaller administrative directorate at Boston Spa. The 'avoidance of duplication combined with reduced record keeping, selective checking and increased delegation to line management will save some forty posts'. Other benefits were the reinforcing of the Departmental Directors' resource responsibilities and the strengthening of the Library's Corporate Services by the inclusion of the Budget Office.

From a services viewpoint the most obvious change was the separation of SRIS in London and DSC at Boston Spa, which were formerly combined as Science Technology and Industry. Henceforward the division is by location and by the nature of the service: reference or lending. On each site subject- and service-based Directorates report to a Director General responsible for those functions to the Chief Executive.

In London SRIS provides a comprehensive reference source of information in science, technology, business and commerce by means of its extensive collections of books, journals, business reports, and patents. H&SS holds the Library's printed reference material in English and other European languages. Much of its collection consists of material published in the United Kingdom acquired by statutory deposit, forming in effect the 'National Printed Archive'. The Newspaper Library, the National Sound Archive, the British Library Information Sciences Service (formerly the Library Association Library), and the Centre for the Book, also fall within H&SS's ambit. Special Collections comprise six separate collections: Western Manuscripts; the Oriental and India Office Collections; the Map Collection; the Music Collection; and the Philatelic Collection. Public Services, with which is allied St Pancras Planning (Operations and Services), includes under its umbrella exhibitions and educational services, the bookshop, the publishing service, general information sources, and readers' admission. Collection and Preservation's field is storage management, space allocation, retention policy, book delivery services, preservation and conservation, the bindery and workrooms, and H&SS photographic and reprographic services. The St Pancras Occupation Project is responsible for the Library's move into the new building and the setting up of operations and services there.

At Boston Spa the DSC provides a national and international loan and photocopy service from its collections of monographs, conference proceedings, scientific reports, and 53,000 currently taken journals. Computing and Telecommunications is a service directorate that develops and operates computer and telecommunications systems which support reading room catalogues, external document supply, BLAISE-LINE retrieval services, cataloguing, acquisitions, personnel, and finance. Acquisitions Processing & Cataloguing's (AP&C) responsibilities include the Library's legal deposit operations, the processing of the majority of modern English-language material acquired for the reference collections, and the scope and content of the records held in the Library's catalogue databases. The National Bibliographic Service (NBS) develops and markets bibliographic publications and services based upon the *British National Bibliography (BNB)* and the catalogues of the Library's collections. It provides information retrieval, selection, and record supply services through CD-ROM and the BLAISE-LINE online system as well as through printed publications.

Two directorates are independent of the two main fiefdoms and report directly to the Chief Executive: Research and Development Department, the principal UK funding agency for library and information research; and Administration, responsible for financial management, budgetary control, personnel policy, and the supervision of the British Library's estate. A full outline, including head-and-shoulder photographs of the current Directors and Directors General, and a directory of all corporate and separate departments, is readily available in a fold-over leaflet, *Structures & Functions.*

PART II
LONDON

4

HUMANITIES AND SOCIAL SCIENCES

Humanities & Social Sciences Collections (H&SS) – formerly British Library Reference Division, and before that the Department of Printed Books, British Museum Library – offers a wide range of services in its reading rooms in the British Museum and elsewhere in London. Scholars and students, writers and media researchers, and innumerable others all benefit from its collections. Outline details of its usage and accommodation, acquisitions, cataloguing system, preservation activities, information and reprographic services, organization, and financial resources are set out in an annual, six-page folded A4 leaflet, *Facts and Figures*. Information on opening hours and admission procedures is available from the Reader Admission Office in the British Museum building.

Apart from Arundell Esdaile's *The British Museum Library* (Allen & Unwin, 1946), still the primary source for a reasonably detailed outline of H&SS collections, and various essays in *Treasures Of The British Library* (1988), there is no composite descriptive record of its immense resources. Nevertheless, a number of pamphlets and isolated articles, mostly relating to specific collections, draw the threads together and present at least a partial picture of the diverse materials safeguarded in the natural reference collections. For example, three recently issued A5 pamphlet guides shed light on the Slavonic and East European material. *Polish Collections in The British Library* (n.d., 12pp.) remarks that H&SS holdings are believed to be the largest in Western Europe although this cannot be reliably established because, like other country or language collections, they are dispersed, there is no central catalogue, and the keeping of relevant statistics only started after 1945. There are notes on the earliest items in the collection, including four incunabula published in Cracow, and nearly 300 sixteenth-century books, some of the utmost rarity; on nineteenth-century material published in Poland and by Polish émigrés abroad, notably in Paris; and on the 'Solidarity' collection, consisting of clandestine books and periodicals issued by the political opposition to the Communist regime in the 1970s and 1980s. A final section lists basic Polish bibliographies and other reference works with their H&SS shelfmarks. *Czechoslovak Collections in The British Library* (n.d., 23pp.) adopts a similar pattern. Both collections were enlarged by the books and periodicals issued by the exiled governments in London during the Second World War received under copyright deposit. Vladimir Il'ich Lenin visited the British Museum Library at least five times between 1902 and 1911. His requests for a reader's pass and other correspondence are chronicled and illustrated in *Lenin at The British Library* (n.d., 23pp.) which also records, with their shelfmarks, the books he donated to the Library and, by some sharp detection work, many of the books he consulted in the Library in the course of his writings and research.

German-language collections in H&SS are well represented in *German Studies: British Resources: Papers presented at a colloquium at the British Library 25–27 September 1985*, edited by David Paisey (British Library, 1986, 321pp.). Essays include Paisey's 'The non-current German collections of the Department of Printed Books' (pp.19-21); P. R. Harris' 'The Acquisition of German material in the mid-nineteenth century' (pp.21–6); Brian Holt's 'German studies in the context of the Reference Division's collection development policies' (pp.26–30); Tom Geddes' 'Acquisitions policy and practice: currently published material Federal Republic of Germany' (pp.31–6); and Lotte Hellinga's 'Incunabula' (pp.40–4).

In 1992, with the help of generous subventions from the National Heritage Memorial Fund (NHMF) and the Kulturstiftung der Länder, British Library acquired the Todd-Bowden collection of Tauchnitz editions of literary works by British and American authors, all in their original English text, published by Tauchnitz in Leipzig and Stuttgart 1841–1955. No fewer than 780 authors were represented in the series. Elizabeth James' 'Tauchnitz Editions at the British Library', *Rare Books Newsletter*, **43**, March 1993:24–9, includes Todd's and Bowden's verbatim remarks made at the presentation ceremony, explaining how they assembled the collection and the significance of the series in English literary history.

Although largely concerned with the Department of Printed Books' collections of Africana acquired in four periods of its history – from the foundation collections to the establishment of the British Museum Library's regular book fund in 1846, from 1847 to the first of the cuts in government expenditure in 1887, from 1847 to the period following the

Second World War, and from the African independence period onwards – Ilse Sternberg's 'The British Library African resources (1) printed materials', pp.119–40, *African Studies. Papers presented at a colloquium at the British Library 7–9 January 1985*, edited by Sternberg and Patricia M. Larby (British Library in association with SCOLMA, 1986, 332pp.), also covers other departments now in either H&SS or Special Collections. Patrick B. O'Neill's 'Canadiana deposited in the British Museum Library between 1895 and 1924', pp.83–90, *Canadian Studies: Papers presented at a colloquium at the British Library 17–19 August 1983*, edited by Patricia McLaren-Turner (British Library, 1984, 210pp.) indicates that the Library's collections for that period are almost complete.

More so than previously published colloquia, *Women's Studies. Papers presented at a colloquium at The British Library 4 April 1989*, edited by Albertine Gaur and Penelope Tuson (British Library, 1990, 189pp.) involved all categories of the Library's holdings, expanding in its two main sections on printed books and newspapers, and on archive and manuscript resources. Barbara James' and Ilse Sternberg's 'The English Language Branch and women's studies' (pp.7–15) is a historical overview of the British Library's integrationist approach to defining women's studies and collection development in H&SS, and of retrieval methods through conventional printed sources and the newer computer databases: 'Measures include carefully constructed thesaural strategies and cybernetic serendipity.' Carole Holden's 'Nineteenth-century black American women's writing' (pp.23–32) finds British Library holdings to be very uneven and unpredictable, whilst Eamon Dyas's 'Newspapers as source material for women's studies 1830s–1930s' (pp.33–45) examines newspaper coverage of women's issues (financial dependence, widows and deserted wives, etc.) and of various social aspects (e.g. women at work, women and sport, women readers and the new journalism), and concludes with a list of newspapers most likely to be of use to readers pursuing women's studies.

Morna Daniels's 'French resources for women's studies', Christine Burden's 'Holdings on women's studies in Italy', Rosomond Eden's 'Resources for a study of the women's movement in Germany until 1945', Brigid Haines' 'Women's studies in West and East Germany', Janet Gilbert's 'Dutch resources', Tom Geddes' 'Scandinavian publications since the mid-1970s', Janet Zmroczek's 'Women in the Soviet Union from 1917 to the present: sources for research', and Barbara Hawes' 'Norwegian women writers' are all bibliographical essays based on and highlighting British Library collections, in some cases with shelf-marks added to individual items.

Sternberg's 'The British Museum Library And Colonial Copyright Deposit', *British Library Journal*, **17** (1), Spring 1991:61–82, 'an outline of the complicated history of the relevant legislation, the attempts to enforce it and a preliminary evaluation of the benefits these brought to collection building in the British Museum Library', is a valuable, author-itative and detailed study of a previously obscure episode in the history of the collections.

Based on the author's time as consultant to British Library to advise on drawing up lists of American materials to be purchased with funds provided by the American Trust for the British Library, Gregory Palmer's *A Guide to Americana: the American collections in the British Library* (K. G. Saur, 1991) is arranged in two main parts. Part 1 looks at early Americana in the British Library's collections; the acquisition of nineteenth-century American material; and the copyright deposit of American books after 1886. Part 2 is concerned with the Library's cata-logues, the microfilm research collections, picture research, American maps, American music, Americana in languages other than English, offi-cial publications, newspapers and periodicals, American manuscripts in the British Library, and the Manuscript Collections. Appendices list sam-ple catalogue entries for Americana, British Library books relating to America published 1493–1525, American books acquired in 1837, American publishers depositing books in the British Library 1850–1950, and British Library holdings of original files of American newspapers published before 1820.

Another major work, D. J. McTernan's *French Quebec: imprints in French from Quebec 1774–1990 in The British Library Volume 1* (1992, 542pp.) includes all works published in Quebec, wholly or partially in French, collected by the British Museum and the British Library from the 1830s to the present. This first volume covers Quebec's creative and artistic output; volume two (1993, 616pp.) includes publications relating to its social and political institutions, history, social order, and geophysi-cal features. An introduction reviews Quebec's published output and its acquisition by the Library. For Australian material James D. Egles' and Graham P. Cornish's 'Australiana in the British Library', pp.177–96, Gorman, G. *ed. Acquisition and Collection Development for Libraries* (Mansell, 1992) provides an exhaustive study.

What appears to be the first issue of an intended annual publication, *London Services Research Register 1993*, describes both the research undertaken by British Library staff in their professional work in the Library – either relating to or based on specific collections, or undertaken to improve services and access to the collections, especially in the fields of IT and automation – and that pursued in their own time as private individuals. At times, no doubt, the two categories are hard to distinguish. Arranged by London-based directorates, the *Register* notes current research and staff publications.

In 1985, in an effort to improve joint collection planning on a sound documentary basis, British Library adopted the Conspectus system, recently developed by the Research Libraries Group of Stanford, California, which 'enable libraries to record and compare quantified data on the strength of their collections and collecting practices in particular subjects. It serves both as an information file and as a basis for collaborative collection development' (Stephen Hanger, 'Collection development in the British Library: the role of the RLG Conspectus', *Journal of Librarianship*, **19** (2), April 1987:89–107). Hanger reported that the Library 'remains optimistic about the scheme as an aid to collection development . . . Conspectus records now encompass the lending as well as the reference collections, thereby giving an overall picture of the level of resources and of their maintenance. For the first time all collections and collecting policies are described and assessed in a single document.' In the past seven years the Consortium of Scottish Libraries (i.e. the National Library of Scotland, eight university libraries, and Edinburgh and Glasgow public libraries) have completed Conspectus surveys. So, too, have the National Library of Wales and the National Art Library. Data collected are registered in the British Library's National Conspectus Office, which not only provides information and advice to libraries planning Conspectus surveys but also maintains the Conspectus database.

British Library regards the Conspectus system as being of prime importance in resource sharing in collection development in areas where coverage is weak: 'Conspectus provides the broad statements of holdings which will form the basis on which acquisitions policy may be redefined in relation to others, or discussions on a joint approach to coverage may be undertaken' (Andy Stephens and Stuart Ede, 'The role of British Library in cooperation', chapter 5, *Handbook of Library Cooperation*, edited by Alan F. MacDougall and R. J. Prytherch, Gower, 1991). For this reason the Library hopes for a close collaboration with other UK national libraries and large public library systems, and is intent on exploring the possibility of resource sharing with major European libraries. Conspectus data also offer a method for co-operation in conservation policies and practices. Within British Library Conspectus data have revealed potential areas of overlap between SRIS and H&SS collection policies and a well-defined map of responsibilities has been drawn up. Conspectus has also identified subject areas which the Library does not intend to cover in depth, thus establishing whether coverage of those subjects could be reduced still further with consequent savings in resources which could be exploited elsewhere.

Crispin Jewitt's 'Conspectus. A means to library cooperation', *Library Conservation News*, **22**, January 1989:4–6, and his 'Developing Conspectus', *ibid.*, **23**, April 1989:2–3, 6, can be recommended to those who want to find out more about exactly what the Conspectus system comprises and how it has been developed in North American and Western European libraries. Ann E. Wade's 'Conspectus: A Reappraisal', *Issues In Focus*, **6**, 1993:1–2, brings the story up to date.

The overall problem facing British Library in collection development not only stems from the unrelenting flow of legally deposited books, reflecting the growth in the annual number of books published in the United Kingdom, but also in the worldwide growth in literature of importance of which, because of the steepling rise in acquisition and preservation costs, the Library is acquiring less and less. If Panizzi's principle of universality in acquisitions were ever attainable in the nineteenth century, nobody should be in any doubt that at the end of the twentieth it is totally beyond reach. The ways in which the Library is coming to grips with the realities of this situation – including the 1988 Review of Acquisition and Retention Policies; greater discrimination in fringe areas of 'popular' literature, possibly in co-operation with other national copyright libraries; the increasing use of microfilm holdings; rapid access to material via online data banks; and full text retrieval systems – are all expounded in Michael Smethurst's 'The British Library: A Response to a Set of Questions . . . ', *Collection Management*, **15** (1/2), 1992:31–8.

A study of library provision for the culture of science, technology, and medicine was set up within British Library in 1986 with the following terms of reference:

> There is material in the British Library which is relevant to the study of the history of science and technology, broadly defined, but this material is acquired, recorded, and made available through a number of separate departments with no central focus of responsibility. Moreover, although we know that the collections are used by scholars in these disciplines, the question of the role which the Library actually

plays, or ought to play, in meeting their needs has never been properly investigated.

Its aims were:

(1) To identify significant bodies of material in the Library which are, or might be, of value for the study of the history of science, including the tools – catalogues, indexes etc. – which are available to assist in using them.

(2) To review the current policies and practices for the development of these bodies of material, including the associated tools, and to estimate, as far as possible, the resources – money, staff time, space, etc. – involved.

(3) To review the current activities of libraries and users in the UK in this field, the kinds of material needed, and the extent to which the Library is meeting those needs. This review should also investigate any difficulties posed by current Library policies and any materials in the Library's collections which appear to be under-exploited.

(4) In the light of findings of (1)–(3) above, to recommend any changes to the Library's present policies on acquisition, recording etc., and any other initiatives which might assist workers in this field, and to promote the use of the collections, having regard to the constraints on the Library's resources.

(5) To publicize the work and publish the results.

R. B. Parsons's Report Of The Study On Library Provision For The Culture Of Science Technology And Medicine (CSTM) was published by British Library as a R&D Report in an 153-page spiral-bound document in 1989. Specific topics considered in the course of the study included information already available throughout the Library, its coverage of sample items, and the reasons for non-acquisition in H&SS and SRIS. Among its recommendations were that in the existing financial climate the Library should not enter into major new commitments but should concentrate on increasing the effectiveness of its present activities and making its holdings more widely known and more easily available. Probably the only way of meeting the desired objectives would be for the Library to adopt a corporate approach to its resources and responsibilities in this field, especially in view of its forthcoming concentration of reference facilities at St Pancras. And the Library should appoint a CSTM subject specialist, very much along the same lines as specialist appointments elsewhere in the Library, to advise on the retention, relocation, and disposal of primary material no longer of current scientific, technological, or medical importance; to advise on the acquisition of material; and to compile a guide to CSTM materials in the Library.

In response to readers' suggestions, *London Services – Bloomsbury Newsletter* has introduced a news feature providing details of some notable recent purchases for the Bloomsbury-based collections, starting with a substantial collection of comic-strip magazines dating from the early 1970s to the late 1980s and ranging from 'traditional' science fiction and fantasy stories to gay, feminist, and political publications. 'Because many of these "comix" or "zines" were produced by underground publishers or by individual enthusiasts (perhaps unaware of the legal deposit requirement) they have not been as well represented in the Library's collections as they should have been.' Numerous purchases of British small-press poetry of the period from the 1960s to the mid-1980s have enhanced the British Library's holdings in this area. 'The poets represented constitute a significant perhaps neglected part of the literary culture of the United Kingdom . . . As well as individual books from this period published by little-known presses in limited editions, the Library has been buying small-press poetry magazines which published the work of many of the poets' ('Acquisition News', *London Services – Bloomsbury Newsletter*, 7, Summer 1993:6).

Also in this issue of the *Newsletter*, Moira Goff's 'Dancing In The British Library' (pp.2–3) outlined the Library's dance collection, which includes such early items as *Antonius Arena ad suos compagnones studiantes . . . bassas dances in galanti stillo compositas* (Lyons, 1529), Arbeau's *Orchesographie* (Lengres, 1528), and John Playford's *The English Dancing Master* (1651).

CATALOGUE OF PRINTED BOOKS
Published by K. G. Saur the current printed catalogue of H&SS's collection now extends to over 500 folio volumes.

1   *The British Library General Catalogue of Printed Books to 1975* (360 vols., 1980–7), which lists more than 8.5 million titles in all European languages. It includes all entries for pre-1975 imprints acquired and catalogued prior to 1976 and all pre-1971 imprints acquired and catalogued since 1976 to within two months of publication of the relevant volume. Entries are listed in a single alphabetical sequence by author.

In addition there are five separately bound sequences:

- *The Bible* (3 vols., 1981–3), in which entries are arranged according to the language of the original text.

- *England* (6 vols., 1982), which includes royal proclamations, official reports, leaflets, memoranda, and documents issued by corporate bodies from Magna Carta onwards.
- *England Titles Index. Subheading Index* (2 vols., 1982). Regular users who have come up against the tortuous vagaries of 'England' headings, 'including every variety of publication imaginable covering England, Wales, Scotland and, to a certain extent, Ireland and the Commonwealth' will appreciate the provision of these indexes.
- *Liturgies* (2 vols., 1984).
- *Russia* (1986), which includes a comprehensive index of subheadings in the Cyrillic script.

2 *Supplement* (6 vols., 1987–8), 84,000 entries pertaining to pre-1071 titles acquired and catalogued too late for inclusion in the main sequence. Others are reprints of entries previously listed but with revised bibliographical data, in some cases involving a new shelfmark.

3 *1976–1982* (50 vols., 1983). Entries in this and subsequent volumes are derived from MARC (machine-readable catalogue) records compiled according to the Anglo-American Cataloguing Rules 2nd edition (AACR 2).

4 *1982–1985* (26 vols., 1986). Also on 177 microfiches with binder.

5 *1986–1987* (22 vols., 1988). Also on 92 microfiches with binder.

6 *1988–1989* (28 vols., 1990).

The British Library awarded a contract to Saztec Europe Ltd in January 1987 for the conversion of the *British Library General Catalogue of Printed Books to 1975* (*BLC*) to machine-readable form, an essential prerequisite to the opening of the St Pancras library, where users of the reading rooms will have direct access to the catalogue which will be linked to the automated book ordering system. Why this operation was regarded as the British Library's second most important objective, ceding absolute priority only to its removal to the St Pancras building, is explained in Pat Oddy's 'British Library Catalogue Conversion', *Bibliographic Services Newsletter*, **43**, June 1987:4–6. This authoritative essay sets the conversion into its historical context, examines the printed catalogue's form and structure, and outlines the processes involved in its conversion. 'Machine-readable files, especially those with a separately-linked authority file, made global editing and rapid correction a reality.' What is more, 'the increased search capabilities of a machine-held file will cut across the restrictions of the present printed form by offering such basic possibilities as search on title word, or search on publisher which will open up the catalogue not only to clients accessing the database, but also to those in the Library concerned with more efficient collection management'. Additional benefits were that the machine-readable catalogue would take up less space and would be more cost-effective and efficient to maintain.

It was necessary first to restructure *BLC*'s data to a format compatible with British Library's other UKMARC databases. This involved three processes: data capture by Saztec at their Ardrossan site in Scotland; data manipulation to produce unit records coded to conform with the UKMARC exchange record format; and data output to magnetic tape. Further discussion of the conversion, including the complexities presented by non-Roman scripts and the pioneering nature of the whole operation is printed in 'Background to the British Library Catalogue conversion', pp.248–50, *Hebrew Studies: papers presented at a colloquium in September 1989* (British Library Occasional Papers, 13, 1991). Oddy's 'Problems of Retrospective Conversion in National and Research Libraries: The Conversion of the British Library Catalogue to Machine-Readable Form', *IFLA Journal*, **16** (1) 1990:85–6, goes into detail on the data conversion specification.

A test-file of some 1.2 million *BLC* records converted to machine-readable form, representing books corresponding to volumes A–HALL of the printed catalogue, was launched on BLAISE-LINE on 1 November 1988, and the four-year project was completed on time in April 1991. *BLC* was the first of the great library catalogues to be successfully converted in this way and it was immediately available online and on CD-ROM. Following a test period early in 1993, British Library made its OPAC system, including *BLC*, available on the Joint Academic Network (JANET), whose users now have on-desk information on the Library's collections. Searching is possible by author, title, subject, publisher, place or date of publication, shelfmark, International Standard Book Number (ISBN), International Standard Serial Number (ISSN), or by control number. A *BLC* factsheet providing instructions on bibliographic checking, on personal author, corporate author, and keyword searching, and on the specially extended character set used for the *BLC* file, is printed in *BLAISE-LINE Newsletter*, **1**, January–February 1993:5.

Saztec Europe and Chadwyck-Healey announced in September 1988 that they had agreed to enter into a contract for the worldwide sale and distribution of the CD-ROM version of *BLC*. Saztec, who hold the exclusive CD-ROM publishing rights until the year 2001, would design and put together the product whilst Chadwyck-Healey would act as marketing and distribution agents. *BLC on CD-ROM* was launched in November 1989 in a set of three discs, conforming to the High Sierra format, in a storage box, with software on floppy disks and accompanied by a user's manual. An informative six-page glossy brochure, answering a wide range of queries, *British Library General Catalogue Of Printed Books To 1975 On CD-ROM*, blazoned with the legend 'The Most Famous Library Catalogue In The World. The Most Important Development In Its History' was circulated to potential customers. The advantages of *BLC*'s publication on CD-ROM are enumerated and annotated – improved research results, subject access, adjacency searches, searching by date, speed of searching, speed of transcribing citations, combination with other tests, sort and rank lists, download cataloguing records, transfer of data to other sites, saving in time and handling, and value for money. Instructions for searching the CD-ROM catalogue under nine different headings, refining the search by combinations with other heading and truncated terms, and on searching by epithets and pseudonyms are pleasantly laid out in colour blocks. There is also information on using *BLC on CD-ROM*, including Boolean searching, browsing, subject access, and catalogue record display. Conrad Lealand's 'Production Of The CD-ROM Version Of The British Library Catalogue', pp.85–91, *Optical Info '89*, describes the conversion of the printed catalogue to machine-readable form and the subsequent design and production of the CD-ROM version. The functional requirements of the software and marketing plans and pricing decisions are also touched upon.

Catalogues for readers' use in the Bloomsbury reading room include the formidable extended lines of the manually maintained loose-leaf guardbook volumes, which incorporate all revisions up to the time when British Library began to catalogue accessions in machine-readable form, and which are apparently positioned to serve as the outer defences of the Superintendent's enclave. Entries for works acquired before 1955 are arranged in the left-hand columns, those acquired 1956–70 are mounted to the right. Those acquired 1971–5 are recorded on blue paper in a separate sequence at the end of each volume. A personal account of the procedures and practices for incorporating new and revised entries to the guardbook catalogue in the 1930s, which had remained virtually unaltered since the 1880s, can be read in Alec Hyatt King's 'The Traditional Maintenance Of The General Catalogue Of Printed Books', chapter 5, *The Library of the British Museum*, edited by P. R. Harris (British Library, 1991). Sets of K. G. Saur's printed catalogues are placed in the North Library, in the Official Publications and Social Sciences Service (OP&SS) reading room, and also in the annexe to the main reading room. *BLC on CD-ROM* is available on a long line of desks just inside the south entrance. Close to hand are copies of the *Revised Users Guide* (Windsor, Saztec Europe, 1992), which contains instructive notes for the bemused reader on starting up, tools of the program, searching and browsing, using results, action menu, and options menu. An A4 factsheet, *General Information About The British Library Catalogue Of Printed Books to 1975 On CD-ROM. Assistance In Using The CD-ROM*, is also prominently displayed. For items acquired after 1975 recourse must be made to the microfiche catalogue situated adjacent to the CD-ROM version.

Guide to Catalogues. An Introduction to the British Library's catalogues and how to use them, a 12-page A5 leaflet, provides a brief introduction to British Library's printed book catalogues, and information on catalogues of other British Library collections and on other libraries' catalogues that can be found on the shelves of the Bloomsbury reading rooms. *The General Catalogue. A quick guide to help you find entries in the General Catalogue of Printed Books* (8pp.) concedes that it is sometimes difficult to use but offers some basic information and a few short cuts.

Replacing an interim online catalogue system, introduced in 1991 for the dual purpose of enabling readers to gain enhanced access to the Library's collections, and allowing Library staff to become familiar with the problems of operating this type of catalogue, a new online system was installed in the Round Reading Room in the autumn of 1993. Using industrial-standard hardware and software, the files available include the General Retrospective Catalogue of Printed Books, containing material published up to 1975 relating to the humanities, the social sciences, and the history of science, technology, and business; the General Current Catalogue of Printed Books for the material published in these fields since 1971; the Printed Music Current Catalogue, of material published since 1980; and the Science Technology And Business Current Catalogue, which contains post-1974 monographs and all periodicals held in SRIS.

These four files, held separately on the system, will offer a greater number of ways of searching. Search types include name, title, subject, date and place of publication, publisher, language, and type of publication. Thirteen catalogue terminals are available in the Round Reading Room, and another in the OP&SS reading room; existing printed catalogues and corresponding microfiche catalogues will be retained. Scheduled future developments include mounting the Printed Music

Retrospective Catalogue and the DSC Monographs Catalogue on the system and, possibly, the facility to search more than one file simultaneously. 'The results of evaluating the new system in operation, together with feedback from users, will also play an important part in deciding the future course of its development' ('The Online Catalogue Up To The Opening Of St Pancras', *London Services – Bloomsbury Newsletter*, **7**, Summer 1993:1–2). At St Pancras the new system will be linked to the Automated Book Request System and the Reader Admission System. Those who delight in detailed descriptions of computer cataloguing processes will find much to please them in Paul Fisher's 'Digital story of a nation', *The Guardian*, 12 October 1989:37, which explains how, for the first time, technology 'will freeze a national catalogue into absolutely and undeteriorating digits'.

Compiled from manuscript and printed sources by R. C. Alston, *The Arrangement Of Books In The British Museum Library 1843–1973* (1986, 48pp.), published by Chadwyck-Healey in association with British Library and other major research libraries in Britain and the United States, and with Avero Publications, outlines the classification system devised by the British Museum Library from its early days in Montague House, listing pressmarks, subject headings, and their subsequent extensions and sub-divisions. Also compiled by Alston, *Handlist of unpublished finding aids to the London Collections of The British Library* (1991, 136pp.) is a consolidated handlist of the many hundreds of finding aids which have been compiled throughout the Library's history to supplement the printed catalogues. Some are very early, belonging to the period before the founding of the Library: notably the manuscript lists of the Old Royal Library, various lists of the materials in the library of Sir Robert Cotton, and Humfrey Wanley's lists of printed books and manuscripts in the Harleian Library – all foundation collections of the British Museum Library, but most of the 1,500 lists and indexes recorded here belong to the nineteenth or early twentieth century. Many were compiled by specialists as working tools to facilitate the routine work of the various departments; others were put together with an eye to publication but never actually reached print. An interleaved copy is kept at the enquiry desk in the Bloomsbury reading room in which additions and corrections are marked. A similar handlist to the 2,000-plus published finding aids is in preparation.

ESTC

The aim of the *Eighteenth Century Short Title Catalogue* (*ESTC*) established in British Library in 1977, is 'to create a machine-readable bibliography of books, pamphlets and other ephemeral material printed (or purporting to be printed) in English speaking countries currently based on the collections of over a thousand libraries world-wide'. British Library and the Center for Bibliographical Studies and Research, University of California, Riverside, are jointly responsible for all except North American imprints; responsibility for those rests with the American Antiquarian Society, Worcester, Massachusetts, through its North American Imprints Program – now virtually complete, and fed into ESTC. Libraries and archives the world over have pledged to report their holdings of eighteenth-century material to ESTC's editorial offices, thus providing additional locations for existing records or entirely new catalogue entries.

Publication of *The Eighteenth Century Short Title Catalogue. Catalogue Of The British Library Collections* on microfiche in December 1983 completed the project's first phase. It was superseded in 1990 by the worldwide *The Eighteenth Century Short Title Catalogue 1990 microfiche edition* (1990 booklet of 30pp. + 220 fiches) which followed the format of the earlier title; viz. one main author/title sequence and a series of special indexes for date, place of publication other than London, and five genres. Some 284,000 bibliographic records are listed with all known locations (1 million in total) in more than 1,000 libraries contributing to the project. The accompanying booklet outlines its history and rationale, the conventions adopted in the form and arrangement of the entries, and prints a key to the library location symbols. *The Eighteenth Century Short Title Catalogue on CD-ROM* (1991) comprises an extensive user's manual compiled by British Library's editorial team, one CD-ROM, software on 5.25-inch and 3.5-inch floppy disks, and a tough library case. Because of the delay in releasing the CD-ROM version, a further 10,000 bibliographical records and many more locations were able to be incorporated. In his 'Eighteenth Century Short Title Catalogue on CD-ROM', *CD-ROM Information Products: The Evaluative Guide*, **4** (1) January 1993:27–35, David Stoker remarked that it 'will be seen as a milestone in eighteenth century scholarship, and will generate further interest and research into the period. The designers of the software have gone to some trouble to provide a range of functions and facilities appropriate to the specialist material on this database', but added, 'there remain some problems with the retrieval software'.

It was announced in March 1989 that:

> after months of negotiation, ESTC had secured the agreement of the copyright holders of STC and Wing, the short title catalogues cover-

ing 1475–1640 and 1641–1700 respectively, to augment ESTC by incorporating their records in the file. The metamorphosis from the Eighteenth-Century Short Title Catalogue to the English Short Title Catalogue has already begun . . . Records for the period 1475–1700 will not be publicly available on ESTC for a few years to come, but our ultimate aim is to produce a comprehensive file 1475–1800 with all records upgraded to the full ESTC standard in terms of titles, headings, notes and locations. We hope to see this published on CD in 1995 ('ESTC News', *Factotum*, **33**, March 1991:1).

ESTC was first made available on BLAISE-LINE as one of its antiquarian databases in 1982. M. J. Crump's *Searching ESTC on BLAISE: a brief guide*, issued as a Factotum Occasional Paper in January 1989, gives a simple explanation of the structure of an ESTC computer record and of the way in which the computer handles ESTC data. Research Publications Inc. of Woodbridge, Connecticut, in association with British Library and other contributors, started publication in 1982 of a microfilm edition of some 200,000 eighteenth-century texts recorded by ESTC. This major project is expected to take until 1997 to complete. ESTC acts as an index to the series, recording the relevant reel number when an item has been filmed. *The Eighteenth Century Short Title Catalogue: the cataloguing rules* (2nd ed., 1991) is published for the benefit of rare books librarians contemplating the automation of their catalogues. Latest ESTC information is printed in *Factotum: Newsletter of the XVIIIth century STC* (March 1978–), an occasional publication intended for circulation to all those interested in the project and, more especially, to those librarians giving practical assistance by contributing catalogue entries for relevant material in their own libraries. Compiled by Ann Lennon, *Index to Factotum numbers 1–30* (1990) cumulates two previous indexes. Crump's 'The Eighteenth Century Short Title Catalogue (ESTC)', *Liber Bulletin*, **34**, 1989:93–8, outlines its history; sets it in the context of A. W. Pollard and F. R. Redgrave's *A Short-Title Catalogue of Books printed in England, Scotland and Ireland 1475–1640* (1920) and D. Wing's *Short-Title Catalogue of Books printed in England, Scotland, Ireland, Wales and British America 1641–1700* (1945–1951); explains its cataloguing style; describes the problems involved in the MARC format; and reports on the latest developments, including the suggestion that the two previous short-title catalogues should be automated.

ISTC
Both a bibliography of fifteenth-century books and other material printed

from moveable type, and a location register of copies, 'the British Library's Incunable Short Title Catalogue sets out to conflate existing knowledge of fifteenth-century printing into a computerised database that will in time provide a complete survey of the field, one that may be accessed from any point of the record and whose information may be strung together in practically any combination' (M. C. Davies, 'The Incunable Short Title Catalogue (ISTC)', *Bulletin of the Society for Renaissance Studies*, **7** (2) May 1990:1–7). Applying the electronic cataloguing procedures devised for the ESTC, ISTC began as an experimental project in 1980 when the complete text of F. R. Goff's *Incunabula in American Libraries: a third census* was keyboarded into British Library's mainframe computer. At intervals since then the bibliographic records of the incunabula listed in the union catalogues of Italy, Belgium, Holland, and other countries worldwide, have been keyboarded and interfiled to make ISTC a truly international project.

From the outset it was intended that eventually ISTC would form a compact union catalogue of UK-held incunabula and this is gradually being achieved as the holdings of British Library and other UK libraries are entered. A special field is reserved for the Library's incunabula, the most comprehensive collection held anywhere, so that in time a complete handlist of its holdings can be produced. By July 1992, 25,300 editions, estimated to be 83% of the total incunabula still extant, were in the file, making ISTC by far the largest bibliography of incunabula in existence. The project is expected to be completed by 1994. 'The prime current object of ISTC is to incorporate new entries for incunabula not yet listed', writes John Goldfinch in his 'Searching the ISTC on BLAISE-LINE', *Searching ISTC*, September 1991:1–22, which includes notes and examples of the basic information contained in ISTC records, on the simple searching and printing system by which records can be retrieved, on combing search terms, and on other search facilities.

The first issue of *News from ISTC*, which started publication in August 1992, provided a global overview of ISTC's progress; including information on Research Publication's *Incunabula: the Printing Revolution in Europe 1455–1500* microfiche project to provide:

> complete texts of a large selection of incunabula, presented in units each covering an aspect of printing, which may be either a geographical or subject area . . . Each unit will be accompanied by a guide with an introduction and the ISTC records for all the items in the unit, followed by indexes. The microfiches will be recorded in ISTC as the project progresses.

General editor is Lotte Hellinga, whose brainchild ISTC was.

Bibliography and the Study of 15th-Century Civilisation. Papers presented at a Colloquium at the British Library 26–28 September 1984, edited by Hellinga and Goldfinch (British Library, 1987, 260pp.), provides a permanent record of the ISTC project 'at a time when the file stood at 18,000 records and was still in a fairly early stage of editing and, even, proofreading'. Papers of relevance here – that is to say, of the ISTC project as part of British Library's activities, not of its application to the study of early printing, or to bibliographical scholarship – include Hellinga's 'Introduction' (pp.1–5) and Goldfinch's 'Searching the ISTC on BLAISE-LINE' (pp.12–33). 'Editions of Petrus Hispanus as recorded on ISTC' (pp.99–123) and an appendix to Severin Corsten's 'Universities and early printing', admirably display the layout of ISTC records. Hellinga and Goldfinch's 'Ten years of the Incunabula Short-Title Catalogue (ISTC)', *Bulletin du Bibliophile*, part 1, 1990:125–31, is valuable for its international extension, its momentum, the benefits of computerization, the limitations on the contents of ISTC records imposed by resource constraints, and the advantages ISTC offers scholars and bibliographers. Goldfinch's 'ISTC: Reading the Renaissance', *Select*, **11**, Winter 1993:10 includes a section on full text and CD developments.

OFFICIAL PUBLICATIONS AND SOCIAL SCIENCES SERVICE
Based in the Official Publications Reading Room, close to the British Museum's north entrance, the Official Publications and Social Sciences Service (OP&SS) provides a reference and bibliographical enquiry service. A reference collection of some 2,000 volumes is on the open shelves, including the principal parliamentary collections, and reference works on the official publications of overseas countries. With the accession of the HMSO database on BLAISE-LINE from April 1989 a fast new way to track down UK government publications is now available. The file includes all items listed in HMSO's daily, weekly, and annual catalogues since 1976; and encompasses both parliamentary and non-parliamentary publications, and also material published by HMSO on behalf of government departments and other national bodies.

OP&SS is a depositary library for the United Nations and its various agencies and also for the European Community. Its continuing importance in current information provision is confirmed by its computer search services and its participation in the Business Information Service (BIS), for which it provides a back-up service for legal and statistical information.

Following the 1989 Review of Acquisition and Retention Policies, which argued that the British Library was uncritically accepting foreign material of little or no intrinsic interest, many OP&SS former exchange agreements have been allowed to lapse. Nevertheless, many thousands of items continue to flood in, overwhelming staff cataloguing resources. At the moment OP&SS relies to a large extent on the knowledge and experience of its professional staff to locate many categories of official publications which elude exact bibliographical control and escape cataloguing altogether. 'Official Publications Library', *British Library News*, **67**, August 1981:2, summed up its peculiar quandary: 'Special difficulties exist for the user and the librarian in retrieving material from the vast inadequately controlled field of official publications. The sheer numbers of documents issued means that potentially interested users can remain unaware of specific titles that are part of a large series as no library has the resources to catalogue analytically.' To assist readers a number of introductory guides in the British Library's familiar A5 pamphlet format are issued. *Using The Official Publications And Social Sciences Reading Room* (n.d., 8pp.) provides helpful notes on the catalogues, the accessibility of the collections, and application procedures, with a decidedly useful plan of the OP&SS reading room.

A collection of Acts of Parliament, dating back to 1551, is shelved in the reading room, providing a rich source of historical and current information. *Parliamentary Papers. British Parliamentary Publications And Procedural Records Of Parliament in The Official Publications And Social Sciences Reading Room* (n.d., 16pp.) contains notes on The Parliamentary Or Sessional Papers of the two Houses, Lords and Commons; the Procedural Records (journals, debates, daily business papers); the Statutes; Post-1921 Publications; and Parliamentary Archives, with text references to the most applicable finding aids.

Many enquiries relate to OP&SS's comprehensive selection of UK electoral registers from the nineteenth century onwards which is virtually complete from 1947. Replacing an earlier pamphlet, *Using Electoral Registers in The British Library* (n.d., 8pp.), a four-page A4 information sheet, *Finding Electoral Registers in The British Library* (1989), clarifies what registers exist and what the Library holds, their arrangement and contents, and how to locate and request them. It is emphasized that the registers are seldom suitable for tracing the whereabouts of known individuals, although they can be consulted to find or to confirm the residents of a known address when the register was compiled.

United States federal government publications in OP&SS date from the late eighteenth century and, in the case of the New England states, from the seventeenth century. Since 1883 most of the publications that the federal government deposits with libraries have been received and many state government publications have been acquired by purchase, exchange, or gift. *United States Government Publications* (1990, 36pp.) outlines the main categories of material available, the indexes and bibliographies that need to be consulted, and the arrangement of the collections, with shelfmarks for the most important collections. Federal publications held include Congressional Publications; Journals, Records and Proceedings of Congress; Congressional Committee Publications; Congressional Hearings; Presidential Publications; Executive Department Publications; and US Federal Law And Publications Of The Judiciary. An appendix explaining the Su Docs classification system, devised in the Library of the Public Documents, 1895–1903, now quoted in the *Monthly Catalog of United States Government Publications*, is not the least valuable feature of this indispensable guide.

Arranged by broad area and country groups, *Microform Collections Government Publications And The Social Sciences* (British Library Humanities and Social Sciences, 1992, 28pp.), compiled by Dorothy Walker, is a descriptive guide to 228 major microform holdings in the Library's London collections with the exception of those in the Western Manuscripts and Oriental and India Office Collections. The location and shelfmark of hard-copy guides is noted.

Compared to that surrounding other British Library directorates, departments and collections, up-to-date documentation on OP&SS is sparse and meagre, although Janice Anderson conveys a sharp impression of its global importance in *The British Library Humanities & Social Sciences Collections* (2nd ed., 1990).

NATIONAL SOUND ARCHIVE

Opened in 1955 as the British Institute of Recorded Sound, the National Sound Archive (NSA) entered the British Library in 1973. One of the largest collections of its kind in the world, it holds approximately 900,000 discs, 125,000 tapes – including copies of all current commercial records, presented by the British Phonographic Industry in the absence of a legal deposit scheme – and a vast number of recordings dating back to the 1890s, when the first gramophones were imported into Britain. Its current intake is in the region of some 50,000 items a year. NSA's collections encompass the whole world of music, oral history recordings, wildlife sounds, literature and drama, and industro-mechanical sounds. Their exploitation for education, commercial, and information purposes plays an increasingly significant role in its day-to-day activities.

Because classical music was one of the British Institute of Recorded Sound's two prime concerns (the other was opera), NSA's Western Art Collections are unparalleled and include many recordings of BBC broadcasts specially made for the Archive which constitute the only available public reference resource. Alan Wood's 'on the radio at the nsa'. *Playback*, **3**, Autumn 1992:4–5, provides a full outline of NSA's collection of recorded radio programmes, and radio-related material – which includes BBC plays and poetry broadcasts, BBC Transcription Services for overseas radio stations, and recordings of the BBC Natural History Unit in Bristol. Recordings and cassettes published worldwide in the country of origin, and a wide selection of specialized European and North American labels, are gathered in the World Music Collections which include folk, ethnic, traditional, and non-Western popular and classical music. The music of Africa and South-east Asia is strongly represented.

All styles of jazz, from all periods and locations, from roots to the present, are represented in the Jazz Collections, which now contain in excess of 30,000 recordings on all formats, mostly commercial but with an increasing number produced privately or by NSA curatorial staff. Ragtime, dance bands, and blues are also prominently featured. The Jazz Collections also accommodate the Oral History of British Jazz, which includes unique interview material, and which is the subject of Chris Clark's 'Jazz Oral History at The British Library National Sound Archive', *Fontes Artis Musicae*, **36**, July 1989:185–94. This ends with an alphabetical list of interviews conducted up to April 1989. Ranging from early music hall to the most modern styles, the Pop Music Collections include live performances recorded by NSA, recorded interviews and seminars, and a burgeoning collection of commercial and promotional videos.

The Spoken Word Collections (i.e. drama and literature) preserve recordings of poetry readings, stand-up comedy, radio drama, and live theatre performances from the National Theatre and the Royal Shakespeare Company (since 1964); the Royal Court Theatre (since 1971); and many other London and provincial theatres. The nature of this type of material, the development of techniques used to capture performances effectively, and some recordings of particular interest are featured in Toby Oakes' 'recorded drama and literature', *Playback*, **4**,

Spring 1993:3–5. Commercially issued foreign-language recordings, language courses, and specialized recordings of social and regional accents are brought together in the Language and Dialect Collection. Jonathan Vickers's 'British Library African resources: (2) archival. The National Sound Archive – spoken recordings' (pp.231–7) and Lucy Duran's 'Traditional African music', (pp.238–44), *African Studies* (1986) outline NSA's rich holdings in African material, its acquisition methods, and possible developments in the systematic collection of African sound recordings.

Recent additions to the Oral History Collections include three Exeter University projects, *Family Life and Work Before 1918*, *Life Stories and Ageing* and *Families and Social Mobility*; the British in India archive; the Methodist Sound Archive; the British Council Recording Unit Archive; the London History Workshop Centre recordings; and material from the Survey of English Dialects. An oral history of the recording industry has just been completed and a similar project covering Glyndebourne, the Sussex country opera-house, is in progress. The National Life Story Collection, an independent charitable trust based at the Archive, carries out life story interviewing projects and collects life story manuscripts. It is centred around two core collections: Leaders of National Life, interviews with people not normally covered by biographers or the mass communications media; and a National Cross-Section which aims to interview working people from all parts of Britain. A leaflet, *Oral History*, details NSA oral history collections and services.

Worldwide in scope, the British Library of Wildlife Sounds is based on the wealth of material bequeathed by Ludwig Koch, the German pioneer of wild birdsong recording in the 1890s. It now boasts 60,000 recordings of the sounds of some 6,000 species of birds, mammals, amphibians, insects, and fish. In contrast, the Industro-Mechanical Sound Collection contains commercial and unpublished recordings of transport and machinery, including steam locomotive manufacture, aircraft, and the sounds of antiquated crafts and industries. Railway sounds, the largest section, includes stereo recordings of every class of modern British Rail diesel locomotive. Aircraft sound includes surviving pre-First World War aircraft and the sound of *Concorde*'s first flight. Road transport sounds cover steam and the internal combustion engine, classic cars, historic buses, tractors, and motor cycles. Military and Battle sounds begin with an HMV record of a First World War artillery barrage and include a range of material from more recent land and sea conflicts. Sound Effects include a historic collection of effects made by the Bishop

Sound Company, for many years suppliers of sound effects to London's West End theatres, and rare long-deleted items from specialist company recordings going back 60 years.

The developing Artefacts Collection – based on the George Frow collection of phonographs, gramophones, radiograms, tape recorders and other artefacts, together with relevant research and display documentation – is also maintained. Items of particular interest include a modern copy of Thomas Edison's Tinfoil Phonograph of 1877, a German gramophone of 1890s vintage, the original version of the famous HMV painting, and a Pathe Majestic disc phonograph designed to play 20-inch records at over 100 r.p.m. Sponsored by the British Phonographic Industry and by JVC, an exhibition to celebrate the centenary of the gramophone by Emile Berliner, tracing the development of the gramophone and the gramophone record, was held at NSA from May 1988 to the following spring. To accompany the exhibition NSA published *Revolutions In Sound: A Celebration Of 100 Years Of The Gramophone*, a 24pp., A5 illustrated booklet which neatly combines social and business history and technical detail. An attractive leaflet, *Industro-Mechanical Sound/Artefacts* describes the Archive's resources and services in this area.

Conservation of its older materials is a constant preoccupation. 'The main problems, most frequently encountered, are the intrinsic fragility of the carrier, the potential for chemical breakdown in the constituent materials, mechanical damage due to rough handling, inappropriate equipment, and of course from adverse environmental conditions.' Fortunately, 'audio technology is such that it has for some time been far easier to produce a convincing authentic copy of an audio recording than it has, for example, of a medieval bible'. Fully aware of the delicate and unique nature of its collection, NSA has instituted 'a continuously researched long-term audio preservation programme', expertly expounded in Jeremy Silver and Lloyd Stickells's 'Preserving Sound Recordings At The Library National Sound Archive', *Library Conservation News*, **13**, October 1986:1–3, which expands on the technical problems involved and the processes used to solve them. Basically, the theory is simple: once a vulnerable or deteriorating carrier is identified, it is transferred to a more durable carrier which from then on is used for audio playback whilst the original is stored for museum purposes. NSA has taken this simple transaction a stage further by producing two copies: one is taken directly from the original, keeping its attendant noise and interference; the other is subjected to a number of filtering, compression, and processing techniques so that it conforms as nearly as possible to modern sound standards. New techniques for the bulk drying of water-damaged tapes are outlined in 'Freeze-Drying Of Tapes', *ibid.*, **34**, January 1992:4–5.

NSA is also involved in all areas of recording and research. Curators of the various collections provide advice and promote relevant activities within their special field of expertise. Its technical resources include a sonograph, advanced digital and sound laboratories, a Neve DSP desk, and a conservation laboratory. A listening and viewing service is available free of charge to individuals and to small groups by appointment. Although primarily intended for reference use, a commercial Transcription Service is offered, provided that copyright clearance has been obtained. The Library and Information Service provides catalogues, discographies, reference works, and expert staff to assist researchers.

Peter Copeland's 'Sound Recordings on Optical Discs', *Library Conservation News*, **38**, January 1993:7, recounts NSA's search for a sound-recording medium with greater longevity. Its needs are:

(1) a medium to store sound which would accept all current sound recordings without dropping the quality;
(2) the sound should be stored as a digital code, so it could be duplicated indefinitely without dropping the quality;
(3) the lifespan should be measured in decades rather than years;
(4) digitized text should be stored alongside the sound in order to record catalogue data; and
(5) pictorial storage is also essential to act as a substitute if the original should decay.

The answer seems to be a type of optical disc technology known as 'moth's-eye' because, when under a suitably powerful microscope, the information-bearing layer comprising separate shaped cells has all the appearance of the magnified eye of a moth. Having arrived at this point, NSA has to decide what to put on it – the original sound waves in the studio, or the sound mixer's interpretation. 'It may in the end prove necessary to copy a recording several times, in different versions for different needs. Clear documentation would have to be appended to explain the differences between the versions.'

In March 1992, alarmed by the low use of NSA's collections – as few as 35 people a week, *The Times* reported – the British Library invested £500,000 in an attempt to prevent the NSA from sliding into complete disuse. Work began on an automated catalogue which would form the basis of NSA's services and would eventually provide a link with readers at St Pancras. Crispin Jewitt's 'no catalogue at the nsa?', *Playback*, 2, Spring 1992:4, pointed out that only between 50% and 60% of NSA's collections was catalogued, although most of the uncatalogued material was findable through a variety of secondary sources. An ambitious target of 75% of the collection being on a single integrated database by 1995, and 95% by the year 2000, was set for a project being developed in consultation with a Touche Ross management team. The plan is to integrate catalogue information from National Discography covering UK published recordings of broadcasts taken off-air and theatre recordings since 1984, and from its own manual pre-1984 catalogue. When the automation project is completed NSA will have a single integrated catalogue of some 900,000 recorded items available for public use.

A penetrating analysis of the early days of cataloguing at the British Institute of Recorded Sound when a 'mushrooming collection of biscuit tin indexes, prepared sporadically and inconsistently by staff with varying degrees of subject expertise and bibliographic skills', and the advent of a precise cataloguing code based on 'the fusion of well-established bibliographic practice (rigorous analysis and consistency of expression) and the tradition of the private discographer – the enthusiast, expert in the medium and subject, but usually unburdened by any professional training in documentation ', is presented in Diana D. Hull's 'The National Sound Archive And Its Relation To The National Discography', *MARC Users Group Newsletter*, **88** (1), January 1988:13–20. Characteristics of the catalogue, the individual unit of intellectual content, its single sequence dictionary architecture, the depth of its analysis and indexing, the fullness of its description, and the compatibility of its records are examined in detail.

'The original plan was to produce a single catalogue containing all material in the collection and to maintain a database of consistently-created records from which all of the Archive's information and catalogue publication needs could be cheaply produced.' Unfortunately, shortage of cataloguing staff and increasing acquisitions resulted in a gap opening up between intake and cataloguing capacity, with a consequent reversion to the bad old days of private office card indexes. Hence the need for a systematic and adequately resourced project to remedy a totally unacceptable and outdated shortfall in NSA's public services.

Because of its urgent need to preserve its extensive collection of 78 r.p.m. records, NSA has been actively involved from the beginning with Cambridge Sound Publications' Computer Enhanced Digital Audio Restoration (CEDAR) project, an entirely new process for restoring sound recordings to their pristine form by the use of the latest developments in digital sound processing and microcomputer technology. Four main processes remove unwanted hiss or crackle caused by wear and tear without interfering with the recording's signal content. First, the recording is scanned for gouges, or even breakages; then the signal content is analysed to identify protracted surface noise. Next, clicks and scratches are located and, finally, the unwanted noise content is analysed. Separate signal processing techniques are then brought into play and each category of noise is removed to leave the original audio signal content unimpaired. No attempt is made to remove imperfections caused by the current state of recording technology at the time of performance, so the recording is restored to its original state.

John Windsor's 'Revolutionary inventions put 78s back on the turntable', *The Independent*, **988**, 9 December 1989:39, is a not too technical report on progress to date. In the summer of 1989 British Library signed an agreement with Cable & Wireless to work together in a new company with long-term plans to make CEDAR available to customers worldwide through Cable & Wireless' Global Digital Highway of fibre optic cables. A notable instance of NSA's leadership in state-of-the-art technology occurred when a 103-year-old coated cardboard gramophone cylinder was rediscovered in the Science Museum and passed to the Archive's conservation unit. After applying CEDAR, a voice thought to be Queen Victoria's was revealed. The full story is told in Paul Tritton's *The Lost Voice of Queen Victoria* (1991).

NSA continues to sustain an archive publishing programme. Following a 1984 nationwide survey when questionnaires went to various institutions and businesses, the responses were entered on to a database, the National Register for Collections of Recorded Sound, from which Lali Weerasinghe compiled and edited the *Directory of Recorded Sound Resources in the United Kingdom* (1989, xxii, 173pp.). Listing 489 numbered collections covering all subject areas, the information provided on each collection includes full address, opening times, conditions of access, details of the collections, named special collections, finding aids available, published indexes or catalogues, and other print or audio publications associated with the collection. An index comprising subject, individual persons, and named collection headings allows research access in the form of a selective guide rather than a definitive analysis of topics.

Popular Music Periodicals Index (POMPI), now published biennially, is currently available in three volumes: *October 1984–September 1986*

(1988); *October 1986–September 1988* (1989); and *October 1988–September 1989* (1991). To all intents a catalogue of NSA's English-language periodical holdings, this easy reference guide provides subject access to the feature articles and interviews in popular music and jazz periodicals and is compiled by three members of NSA's curatorial staff, Chris Clark (jazz), Andy Linehan (popular music), and their assistant, Paul Wilson, with additional input from Exeter University Library staff. A brief history of the POMPI project, the need for such a publication, its indexing policy, and future possibilities – which include publication in CD-ROM format and the extension of POMPI to non-English language periodicals and to material printed to 1984 – are all covered in Chris Clark's 'POMPI: Popular Music Periodicals Index', *Fontes Artis Musicae*, **38** (1), January–March 1991:32–7, which ends with a classified list of periodical titles already indexed.

Robert Perks' *Oral History: An Annotated Bibliography* (1990, 183pp.) includes 2,132 numbered and annotated items relating to print and audio publications, ranging from practical guides, community histories, project catalogues, and teaching materials, to transcribed life stories and academic studies. Coverage is comprehensive for the United Kingdom and selective for the rest of the world. A well-structured index contains names, topics, places, and concepts. *Developments In Recorded Sound: A Catalogue of Oral History Interviews* (1989, xviii, 59pp.) is a synopsis of over 100 interviews with artists, engineers, and managers involved in the recording industry.

Notable audio-wildlife publications include Ron Kettle's *British Bird Songs & Calls* (1987, two cassettes and booklet in slipcase), a set of tapes for identifying the sounds of 119 frequently heard birds, and the same compiler's *More British Bird Sounds* (1990, cassette with recording notes), identifying a further 52 species, including many to be found only in remote areas or whose survival is threatened by the destruction of their natural habitats; and Kettle and Richard Ranft's *British Bird Songs on CD* (1992, two CDs and booklet in slipcase).

Described by the author, Conservation Manager at the NSA, as a collection of information and anecdotes, Peter Copeland's *Sound Recordings* (British Library, 1991, 80pp.) is a pleasant introductory survey of the history of sound recording which not only considers the highways of the progress of recording techniques but also delves into the byways of the development of sound recording documentation, the faking of recordings, and some technical freaks and follies of the recording companies. Timothy Day's well received *Discography of Tudor Church*

Music (1989, 320pp.) documents the rediscovery of this type of music in recorded performances.

Playback: The Bulletin Of The National Sound Archive (Spring 1992–) is issued three times a year. Its contents include details of NSA's current and future activities, news from the world of sound archives and audio preservation, and informative historical articles. *Introducing The National Sound Archive* is a twice-folded A5 illustrated leaflet outlining its services, resources, and collections. NSA is spared two pages in Janice Anderson's *The British Library: Humanities & Social Sciences Collections* (British Library, 2nd ed., 1990).

In 1986 NSA joined forces with the Mechanical-Copyright Protection Society (MCPS) to produce a centralized online discography of all UK commercial sound recordings. For its part MCPS (the owner of the National Discography) needed to identify the copyright owners of every recording issued, either currently available or long deleted, whilst NSA was anxious to catalogue its immense holdings of discs and tapes. Although it was at first hoped to have the database available in 1991, it was eventually decided to delay its launch until negotiations with the UK music publishers and record companies persuaded them to turn the National Discography into a joint venture. Priority was given initially to 'currently' available recordings – that is, from the date of the signing of the agreement between NSA and MCPS in 1986. Once this information is fed into the database the plan is to tackle the immense task of retrospectively capturing NSA's historical collections. Two documentary sources feed information into the system: the label copy that a record company sends to a printer for the creation of a label, and the statutory notice which notifies MCPS or a music publisher of the royalty entitlement on the product issued. NSA holds the print rights to the National Discography (the online rights are retained by MCPS). When the project was first announced, it was reported that 'the Archive plan to develop its services with the printed publication of the national discography, exploiting British Library's considerable experience in producing national catalogues of different forms of material' ('Work begins on national discography', *British Library News*, **14**, February 1986:1). Sadly these plans appear either to have been shelved or to have receded into the distant future.

The National Discography database comprises seven large computer files linked together to allow access via every conceivable route. A products file includes titles, performers, formats, UK and international catalogue numbers, barcodes, music classification, distributors, and current dealer prices. A recording file gives performer details (including the instrument being played), track timings and sequences, medley details, recording details (venue, date, owner), composers, arrangers, and publishers. Performers include vital statistics, country of origin, styles of music, roles and instruments played, and of which groups the performers are or have been members. Separate files for composers, writers and publishers; record companies and labels; and distributors, can be searched at several levels: Quick Search takes words from all of the files in any combination; Basic Search can be made by title, performer, composer or arranger, record company, label, catalogue number, barcode, release date, and by price; Combination Search uses any combination of the Basic Searches; Customized Search provides precision searching; and Linked Searching, developed specifically for the National Discography, enables the searcher to move from one aspect to another within a single long continuous search sequence. Originally the National Discography was to be available in two forms, CD-ROM and online text, but in the event only the online service is offered.

Supported by a database of more than 200,000 products, the National Discography became fully operational in 1993, offering three new information services. A catalogue service started in February with a 'shopping' facility which supplies customers with the level of information they require from whatever details – catalogue numbers, record company, or artist – they may have. From March an information desk, open during normal office hours, provides a fast response service answering specific music queries by phone or fax. A new release service came on song from April, providing a regular weekly, fortnightly, or monthly update on all forthcoming UK music product releases, supplied on computer disk or tape to run on subscribers' own systems, giving full commercial information including scheduled release dates, distributors, and trade prices.

Although preliminary articles had appeared in specialist journals, the National Discography was generally introduced to the library and information world at the Library Association UmbrelLA Conference in Leeds in 1991 when an A4 brochure, *The CD with an IQ*, provided details of what the database contained, how it worked, and how it could be used. Historical notes on the project; on the purposes of its two funding sponsors, NSA and MCPS; and sections on how it is compiled, with reactions from all areas of the British Phonographic Industry, were printed in a separate eight-page glossy brochure, *National Discography. The Sound Recordings Information Bureau*, inserted in an inside cover pocket of the main brochure. *ND News* (Spring 1991–) is a very occasional update on the project published by MCPS. Malcolm Tibber, General Manager of the National Discography, writes authoritatively of its origins and operations, its potential users, and its perceived pattern of future services, in his 'The National Discography', *Audiovisual Librarian*, **15** (1), February 1989:25–8.

NEWSPAPER LIBRARY

Located at Colindale in north-west London, the British Library Newspaper Library (BLNL) has been described as 'unique among the world's great research libraries for its integration on a separate site of all activities associated with the acquisition, organisation, preservation and use of newspapers' (Geoffrey Hamilton, 'Newspaper preservation and access: developments and possibilities', *Interlending & Document Supply*, **20** (2), April 1992:43–8). Its collections comprise some 600,000 bound volumes and parcels and 250,000 reels of microfilm, of English, Irish, Scottish and Welsh provincial newspapers from 1690, London daily and weekly newspapers (comprehensive from about 1840 onwards), and long runs of Commonwealth and foreign newspapers. About 6,000 volumes and 11,000 reels are added annually. Newspapers requested are delivered from the closed-access stacks to the reading room, where full reference and photocopying services operate. The photocopying services are also available to off-site users. Admission is by either a BLNL reader's pass or by a general British Library reader's pass. Two informative A5 leaflets, *Admission and Regulations*, and *Notes for Readers Using the Newspaper Library Reading Rooms & Copying Services*, are issued for the benefit of users.

BLNL's objectives are:

(1) to maintain the research collections of newspapers within the framework of the Library's collection development policy, including responsibility for the legal deposit of UK and Irish newspapers, selection of overseas newspapers and microfilm purchasing to ensure the most effective use of preservation resources;

(2) to provide the public services to exploit the collections and to act as a focus of expert knowledge of newspapers;

(3) to ensure the preservation of the newspaper stock through planning the microfilming and binding programmes; and

(4) to co-operate with other parts (of H&SS) in assuming the most effective provision of services in the St Pancras building.

(From 'The Objectives of the Newspaper Library', *BLNL Newsletter*, **8**, June 1987:4).

When the former Copyright Receipt Office was reorganized, relocated, and renamed as part of the British Library's strategy to move out of central London as much of its activities and operations as possible, the Newspaper Library assumed responsibility for the Newspaper Legal Deposit Office as from January 1991. Situated in a large warehouse building a short distance away from the Library in Colindale, the Office currently receives over 2,500 titles on legal deposit, about 85% of the total intake, whilst the other 15% consists of 500-plus foreign titles. In addition to daily newspapers, the Newspaper Library generally holds weekly and fortnightly periodicals; less frequently published material is stored with the main H&SS collections at Bloomsbury, although these dividing lines have become blurred in recent years. The detailed work of the Office, how material arrives, how it is processed, how 'missing' issues are recovered, microfilming arrangements, and plans for staff access to microcomputers in a local area network are all revealed in 'The Newspaper Legal Deposit Office', *BLNL Newsletter*, **15**, Spring 1993:1–2.

A reader survey in April and May 1989 was designed to find out who its readers were, why they visited the Library, how many times they came, how long they stayed, and what types of new services they would like to see introduced. Based on a response rate of 48.6% (437 readers out of 900 returned their completed questionnaires), nothing very startling emerged: two-thirds of readers came from London and the Home Counties; over one-third of the respondents were academics, others were freelance journalists or professional media researchers. Of possible new services, telephone ordering excited most interest, closely followed by a general research service, a family history service, and an in-depth advisory service. A quickening-up of delivery times to the reading rooms was the improvement most desired, with longer opening hours, improved catering, fewer microfilm readers out of service, and various copying services complaints also finding a voice; whilst the friendliness and helpfulness of the staff, satisfaction with the collections(!), and the overall efficiency of the service attracted most plaudits.

Perhaps the most surprising statistic was the number of first-time users (39%) included in the survey. Two explanations immediately leap to mind: either that first-time users might be more inclined to return their questionnaires, flattered to be asked, or else many come once for specific information and have no reason to make return visits. The only other conclusion – that some arrive, are not impressed or are frustrated, and are not encouraged to make further visits – is too horrendous to contemplate. All is revealed in Geoff Smith's 'Results of Newspaper Library Survey', *BLNL Newsletter*, **11**, July 1990:2–3.

This survey was followed up by an analysis of all reading room requests for 30 days in the financial year 1990, by category of material, by date, and by specific title requested. Again, the results were not exactly earth-shattering: UK and Irish local and regional titles were most often requested (36% of items delivered), followed by national daily and Sunday titles (32%). Of the national dailies, *The Times* was most in demand (over 20% of requests), twice as many as its nearest rival, *The Daily Telegraph*, with 9%. Requests were divided into three date groups (pre-1900, 1900–49, 1950 to date) with usage being fairly evenly divided. 'The information gathered in the survey will be useful to help plan the most efficient use of the Newspaper Library's storage space. It also raises some questions about whether some parts of our collections (overseas titles, for example) are less used because readers and potential readers are less well aware that they exist' ('Reader Ticket Survey', *BLNL Newsletter*, **13**, Autumn/Winter 1991:12). A survey of the use of the CD-ROM databases available in the reading room at Colindale by asking users to fill in a short questionnaire, and its results, are reported in 'Evaluation of Newspapers on CD-ROM', *ibid.*, **15**, Spring 1993:5.

A fascinating insight into the work of BLNL's binding operations is contained in R. A. Russell's 'Colindale Newspaper Conservation Bindery', *BLNL Newsletter*, **10**, June 1989:12–13, where the problem posed by the use of chemically treated wood-pulp paper by the newspaper industry is graphically confirmed. The bindery was established in the early 1940s by the HMSO, who managed it until British Library took it over in 1983. Preservation treatment up to then consisted of flattening the papers, sewing sections on to tapes and webbing, and binding them in quarter bound double warp linen buckram. New techniques have been harnessed and 'the bindery now has a system that deacidifies wood pulp paper in a way that tests have shown enhances the permanence of the paper by roughly 100 years, provided that good housekeeping is carried out in the storage areas'. It is now possible to deacidify around 6,000 x 8-page newspapers (448 bound volumes of a newspaper) per month; the full capacity of the bindery is in the region of 2,160 volumes a year. Mathematicians will no doubt be able to compute how long it will take for Colindale's vast holdings to be conserved in this way, taking into account newspapers added while this process continues.

The microfilm unit, whose objectives in the early days were to film bomb-damaged volumes and volumes borrowed from other libraries to remedy the gaps resulting from air-raid losses, is now an instrumental factor in implementing the Library's preservation policy for newspapers, and also a far from insignificant revenue earner for copies requested from external customers. The master negative becomes part of the British Library's preservation archive and, as such, is recorded in the National Register of Preservation Microfilms (RPM). To meet a Cabinet Office scrutiny team's recommendation that all British newspapers should be filmed on receipt and the originals should be wrapped and not available to readers, all local newspapers published since 1985 go through that process. Microfilming is also extensively used in preserving older British newspapers, although if commercially produced films of acceptable quality exist then the British Library does not hesitate to make appropriate purchases.

What happens after microfilming is explained in 'Retention of United Kingdom newspapers After Microfilming', *BLNL Newsletter*, **15**, Spring 1993:9–10. A policy decision taken by the British Library Board in July 1990 for the disposal of some foreign newspapers (for which the British Library has no copyright responsibilities) has already released shelving equivalent to 18 months' intake of UK legal deposit material. Because of the British Library's legal requirement to maintain the national printed archive, a recent review of retention policy has decided that original copies of UK newspapers should be retained, not least as an insurance policy against the loss of or damage to microfilm negatives. A number of measures and recommendations to cope with the implications of this decision, including the storage aspect, are enumerated:

(1) the Newspaper Library should implement fully the policy already agreed for disposing of some foreign newspapers after microfilming;
(2) national newspapers will continue to be retained in the original at Colindale even after the intended provision of duplicate microfilm (or possibly CD-ROM) for use in the St Pancras reading rooms;
(3) the Newspaper Library should explore with the national libraries of Scotland and Wales the further scope for their retention of original copies of current local newspapers published in their countries;
(4) low-cost off-site storage should be sought for wrapped originals (post-1986 legal deposit material and weakened bound volumes wrapped after microfilming);
(5) the Newspaper Library should discuss with newspaper publishers arrangements for providing the variant content of local editions; it

should also discuss with other libraries the practicalities of the Newspaper Library's discarding of local variant editions when an original copy is held locally and the changed pages are available on microfilm;

(6) the Newspaper Library should work closely with its partners in the NEWSPLAN project to ensure that for material where the Newspaper Library's original copy is unusable and irreparable, a master negative and positive microfilm copy are available and another original copy is located and the owner notified that this is now to be held as the national archive copy;

(7) the Newspaper Library should also discuss with NEWSPLAN partners the scope for an optimum national strategy for retention arrangements that will meet local and national needs economically and effectively.

BLNL does not figure prominently in *Gateway to Knowledge* (1989), except that a definite intention is stated that it would establish a Centre for the Study of the Press along the same lines as the Centre for the Book at St Pancras. At the time of writing, this intention seems to have fallen by the wayside, although it remains a long-term aim when circumstances (and resources, no doubt) permit.

Intended 'to encourage an exchange of information about all aspects of newspaper collections', *BLNL Newsletter* first appeared in August 1980 as a twice-yearly publication. In the event its appearance has been rather more erratic but, along with *OIOC Newsletter*, it is undoubtedly one of the most readable of the British Library's stable of newsletters, carrying informative features not only on the Library's history but also on some of the titles represented in its collections. Two articles by Eamon Dyas deal with the history of the collections and investigate their diverse nature. 'The Early Development Of the Newspaper Library' (**10**, June 1989:4–6) investigates the early history of newspapers in the British Museum Library. This includes the conscious introduction of a collection building policy by the Trustees in 1822, when they entered into an agreement to acquire the newspapers deposited at the Stamp Office; the decision in the 1880s to reconstitute the newspaper collection as a distinct category in the Library; the problem of storage space at the end of the century; the drastic nature of the solution put forward by the government, which could have led to the destruction of all post-1837 provincial newspapers, and the orchestrated outcry this caused; the eventual building of a special depository at Colindale; and the arrival there not only of newspapers but of all types of serious and popular journals and periodicals.

'Hidden Collections At The Newspaper Library' (**11**, July 1990:5–9) begins with an attempt to define newspapers – more difficult than might appear at first sight – and then proceeds to explore the origins and some notable byways of comics and women's magazines. Finally, Dyas draws attention to draft, unrevised subject title lists available from the Information Officer at Colindale – Caricature and Satirical, Children's and Youth, Cinema, Humorous, Labour and Women's Magazines – and also to the work already carried out on identifying and listing indexes bound with periodicals on the shelves. 'The Newspaper Library at War' (**12**, Spring 1991:3) is a much shorter, straightforward account which relates the effects of enemy action in the shape of a high-explosive bomb on one of Colindale's repositories on 20 October 1940. Recent issues have included anniversary features on 'The Observer 1791 To 1991' (**12**, Spring 1991:7), Chaim Bermant's 'The Jewish Chronicle: 150 Not Out' (**13**, Autumn/Winter 1991:11), and 'The Great Survivors (And Some Which Did Not Survive)' (**13**, 1991:5–6), contrasting the mixed fortunes of some very early titles. Graham Cranfield and John Westmancoat's 'The Newspaper Library, Colindale', pp.66–70, *German Studies* (1986), looks at individual titles printed in Germany and in non-German speaking countries, and includes a list of German-language newspapers currently received.

NEWSPLAN, a programme for preserving local newspapers on archival quality microfilm, maintained by the British Library in co-operation with public library authorities, record offices, local newspapers, and the regional library bureaux, began with a pilot project originally put forward by the South West Regional Library System with the objective of establishing the best approach for collecting basic information about surviving newspaper files in libraries, archives, museums, newspaper offices, and private collections; and for inspecting and assessing their physical condition. The pilot project was effected in 1983–4 and a report, Rosemary Wells' *NEWSPLAN: report of the pilot project in the South West*, was published as a Research and Development Department Library and Information Research Report in 1986. In the following months NEWSPLAN hardened into a planned programme with the notional ultimate aim of promoting and co-ordinating the microfilming and preservation of all local newspapers in the British Isles from the earliest times to the present.

The task was both pressing and expensive. Anyone who has researched among the brittle yellowing pages of newspapers printed on chemically-based wood-pulp paper, used in the rapid expansion of the newspaper industry since 1860 onwards, will need no reminding that such newspapers often crumble at a touch. Their large size requires special purpose-built accommodation, copying facilities, specialist handling, and expert management. NEWSPLAN's aims and objectives were:

(1) research into existing preservation effort and the needs of libraries, museums, and newspaper offices;
(2) sizing up the task of a preservation microfilming programme for newspapers UK-wide;
(3) establishing priorities, local libraries and the British Library in co-operation;
(4) action to initiate microfilming programmes and to obtain resources for them;
(5) sharing experiences built up in the British Library on the management and technical aspects of large-scale microfilming; and
(6) Bibliography of British Newspapers assisted by the gathering of bibliographic and holdings information.

('NEWSPLAN Update', *BLNL Newsletter*, 7, April 1987:4–5).

NEWSPLAN covers the British Isles in ten regional projects, each project starting with research to draw up a survey and inspection of newspaper files held. Storage conditions and restrictions on access are noted and the quality of existing microfilming programmes assessed. Once the survey is complete, recommendations are then made on the future course of action to be followed, primarily how, in what circumstances, and in what order, newspapers should be microfilmed. The cost of this research is shared between libraries in the region and the British Library. NEWSPLAN reports published since 1986 include David Parry's *NEWSPLAN: report of the NEWSPLAN project in the Northern region* (1989); Ruth Gordon's *East Midlands* (1989) – her 'Newspaper Hunting In The East Midlands', *BLNL Newsletter*, 10, June 1989:7, is a brief but evocative account of a day's work on the trail; Ruth Cowley's *North Western Region* (1990); Andrew Parkes' *Yorkshire and Humberside* (1990); Tracey J. Watkins's *West Midlands* (1990); James O'Toole's *Ireland* (1992); and Beti Jones' *Cymru/Wales* (1994). Her progress report 'NEWSPLAN Cymru/Wales', *BLNL Newsletter*, 12, Spring 1991:4–6, refers to some of the more engaging Welsh newspapers. Reports for London and the south east, and Scotland, co-ordinated by Selwyn Eagle and Alice Mackenzie respectively, are expected in 1994. With titles listed and located in an alphabetical sequence by town, the reports cumulatively constitute the most comprehensive survey of local newspapers ever attempted. Locations at BLNL are not recorded.

As the NEWSPLAN project progressed it became increasingly clear that the information collected must be transformed into practical programmes for promoting local newspaper microfilming according to nationally agreed criteria. From the beginning it was envisaged that the recommendations contained in the reports should be implemented within a reasonable time-span. In January 1989 proposals previously agreed by NEWSPLAN's steering committee were submitted to the National Committee for Regional Library Cooperation (NCRLC) (reconstituted in May 1989 as the Libraries and Information Cooperation Council) in order to maintain the momentum built up thus far. A set of five agreed recommendations emerged:

(1) There should be a published national policy on newspaper preservation, agreed by the British Library and all other interested bodies, and a plan aimed at comprehensive microfilming programmes (relying on microfilm as the principal medium of preservation and use) within a timespan of 15–20 years;

(2) an implementation committee . . . should be instituted in each Region, succeeding the NEWSPLAN steering committee on completion of the research phase;

(3) a new national body should be set up by the NCRLC, reporting to it, and representing the Regional implementation committees;

(4) a central data-base should be created, recording all the information gathered by the NEWSPLAN projects, and all action taken or to be taken by local library authorities, by the BLNL, or by other agencies, whilst the information on titles filmed should be included on the national register of microform masters. BLNL is prepared to maintain this data-base; and

(5) the development of adequate microfilming capacity, capable of handling old bound volumes, in libraries and commercial bureaux should be encouraged. Cost-sharing arrangements between libraries and other agencies, particularly the newspaper industry, should be developed.

The British Library agreed to contribute to the planned programme by undertaking from its own resources, and as part of its own archival filming programmes, a proportion of the work identified in the NEWSPLAN reports. It aimed to film those titles the project officers considered should be filmed from its own holding, providing it was able to maintain its microfilming capacity at its current level, but it pointed out that its resources were finite. Libraries would have to attract sponsorship from local companies and partnership schemes if the projects were to reach fruition. The British Library would also provide the new subcommittee's secretariat and maintain and update the proposed central database. Full details of the subcommittee's terms of reference and membership are printed in 'NEWSPLAN Update', *BLNL Newsletter*, **10**, June 1989:2–3.

The first national NEWSPLAN conference was held in April 1991, when it was reported that the subcommittee was contemplating a national retention policy for the original copies of newspapers microfilmed and the possibility of commercial sponsorship. British Library's free newspapers research project to examine and quantify the problems associated with free newspapers, and to propose a national strategy for dealing with them, was announced. The root of the Library's concern was the fear of being overwhelmed by the sheer volume of the free newspaper publishing output, realistically acknowledging that local libraries were unlikely to tackle the problems of collecting and preserving free local newspaper titles. NEWSPLAN's developing programme, the pilot research project in the south west, achievements to date, current local newspapers, and future activities – including the role of the national subcommittee – are all considered in Eve Johansson's 'NEWSPLAN: an update', *Library Conservation News*, **25**, October 1989:4–5.

Another volume in the Bibliography of British Newspapers – a project which will eventually cover all British newspapers in a series of historical county or counties volumes – *Cornwall and Devon*, was published in 1991. It joins *Wiltshire, Kent, Durham and Northumberland*, and *Derbyshire and Nottinghamshire*, already published.

The resources, services, and future development plans of BLNL are outlined by Geoffrey Hamilton in his 'A Ticket To History', *British Book News*, April 1990:242–4. Plans to meet the need for more reading room seats to accommodate the increasing number of researchers are in hand but their full implementation is likely to depend largely on external funding. In addition, 'with the high value placed on information today, the Library is looking at ways of providing a full-cost recovery service to users who need a fast information and photographic service, able to retrieve and reproduce from BLNL's huge store of news and illustrations, material relevant to their current projects'. Huw Richards' 'History stored in column inches', *Times Higher Education Supplement*, 1 February 1991:7, presents a realistic assessment of the problems confronting BLNL in terms of collection and readers' accommodation. At times 'Reading Room Full' notices are posted by 11 o'clock, visitors arriving later being forced to wait with as much patience as they can muster until a reader's seat becomes vacant. It was hoped that ten new readers' seats and a further 20 new microfilm places, would soon be available, although replacing the microfilm machines, some of which had been in service for ten years, was problematical. New technology, such as computer scanning, was still some way from the required degree of sophistication and, in any case, was too expensive for consideration in the immediate future. Nor were opening hours likely to be extended. In many ways Richards painted a sombre picture.

BLISS

In 1988 British Library and the Library Association concluded an Agreement replacing the 1974 Memorandum of Understanding by which the British Library guaranteed to maintain in its existing accommodation the former Library Association Library, henceforward to be known as the British Library Library Association Library – surely the most ponderous and ungainly title ever to be inflicted on a long-suffering profession. The Memorandum had worked well enough until 1987 when it had become clear that with the Library's services costing £300,000 a year at a time when British Library was facing a shortfall in grant-in-aid income as opposed to its total expenditure, a renegotiation of the memorandum was vital. Under the new Agreement both British Library and the Library Association reaffirmed their commitment to an appropriate and cost-effective library service to library and information professionals. In time this would involve other collections and institutions but a continuing special relationship was acknowledged. Nevertheless, a change of title to British Library Information Sciences Service (BLISS), successor to the Library Association Library, was deemed appropriate. The duration of the Agreement was to be for a five-year period from 1 July 1988. At the end of this period, or at a time subsequent to it, British Library intended to transfer BLISS and its collections to St Pancras when the new building was open to the public.

British Library undertook to maintain the integrity of the collection subject to normal discarding practices, to continue to keep it up to date (within the framework of its current acquisition policies), and to keep it available on open access with the proviso that some material would only be available in the general collections and so unavailable for loan. Individual Library Association members would continue to have access to the collections and to enjoy basic library services including personal and postal loans, and would also be entitled to a reader's pass to the main

Bloomsbury reading room. Staffing would be maintained at a cost-effective level in terms of the services offered and at a correct professional/executive/clerical ratio to good professional standards. The Agreement established three bodies to review and monitor the work of BLISS: a Consultative Group to advise British Library on the development of BLISS services; a Review Body to monitor the effectiveness of BLISS and its financial position, and to consider any changes agreed to be necessary; and an Agreement Review Team to Monitor its practical arrangements. Full details, including the financial provisions and dispute procedures, are set out in 'Agreement Between The British Library Board And The Library Association', *Library Association Record*, **90** (7), July 1988:412–13.

And so BLISS, still situated on part of two floors of the Library Association's Headquarters, is essentially a service to the UK library and information profession. Its collections cover all current and historical aspects of librarianship and information science, and topics such as cataloguing and classification, computer applications in libraries, library management, and to a lesser extent book production and the book trade, information retrieval, and archival practices. BLISS also houses the Mark Longman Library, a collection of some 4,000 volumes on printing, the book trade, paper making, bibliography, and related topics, which was deposited at British Library by the Book Trust in 1987. This material is shelved separately and is not recorded in BLISS' main current catalogue on COM fiche which contains all post-1976 items together with a large amount of older recatalogued material. From November 1988 this has been available as the BLISS file on BLAISE-LINE. Information on BLISS collections, catalogues, loan, and other services is collected in an eight-page A5 pamphlet, *Notes for Visitors Using the British Library Information Sciences Service* (n.d.). Dave Ferris's 'Ignorance of BLISS?', *State Librarian*, **38** (2), July 1990:25–7, authoritatively untangles BLISS's complex institutional background and describes its collections and catalogues, reading room services, accommodation, and use.

Annual reports on BLISS staffing, accommodation, promotion and marketing, collections, governance, and current thinking on its role when relocated to St Pancras appear in *Library Association Record* in September or October in order to equate with British Library's financial year. 'The Future of BLISS', *Library Association Record*, **94** (1), January 1992:62–3 contains the text of a 'mission statement' prepared by the Consultative Group 'in the context of a realistic appraisal of the budgets and services of the Library as a whole' on BLISS collections, services, resources, and liaison with other organizations. The aim of BLISS is 'to provide access to information on all aspects of library and information science and related topics by (a) responding directly to enquiries, or (b) referring to, or enabling the referral to, other organisations of enquiries, and (c) facilitating the access to, and usage of, relevant materials held at the British Library'. This should be achieved by:

> providing an open access collection of relevant materials, and assisting in the most effective usage of the whole of the British Library's collections by members of the library and information service community; and providing advice and information to enquirers in response to personal, telephone, postal, fax and E-mail requests, and via any new technological advances in communications which may occur.

BLISS collections should place particular emphasis on English-language material and on that of European relevance. Specifically it should include current directories and similar quick reference material, the most recent issues of key professional journals which should at least match the 200 titles currently on display, and a representative stock of significant and recent monographs in its area of interest.

As an information service BLISS should ensure that it possesses the relevant expertise and a wide knowledge of expertise available elsewhere in British Library. It should assume a leading role in the development of an effective referral service which should have an international element and continue to provide a range of information and literature guides 'and other specifically targeted publications in response to perceived needs'. It should consider the development of a fee-based selective dissemination of information service and other services to British Library staff and it 'should work closely with other organisations to ensure the most effective service to the library and information science community'. The other organizations in mind were the major professional institutions, research centres, and the library and information science schools. Within British Library the Centre for the Book was one department where liaison could obviously be of mutual benefit. And then came the crunch: what all this preamble was leading up to in the hope perhaps of camouflaging the statement's main import. 'The Group believes that the resources required to support fully the ambitious range of information services described . . . can best be brought together by the termination of the obligation for Bliss to support a loans service to Library Association members.' Including the purchase of stock, staff activity such as acquisition, cataloguing, issuing and shelving, accommodation costs, and loans, BLISS was costing British Library something in the region of £260,000 a year. 'The Group concluded that the cost of maintaining a loans service for one section of the lis community is disproportionate to its usage, and the existence of the obligation limits the optimal development of Bliss potential.' In essence the message was that the information needs of Library Association members should in future be met by the national interlibrary loans system and the DSC. It says a lot for the current interests and expectations of the library profession that the ensuing debate was as muted as it was.

Russell Bowden's 'Plans for an information future', *Library Association Record*, **95** (6), June 1993:345, confirms that it is assumed both by British Library and the Library Association that no removal of the BLISS collections will take place until some time in 1995. Both parties also assume that the 1988 Agreement will simply be extended.

A number of Library and Information Guides are published by BLISS, such as *Copyright in the UK* (2nd ed., 1991); *Legal Deposit of Audiovisual Material* (1990); *Matter of Fax* (1993), a directory of library fax numbers; *Directory of European Library and Information Associations* (2nd ed., forthcoming); *JANET* (1993); *Censorship* (1993); and many others. Responsibility for the publication of *CABLIS* (*Current Awareness Bulletin For Library And Information Staff*) passed from BLISS to the Research and Development Department in January 1989. It was relaunched, on condition that it recovered its costs within two years, in a new format with new contents, under a new editor, although BLISS remained responsible for a short time for the creation and input of the contents pages of periodicals feature and for providing a list of monographs added to stock. The redesigned monthly *Bulletin* carried a digest of news coverage including overseas news, thematic literature reviews, and a quarterly feature on reprographic technologies, but it never seemed likely to cover its costs and it ceased publication with the December 1990 issue.

FRIENDS OF THE BRITISH LIBRARY

A Friends of The British Library organization to encourage, assist, and promote the work of the Library was announced late in 1987 and was officially launched in May 1989. Its aims are

(1) 'to widen public understanding of the British Library through the provision of information on its collections and services';

(2) 'to improve awareness of the Library's role as a cultural centre and guardian of the national heritage';

(3) 'to provide a means of developing special relationships with the private sector for fund raising and joint venture activities'; and

(4) 'to establish itself as a self-financing revenue and profile raising organisation over a period of two to three years'.

('Friends of the British Library to be set up', *British Library News*, **131**, November 1987:1).

Privileges of membership include use of an attractive Friends' Room known as the Geoffrey Leigh Room after the benefactor who provided the furnishings, a programme of lectures and other events, tours behind the scenes, the right to a Readers' Pass (subject to the Library's normal regulations), invitations to private views of British Library exhibitions, priority booking for British Library concerts, occasional special offers, and *The Friends Of The British Library Newsletter* three times a year. A change of title to *Friends of The British Library News* was effected with the December 1993 issue (no. 14). First issued in September 1989, the newsletter carries notices of events, tours and visits, and exhibitions; news of recent and forthcoming publications; British Library news, including notable recent acquisitions; details of grants made from Friends' funds; and informative articles on the Library's collections. A colourful 9.5cm x 21cm brochure, *The Friends Of The British Library*, containing details of membership application and subscription rates, is obtainable from The Friends Of The British Library, Great Russell Street, London WC1B 3DG. The organization is a registered charity.

AMERICAN TRUST FOR THE BRITISH LIBRARY

The American Trust for the British Library, formed in 1979 to fill gaps in the Library's collection of American material published 1850–1950, and to replace the 9,000 American books destroyed by bombing in the Second World War, successfully completed its programme and was formally wound up on 1 January 1993. Latterly, its acquisition programme centred round the compilation of what were known as the Pew bibliographies in 49 subject fields in science and technology, regional history, social history, political and social science, and the humanities, supported by a grant from the Pew Memorial Trust.

Each bibliography contains an average of 2000 entries primarily for works published during 1880–1950, the period with which the Trust is concerned. The bibliographies are, as their length would indicate, selectively tailored to the particular requirements of the British Library and the American Trust. They include books, journals, transactions of learned societies and, where relevant, newspapers. After each bibliography is checked against the BL's holdings, it is used as the basis of a desiderata list. The majority of the titles on these desiderata lists will then be microfilmed and copies supplied to the British Library.

(Katherine Van de Vate, 'The Subject Bibliographies for the American Trust for the British Library', *American Studies Library Newsletter*, **21**, June 1986:33).

The Trust has reformed as an affiliate to the New York office of the English Speaking Union and will continue to act as a channel for grants and donations to the Library.

DAVID AND MARY ECCLES CENTRE FOR AMERICAN STUDIES

Endowed with a £1 million gift to the Library from Viscount Eccles, the first Chairman of the British Library Board, and his wife, the former Mary Hyde, a scholar of eighteenth-century literature, the David and Mary Eccles Centre for American Studies was established in 1991 to develop and promote the British Library's collections of Americana as a means of increasing understanding and knowledge of North America and strengthening Anglo-American friendship. Its Bibliographical Editor is responsible for the collation of relevant materials from the Library's collections, the setting up of computer databases, including a national electronic communications network and bulletin board, the publication of guides to the collections, and the provision of assistance to scholars, specialists, and the general public.

In December 1992 the Centre published *An Era Of Change. Contemporary UK–US–West European Relations. A Bibliography of Materials held at the British Library*, a 55-page descriptive booklet divided by form (monographs, articles, conference proceedings, reports, and UK and US official publications) and arranged in Political, Economic and Strategic Relations sections. R. Burchell's 'The David and Mary Eccles Centre For American Studies', *American Studies Newsletter*, **34**, January 1992:14–16 outlines the Centre's programme.

5

SPECIAL COLLECTIONS

ORIENTAL AND INDIA OFFICE COLLECTIONS

Oriental and India Office Collections (OIOC) formally came into existence in April 1991, the result of a reorganization of London-based services prior to the transfer to St Pancras. It comprises the former Oriental Collections, established as the Department of Oriental Manuscripts in the British Museum Library in 1867, and the India Office Library and Records, which traced its history back to the East India Company's library, founded in 1801, and which became the British Library's responsibility in April 1982. The combined libraries and archives constitute the world's most comprehensive collection of material in the languages and literature of Asia, and those parts of North and North-East Africa which use a non-Roman script, being particularly strong in the humanities and social and political sciences, and in Indological and modern South Asian material, notably that relating to the history of India in the British period.

Inevitably the transfer of Oriental Collections from British Library's Store Street premises in Bloomsbury to Orbit House, south of the Thames, near Waterloo Bridge, extracted a letter of protest from an illustrious group of academics to *The Times*, urging British Library to cancel the proposed move, 'to take . . . both a courageous and correct decision and place the needs of conservation above administrative convenience and short-term financial savings' ('Moving London's eastern treasures', *The Times*, **63282**, 4 January 1989:11). Specifically they feared damage to 'unique and irreplaceable treasures of international importance' and the disruption of scholarship and academic research. If the transfer and merger of the two collections were driven by the Library's need to reappraise its London accommodation budget and resources following government cuts in its grant-in-aid, the housing of the collections on one site would give more extensive access to readers, allow staff to be deployed more effectively, and save posts in administration and book delivery.

Confirmation of the move came in March 1990 when it was announced that:

> a new reading room will be provided . . . air conditioning will be installed where OC's manuscripts and rare books are to be stored, and compact shelving erected to take printed materials . . . the new purpose-designed reading room on the 1st floor will provide more space and facilities than those presently enjoyed by readers in either Orbit House or Store Street. There will be 76 reader places, with another 6 in the soundproofed area where cassette-recorders and PCs may be used. The use of fax machines will improve the efficiency of document-delivery. There will be more material on open-access and greater scope for displaying current periodicals. Provision has also been made for the future installation of terminals for public access to the Library's on-line catalogues (J. M. Smethurst, 'Oriental Collections To Join The India Office Library & Records, *IOLR/OC Newsletter*, Spring/Summer 1990:1–2).

The story unravels in words and pictures in John Sim's 'New Reading Room To Open in January', *OIOC Newsletter*, **45**, Autumn/Winter 1990:1–2 and 'Move Into Orbit House Completed', *ibid.*, **46**, Spring/Summer 1991:1–2.

Descriptions of the various collections frequently appear in the *Newsletter*. Vrej Nercessian's 'Bibliographical Sources On Armenian Periodicals: A Survey And Guide To OMPB Resources' (**37–38**, March 1987:2-4), the same writer's 'OIOC Acquires Important Armenian Collection' (**47**, Winter/Spring 1991/2:7–11), and D. M. Blake's 'The Verelst Collection' (**41**, September 1988:15), describing a collection of papers relating to British activities in Bengal following Clive's victory at Plassey in 1757, are recent examples. An account of Panizzi's efforts to obtain India Office publications and to enforce the conditions of the Copyright Act, under which the British Museum Library was entitled to receive a copy of all works published in India, is printed in Ilse Sternberg's 'The British Museum Library and The India Office', *British Library Journal*, **17** (2), Autumn 1991:151–66, which brings the story up to the Indian Government's termination of copyright privileges for both libraries in 1948.

OIOC's Stein Collection of manuscripts, mostly in scroll form – recovered from a walled-up library in the Caves of the Thousand Buddhas near Dunhuang, an important administrative and cultural centre in Gansu Province, China – comprises fifth- to tenth-century Buddhist and secular texts translated into Chinese. Hidden in the late tenth century when invasion threatened, they had remained undisturbed until the early years of the twentieth. The circumstances surrounding their discovery by Sir Aurel Stein and other European archaeological explorers are graphically recounted in Peter Hopkirk's *Foreign Devils On The Silk Road. The Search for the Lost Cities and Treasures of Chinese Central Asia* (John Murray, 1980). Despite the best efforts of the British Library conservators, up to a third of the collection remained untapped by scholars, too fragile to be handled or microfilmed. In 1987 visiting scholars from the Institute of History in the Chinese Academy of Social Sciences suggested that a facsimile publication of the secular documents by the Sichuan People's Publishing House should be attempted. The full story of the organization, staffing, and funding involved; and of the formidable technical problems that needed to be tackled, in the UK and China, is related in Frances Wood's 'The Dunhuang Manuscripts Project. A brief review', *OIOC Newsletter*, **45**, Autumn/Winter 1990:11–12; in Beth McKillop's 'A scholar visits China', *ibid.*, **46**, Spring/Summer 1991: 16–17; and in Wood's 'The Dunhuang Manuscripts Project. Reaping the rewards', *ibid.*, **47**, Winter/Spring 1991/92:13–14. Eventually, it might be suspected, the behind-the-scenes story of this extremely delicate and hazardous operation will be the subject of a book-length study. Certainly it was one of the most intriguing and enterprising of all British Library projects in recent years.

South Asian Studies: papers presented at a colloquium at the British Library 24–26 April 1985, edited by Albertine Gaur (1986, 327pp.) includes Gaur's 'South Asian material in the Department of Oriental Manuscripts and Printed Books' (pp.4–12), an overview history of the collections, and a description of some outstanding individual items; and Ray Desmond and Martin Moir's 'South Asian material in the India Office Library & Records' (pp.13–21), which provides valuable notes on finding aids and on the microfilm exchange agreements with the National Archives of India and Pakistan's National Documentation Centre. Richard Bingle's 'Private papers in the India Office Library & Records' (pp.26–36) investigates the origins and growth of the collections, their chronological distribution, and the large quantity of material concerning the end of British rule in India. Mary Lloyd's 'Publications proscribed by the Government of India' (pp.102–5) examines a collection of special interest to historians; and David M. Blake's 'Oral archives at the India Office Library & Records' (pp.128–34) assesses their use and value, outlines the technical support available, and ends with a composite list of the archives held.

Chinese Studies. Papers presented at a colloquium at the School of Oriental Studies, University of London, 16–17 April 1987, edited by Frances Wood (British Library, 1988), includes Anthony Farrington's 'Chinese materials in the India Office Library and Records' (pp.61–70), which is devoted mainly to records of the East India Company's trade with China and to political relations between China and the British government of India; and Wood's 'Curiosities of the British Library Chinese Collection' (pp.97–105), giving the historical provenance of some of the items in the Oriental Collections inherited from the British Museum Library's foundation collections and other more recent acquisitions. Two papers in *African Studies* (British Library in association with SCOLMA, 1986) relate to OIOC material: Penelope Tuson's 'British Library African resources (2) archival' (pp.218–26) points out that the archives of the India Office are a rich source of materials on Africa, outlines their scope and provenance, and suggests ways in which these resources might be more fully exploited; whilst Hugh J. Goodacre's 'The Department of Oriental Manuscripts and Printed Books' (pp.227–30) is mostly given over to the collection of about 600 Ethiopic manuscripts, predominantly biblical and religious in character, but representing all branches of the literature of medieval and early modern Ethiopia. Two specialist papers relating to OIOC appear in *Women's Studies* (1990): Penelope Tuson's 'Suffragettes and saris: resources for women's studies in the India Office Library & Records' (pp.98–108) and Albertine Gaur's 'The life of Asian women as depicted in oriental manuscript illustrations' (pp.109–15).

Illustrating India's architecture, archaeology, ethnology, social life, trade and transport, OIOC's photographic archive ranges from one or two associated items to collections comprising 70 or more albums. An award of £160,000 by the Getty Grant Program of Santa Monica, California, announced in June 1993, will be used to produce an up-to-date catalogue and a computer database, thus allowing researchers much improved access to some 250,000 images.

Because of the wealth and diversity of the collections, the British Library has always been assiduous in printing catalogues and guides. Recent titles in the A5-size pamphlet guides include Yu-Ying Brown's *Japanese Language Collections In The British Library* (1988, 24pp.), giving historical and location details; *India Office Records. The Board's Collections 1796–1858* (n.d., 6pp.), offering advice on tracing material; *Map Collections in The India Office Records* (1988, 15pp.), which contains notes on their historical background and context, their scope, and on related collections in other institutions; *India Office Records.*

Ecclesiastical Returns (n.d., 7pp.), a brief guide to birth, marriage, and death registers sent to the East India Company's London headquarters; and *Political and Secret Department Registers And Indexes 1875–1930* (n.d., 14pp.), outlining effective search sequences when using the records.

John Sims' 'OIOC at St Pancras', *OIOC Newsletter,* **48–49**, Autumn 1993:1–3 is the most detailed study to date of what effect the move there will have on OIOC readers. 'The OIOC reading room is situated on the third floor in the north-eastern corner of the building . . . with high-level natural lighting . . . The catalogue consultation area will be the nearest to the entrance and the reading area beyond with the service counter sited centrally so as to be easily accessible to readers in both areas . . . The appearance of the room will be enhanced by a display of large paintings from the former India Office collection. The graphic collections will be used, as now, in a separate Prints and Drawings room, which will be next-door to the main reading room.' Existing card catalogues of Western language printed books 1936–1983 which will eventually be incorporated in the general OPAC at St Pancras, and the complexities in their use caused by previous weeding of the stock and recataloguing on various occasions, are discussed in 'The Printed Book Catalogues – the future, the interim and some mysteries explained', *ibid.*, pp.4–6.

The intricate and skilled work of OIOC's Conservation Studio is described in David Jacob's 'A simple form of Book Support', *Library Conservation News*, **33**, October 1990:3 + 8, and in Jacob's and Barbara Rodgers' 'Developments in the Conservation of Islamic Manuscripts at IOLR', *OIOC Newsletter*, **45**, Autumn/Winter 1990:17, which outlines its efforts to restore this type of material by using well-tested conservation techniques in ways fully compatible with traditional Islamic book construction methods.

A number of book-length guides to the collections are published. Rosemary Seton's *The Indian 'Mutiny' 1857–58: a guide to source materials in the India Office Library and Records* (1986, 104pp.) outlines its vast archival materials, including records of the East India Company, the Board of Control and the India Office; proceedings of the government of India, the Presidencies and Provinces; and private papers and photographs. Amar Kaur Jasbir Singh's *A guide to source materials in the India Office Library and Records for the history of Tibet, Sikkim and Bhutan 1765–1950* (1988, 187pp.) is a similar descriptive inventory and acts as a companion volume to his *Himalayan Triangle: a historical survey of British India's relations with Tibet, Sikkim and Bhutan*

1765–1950 (1988, 428pp.). Michael Moir's *A general guide to the India Office Records* (1988, 331pp.), designed to help researchers negotiate their way through the bewildering range of records either by their provenance, period, place, or subject, is arranged in two parts. Part 1 explains the Records' administrative background whilst Part 2 is an annotated guide to their provenance. Ian A. Baxter's *India Office Library and Records: A Brief Guide to Biographical Sources* (2nd ed., 1990, 59pp.) is arranged according to categories of people with indications of the different types of source material for each category. Short illustrated surveys of the two former separate collections appear in Janice Anderson's *The British Library Humanities and Social Sciences Collections* (2nd ed., 1990).

As a result of the British Library's uninhibited tendency to change the names of its divisions and directorates at the drop of a new strategic plan, the *Newsletter*, although remaining constant in its format and contents – which include views of current projects, notable acquisitions, reviews of new publications, details of research in progress, senior staff visits overseas to their specialist areas, and longer articles based on the collections – has suffered more than one change of title. *The India Office Library and Records Newsletter* (1974–) became first *India Office Library And Records Oriental Collections Newsletter* in September 1987 and then *OIOC Newsletter* in Autumn/Winter 1990, at which point the editor was gracious enough to offer his apologies to serial librarians and cataloguers everywhere.

WESTERN MANUSCRIPTS

Medieval illuminated manuscripts, notably the seventh-century Lindisfarne Gospels, and the fourth-century Codex Sinaiticus; charters and rolls, and other legal documents; seals; Greek and Latin papyri; the correspondence of politicians, statesmen and diplomats; literary manuscripts and autographs; scripts of plays performed in the UK from 1824 to the present day; music manuscripts; and maps and other topographical material are all numbered amongst the collections of Western Manuscripts.

Daniel P. Waley's 'Resources for advanced research in Canadian Studies in the British Library Reference Division: archival materials', pp.55–7, *Canadian Studies. Papers presented at a colloquium at the British Library 17–19 August 1983* (British Library, 1984) and his 'Materials bearing on Australian and New Zealand Studies in the Department of Manuscripts, British Library Reference Division', pp.166–8, *Australian and New Zealand Studies. Papers presented at a*

colloquium at the British Library 7–9 February 1984 (1985), both edited
by Patricia McLaren-Turner, describe some important collections of
papers available to scholars and researchers. His 'British Library African
resources (2) archival The Department of Manuscripts', pp.215–17,
African Studies (1986), mentions significant items acquired since 1970,
including nineteenth-century maps of Africa purchased from the Royal
United Services Institution, the voluminous papers of the fourth Earl of
Carnarvon, Colonial Secretary 1866–7 and 1874–8, and the papers of Sir
Mansfeldt Findlay, Councillor at HM Agency in Cairo 1903–5. Sally
Brown examines 'Katherine Mansfield's letters in the Department of
Manuscripts', pp.116–23, *Women's Studies* (1990) – which also includes
Frances Harris's 'Rich and poor widows: eighteenth-century women in
the Althorp papers' (pp.125–8). An illustrated feature on the Manuscript
Collections, including brief descriptions of some outstanding heritage
items, is contained in Janice Anderson's *The British Library. Humanities
& Social Sciences Collections* (British Library, 2nd ed., 1990).

By their very nature manuscripts are necessarily and stringently
restricted to readers undertaking research which cannot be carried out
elsewhere, and if they are to be exploited at all they must be adequately
recorded and documented. A students' room, for which a separate reading pass is required, is situated in the south-east corner of the British
Museum building in Bloomsbury and provides a full range of information and photographic services. Four finding aids especially warrant a
mention. Undoubtedly the most useful is M. A. E. Nickson's *The British
Library: Guide to the catalogues and indexes of the Department of
Manuscripts* (British Library, 2nd ed., 1982), an A4 glossy 24-page
booklet listing both published and unpublished catalogues. An explica-
tion of the amalgamated index, a card index of names of persons and
places, compiled from the indexes of the printed catalogues, and a list of
basic reference works shelved in the Students' Room are also included.

After 20 years of close co-operation with the Department of Manuscripts, Chadwyck-Healey launched the ten-volume *Index of Manuscripts In The British Library* in 1984. This major enterprise comprises a
single sequence index of persons and places containing over one million
entries. Search procedures for material accessioned up to 1950 were
immeasurably improved: one index now takes the place of 30 or more
separate indexes. It includes all the indexes to the working catalogues
and reveals the full richness and variety of Western Manuscripts' collections, enabling users to identify quickly individual items and the collections to which they belong. 'BLRD Department of Manuscripts',

pp.138–41, *A Directory of Rare Books and Special Collections In The United Kingdom And The Republic of Ireland*, edited by Moelwyn I. Williams for the Rare Books Group of the Library Association (Library Association, 1985), examines the numerous and varied finding aids to Western Manuscripts' catalogues and indexes, to collections deposited on permanent loan, to major categories of material such as the manuscripts relating to bibliography and the book trade, to sale catalogues, and to over 2,000 offprints and pamphlets relating to individual manuscripts in the collections. *Calendars of Charters and Rolls in the Manuscript Collections of The British Library*, published by Chadwyck-Healey on 18 reels of positive silver halide microfilm in 1989, records over 75,000 documents, deeds, royal letters, Papal bulls, monastic charters, manorial documents, farm accounts, wills, treaties, diplomatic documents, maps, chronicles, and heraldic material.

Produced by the British Library Manuscript Collections in 1989 in an A4 spiral-bound format, *Automated Cataloguing: A Manual* is a guide to the compilation of data for the automated catalogue introduced in the Manuscript Collections. Based on traditional cataloguing practices adapted for input into personal computers, part 1 covers the construction and formatting of word-processed, narrative descriptions of manuscripts, whilst part 2 deals with the preparation of index entries for a database. Both parts are illustrated with examples from current catalogues. It is stressed that the *Manual* is a local solution to local problems and is based on the principle that automated practices should not stray too far from the standards and conventions in preceding *Catalogues of Additions to the Manuscripts*. These catalogues are soon to be superseded by *Summary Catalogues of Manuscripts*, initially in the form of a printout but eventually in published form, for topics such as early modern, nineteenth- and twentieth-century historical papers; the papers of writers, artists, musicians, and scientists; and book trade records. Western Manuscripts' strong pragmatic approach to arranging and cataloguing its archival material is underlined in Timothy Burnett's 'Theory and Practice in Archive Classification at the British Library', *Journal of the Society of Archivists*, **11** (1 + 2), January and April 1990:17–20.

Priorities in the acquisition of manuscripts are outlined in *For scholarship, research and innovation*, their permanent value to the national heritage being the prime criterion.

We shall seek to create coherent and representative collections relating to the twentieth century, developing our strengths in holdings of literary manuscripts and personal political papers, and acquiring selectively archival collections relating to national institutions or associations. We shall remain highly selective and work in close collaboration with other archives, seeking not to duplicate their areas of primary interest, nor to compete for collections of national importance in such a way that the collections are split (para. 42, p.24).

British Library News regularly reports important acquisitions. The Eleanor Farjeon papers, comprising several hundred items of correspondence, manuscripts, printed plays, operettas, magazines, and poetry by this prolific children's writer, were donated to the Library in 1987. The Secret Treaty of Dover papers of the first Baron Clifford (one of the CABAL), relating to the treaty concluded between Charles II and Louis XIV in 1670 behind the back of Parliament and most of Charles' ministers – some 70 documents including the Treaty's protocol, Charles' letters to his negotiators, and autograph letters to Louis XIV – were acquired by the Library in 1988 with the aid of a generous grant from the NHMF after the Library had opposed the granting of an export licence. The Fund also assisted in the purchase of the Trumbull papers, collected in the seventeenth and eighteenth centuries by the diplomat William Trumbull and his grandson Sir William Trumbull; and in the acquisition of the Duke of Wellington's Waterloo despatch, the initial draft of the Duke's account of the Battle of Waterloo written only hours after the guns fell silent.

A feature, 'The Trumbull papers', *Seventeenth Annual Report 1989–90*:21, describes the dramatic withdrawal of the papers on the afternoon of the sale which aroused public expectations which the British Library would have been hard pressed to meet had the NHMF not stumped up 90% of the asking price.

> Trumbull was a success story, but it cannot be too strongly emphasised that the gap between the Library's resources and the potential calls on them for this class of material is now all but unbridgeable . . .
> In the past, consideration for the public interest led many owners to give their archives to the Library . . . Today, however, the impact of estate duties and the soaring cost of maintaining historic property puts great pressure on owners to realise the cash value of their archives.

The Library warned that 'the dispersal of a great British archive is an irreparable national tragedy'. Whether its warning was heeded or not is impossible to determine, but it would be unwise to lay money on it.

Three archives of literary importance were acquired in 1990: the theatrical archive of Sir Terence Rattigan, including correspondence with many famous names in the world of stage and screen; the G. K. Chesterton archive, comprising childhood writings, journalism, poems (some not yet published), short stories, essays, and correspondence with his famous contemporaries H. G. Wells and George Bernard Shaw, acquired with a subvention from the British Museum's Shaw Fund; and the Macmillan Archive, authors' letters and readers' reports from the 1930s to the 1960s, supplementing earlier Macmillan papers 1850–1930 purchased in 1967. Elizabeth James' 'The Macmillan Archive at the British Library', *Publishing History*, **32**, 1992:67–8, reports that it is one of the Library's most heavily used manuscript collections. The Archive was followed, a year later, by Evelyn Waugh's correspondence, an unusually complete collection including some 4,000 letters from Graham Greene, John Betjeman, and George Orwell. In February 1993 it was announced that the papers of Sir William Petty (1623–87), including 103 large-scale maps from the Down Survey of Ireland as well as treatises on economic, scientific, technical, and religious subjects, had been purchased with another generous grant (£700,000) from the NHMF.

Control of the income from the British Museum's Shaw Fund, bequeathed by George Bernard Shaw 'in acknowledgement of the incalculable value to me of my daily resort to the reading room' in the early years of his career, estimated to be worth £500,000 a year in royalties from his works, including the very lucrative *My Fair Lady* musical, adapted from *Pygmalion*, became a matter of some contention between the Museum and the British Library. Although Sir Edward Boyle told the House of Commons in December 1959 that income from the Fund 'would be used primarily for the benefit of the library', the British Library has never received anything like that sum in a normal year. With the Library's departure from the Reading Room now in sight, the Museum is expecting to accommodate its ethnographical collections and departmental libraries there, and agreement about the disposal of income from the Fund is as far off as ever. The background to this peculiar episode in the Museum's and British Library's history is recounted in Michael Holroyd's 'Abuse of Shaw's literary legacy', *The Times*, **64300**, 7 April 1992, Life & Times Section, p.1.

The culmination of a project whose antecedents go back 20 years to the founders of the Strachey Trust – formed to dispose of Lytton Strachey's papers in such a way as to further the cause of scholarship – the *Location Register Of Twentieth-Century English Literary Manuscripts And Letters: A Union List Of Papers Of Modern English, Irish, Scottish And Welsh Authors In The British Isles* was published by British

Library in two volumes in 1988. Based on the University of Reading Library, where it was launched in 1982 following a pilot project and feasibility study undertaken on behalf of the SCONUL Advisory Committee on Manuscripts, the *Register* is a descriptive list of all literary and personal papers of modern poets, essayists, dramatists, and novelists in publicly available collections – although not always on demand without an appointment – which covers not only native British writers but also immigrants and others who have spent a considerable time in the British Isles. Entirely computer generated, and arranged A–Z by author, each entry includes the title of the document, its date, description, location, and conditions of access. Where possible further information is included on local manuscript numbers, the form of the document (i.e. whether typescript, autograph or proofs), and notes about its eventual publication. The time limit of the twentieth century extends to Victorian writers who lived on into the early years of the century. The project's protohistory, including British Library's role, is outlined in David Sutton's 'A highly important paper chase', *Times Higher Education Supplement*, **648**, 5 April 1988:13, and in Michael Holroyd's 'Preface' (pp.v–vi) to the Register's first volume. Details of a similar project covering literary papers 1700–1900 are printed in Sutton's 'The Location Register of English Literary Manuscripts: a second project', *Journal Of The Society Of Archivists*, **9** (3), July 1988:148–9 and in Sally Brown's 'Location Register of English Literary Manuscripts and Letters the second phase: 1700–1900', *Rare Books Newsletter*, **35**, February 1990:18–19.

MUSIC LIBRARY
No British Library department is more eagerly anticipating its transfer to St Pancras than the Music Library, whose readers currently huddle together in the music reading area at the far end of the OP&SS reading room, where reference books, catalogues, a catalogue desk, a supervisor's desk, and a music readers' table may be found. According to the plan in *Using The Music Reading Area*, an eight-page A5 introductory leaflet, music readers must not trespass on other tables reserved for OP&SS readers!

Much of the music collection of 1.5 million items – covering the history of music from the early sixteenth century onwards, with an emphasis on Western art music – has been acquired under copyright legislation, although legal deposit has not proved so effective with printed music as with books and periodicals, principally because of the absence of a music trade list which could be used to check its receipt. Filling the gaps in copyright material is regarded as essential if the Library is to achieve its ambition of holding a near comprehensive archive of music printed in the United Kingdom. But the Library does not restrict its acquisitions to copyright material; its purchases of new and antiquarian music published abroad are extensive although select and it can boast a wide range.

Significant collections recently acquired include the manuscripts of Haydn's 'London' or 'Salamon' symphonies written during the composer's visits to London, 1791–5, which were purchased for £600,000 from the Royal Philharmonic Society in 1988 with the aid of a grant of £400,000 from the NHMF, and with sizeable contributions from the Baring Foundation, the Mercers' Company and the Worshipful Company of Musicians; the pre-1970 business papers of Novello & Co., who pioneered the production of cheap music scores for the choral societies that emerged in the latter half of the nineteenth century; and the music manuscripts of the composer Bernard Stevens (1916–80). The acquisition of important archives such as these is invariably reported in *British Library News*. *Sundry Sorts Of Music Books*. *Essays on The British Library Collections*. (British Library, 1993) includes contributions from leading European and North American musicologists celebrating British Library's outstanding collections of manuscripts and printed music.

A historical conspectus of the various catalogues of the music collections is available in Malcolm Turner's 'Waving or drowning? – the growth of the music catalogues in the British Library', *Fontes Artis Musicae*, **36**, October 1989:297–304, which follows their history from the first catalogue, started in 1840 and completed ten years later, to a glance forward to the new OPAC to be installed at St Pancras. A formidable milestone on the way is K. G. Saur's massive *Catalogue of Printed Music in the British Library to 1980* (62 vols., 1980–7), which unites in a single sequence entries numbering approximately one million in total from all previous music library catalogues. In compiling this comprehensive work the opportunity was taken by a joint editorial/Music Library team to iron out some long-standing inconsistencies in cataloguing practice. For material published after 1980 it is necessary to consult the current catalogue, growing by something like 4,000 records a year and published in three formats: a monthly updated cumulative fiche catalogue for the use of staff; the non-cumulative interim issues and annual volumes of the *British Catalogue of Music*; and a BLAISE online database. This straightforward division between the *Catalogue of Printed Music* (*CPM*) (pre-1981 imprints) and the current catalogue (post-1980 imprints), making life just a little easier for readers, leaves a gap for pre-1981 imprints acquired since 1980 which is plugged by the automated *CPM Supplement.*

Turner goes into technical detail to explain how automated cataloguing using the UKMARC format is regarded by Music Library staff as something of a mixed blessing, proving initially at least to be two or three times slower than the old manual system. Because staff resources would be wholly inadequate for retrospectively converting *CPM* to an online database so that it could be mounted to the St Pancras OPAC, the Library endeavoured to interest an outside publisher who, in return for a substantial investment in the conversion, would be allowed to market the computerized catalogue. In 1991 British Library signed a contract with Bowker-Saur for a catalogue to be published in a CD-ROM format: *CPM Plus Catalogue of Printed Music in the British Library to 1990 on CD-ROM* (1993) brings together on one disc all the data in:

(1) *CPM* (over 600,000 items to 1980);
(2) The Current Music Catalogue (printed music post-1980 consisting of over 4,700 items); and
(3) *The CPM Supplement.*

As opposed to the printed *CPM* which could only be searched by composer or song titles, *CPM Plus* is a multiple access tool searchable on 12 different data elements, any one of which can be combined with any other. Records can be displayed either in catalogue card or MARC format. The basis of a national music catalogue is now effectively in place.

The advantages and disadvantages of automating the music catalogues are further investigated in Turner's 'Jam tomorrow: the present and future state of the British Library's automated music catalogue Part One', *Fontes Artis Musicae*, **37**, January 1990:48–52, whilst the potential of a computerized catalogue in music library networking is explored by Hugh Cobbe in part two (pp.53–6). Traditionalist readers, bemused by these electronic marvels, will no doubt turn with relief to Turner's 'Card Catalogues In The British Library', *Brio*, **25** (2), Autumn/Winter 1988:51–4, which enumerates the catalogues essentially intended for use by staff although they can be made available to readers by special arrangement. Information about each catalogue is given in standardized form: title of catalogue, description, countries and time period covered, selective or comprehensive for British Library holdings, form, number of entries, arrangement, and whether closed or maintained.

Now compiled from computerized records, the *British Catalogue of Music* (*BCM*) is published by the National Bibliographic Service three times a year, the third issue being an annual volume, and is the most complete list of current printed music available. Covering all types of music, it includes new music printed in the UK received at the Legal Deposit Office, foreign music available in the UK through a sole agent, and music acquired by the Music Library overseas. *BCM* is arranged in three sections: a classified list according to the DDC; an A–Z composer and title index; and, in the annual volume, a subject index listing entries by musical forms, musical characters, and performing forces. A cumulation, *British Catalogue of Music 1957–1985*, edited by Michael Chapman and Elizabeth Robinson (K. G. Saur, 10 vols., 1988–9), includes some 60,000 entries and an index of composers, arrangers, editors, lyricists, and titles.

Printed Music Before 1800 Collection One: The Music Collection Of The British Library London. Series 1 British Printed Music Period A Music Before 1650. Part 1 Individual Composers; Part 2: Anthologies And Tract Volumes was published by Harvester Press Microform Publications in 38 reels of 35mm silver halide roll film with a reduction ratio of 12:1 in 1989. A hard copy guide accompanies the microfilms.

MAP LIBRARY
Although not as crowded as the Music Reading Area, more than four or five readers in the Map Room at the same time definitely constitute a crowd. Admission is reminiscent of Hernando's hideaway – readers must press a bell on an uncompromising closed door on the mezzanine floor of the King Edward VII building on the north side of the British Museum. However, because of the specialist nature of the Map Library's collections, and because many researchers regard it as a library of first rather than last resort, access is not dependent on holding a current British Library reader's ticket. The library is open to all those over the age of 18 who cannot find the material they require in their public or academic library.

Including manuscript maps and printed atlases, engraved maps and charts, celestial and terrestrial globes, and aerial photographs, some 1,600,000 items in all, the Map Library is the national repository for both past and present map production, receiving through legal deposit the full range of UK cartographic publications. Most frequently consulted is the almost complete Ordnance Survey file, including the surveyors' original manuscript drawings for the period 1793–1840, deposited by the Ordnance Survey in 1955. *The Original Manuscript Maps of the First Ordnance Survey of England and Wales, from the British Library Map Library* is available on microfilm from Harvester Press, either as a complete set or in five regional subsets, enabling researchers to trace physical features on the ground even before the date of the first engraved maps. The Map Library's information services include an open-access reference library (the Map Room), although its stock of some two million items is on closed access. Well-established links with foreign survey departments and map producers ensure a steady influx of overseas material; more is received through exchange schemes. Its aim is to maintain world coverage on topographical scales appropriate to individual countries and regions and to collect all important general atlases and significant thematic or special purpose maps. Items of historical interest are acquired when opportunities arise. Outstanding acquisitions are noted in the British Library's *Annual Report.* Notes on its collections, catalogues, the supply of maps and atlases, assistance and enquiries, its photographic service, organized visits, and regulations for admission are printed in a revised introductory foldover leaflet, *Map Library*, issued in 1989.

Following the recommendations of the 1984 House of Lords Select Committee on Science and Technology (Remote Sensing and Digital Mapping) report, the Map Library assumed responsibility for making available on open access all forms of remote sensed imagery, from aerial photography to multispectral data from satellite and airborne systems. R. P. McIntosh's 'Remote Sensing Resources at the British Library', *Cartographic Journal*, **23** (1), June 1986:68–9, describes the national Landset colour imagery archive in the Map Library, the Eros Data Center's 'Microcatalog' – a comprehensive microfiche catalogue which shows the availability and characteristics of Landset data worldwide – and other finding aids at the disposal of readers in the Map Room.

A clear distinction has to be drawn between the Map Library and the total map collections of British Library. For example, most of its manuscript maps – notably those belonging to the British Museum's foundation collections, including four thirteenth-century maps of Britain, and the *Boke of Hydrophaphie* (1542) compiled by Jean Rotz, a Dieppe pilot and King Henry VIII's hydrographer – are in Western Manuscripts Collections, which also holds some printed material such as the proofs of Christopher Saxton's county maps produced in the 1570s. Other manuscript material includes medieval copies of Roman maps, fourteenth-century portolan charts; and large-scale civil and military mapping of western and central Europe, the Americas, and Australia up to 1860. Early oriental maps and manuscript maps from the East India Company's records are in OIOC. *The Map Collections of The British Library* (1989), an introductory, 20-page A5 guide, contains notes on the Map Library's services and resources, details of the contents of and access to manuscript collections elsewhere within British Library, and a useful list of references relating to the history of the collections. *How To Find Manuscript Maps In The British Library* (British Library Manuscript Map Guides No. 2), a duplicated six-page, A4 information sheet available in the Map Room, not only outlines the location of various types of maps within British Library but also indicates the holding of the British Museum's Department of Prints and Drawings, the Museum of Mankind (Department of Ethnography), and the Department of Western Antiquities.

Tony Campbell's 'The British Library's map collections and the national topographic memory', *Cartographic Journal*, **28** (1), June 1991:27–9, is especially valuable both for its overview of the Map Library's current concerns and for its perception of its services in the St Pancras building:

> The Map Library is seizing this opportunity to convert to machine readable form all descriptions of cartographic materials, wherever they might be stored in British Library . . . The breaking down of physical barriers to enable the side-by-side comparison that forms so essential a part of early map research will be matched by a single catalogue access, tailored to the needs of map users. Whether searching the interactive catalogue for author, geographical area, scale, cartographic or other elements, a uniform answer will be given, covering the entire cartographic collections.

The development of the Map Collections is briefly chronicled and illustrated in chapter 10, 'Maps and music: the Printed and Manuscript Collections', in *Treasures Of The British Library* (1988) and, on a lesser scale, in Janice Anderson's *The British Library Humanities & Social Sciences Collections* (2nd ed., 1990). A specially prepared British Library Map Collection offprint from *The Map Collector*, **28**, September 1984, described as 'a general introduction to the cartographic wealth of the British Library', contains an account of the collections and four specific articles on manuscript and oriental maps and on various European thematic and special purpose maps.

Helen Wallis's 'Resources for advanced research in Canadian Studies in the British Library Reference Division: maps', pp.59–65, *Canadian Studies* (British Library, 1984), describes maps and charts inherited from the Foundation Collections of the British Museum Library and the King George III Topographical and Maritime Collections which found their way to the British Museum in 1828 (with further sections in 1844 and

1952), and discusses the development of the Map Library's collections, including the Colonial Copyright Collections and the purchase of the Royal United Services Institution Sheet Map Collection in 1968. Her 'Resources for Australian and New Zealand Studies in the British Library Reference Division: Maps', pp.103–15, *Australian and New Zealand Studies* (1985), consists mostly of an annotated conspectus of relevant cartographic materials, with sections on maps and charts of the Dieppe school; Dutch discoveries of New Holland (Australia) and New Zealand; circumnavigators and collections of voyages; Captain Cook's voyages; and exploration and settlements from 1788. Wallis and Peter Barber's 'Cartographic material relating to Germany in the British Library', pp.62–5, *German Studies* (1986), looks at medieval and Renaissance materials, early military maps, eighteenth-century mapping in King George III's Topographical Collection, and appends a list of catalogues and other finding aids. Wallis also contributed 'South Asian maps in the British Library Reference Division', pp.43–55, *South Asian Studies* (1986).

Printed catalogues of the cartographic collections encompass *The British Museum Catalogue of Printed Maps, Charts and Plans* (British Museum, 15 vols, 1967); *The British Library Catalogue of Printed Maps, Charts and Plans Ten Year Supplement 1965–1974* (1978); and *Catalogue Of Cartographic Materials In The British Library 1975–1988* (K. G. Saur, 3 vols, 1989). This latest catalogue, also available in a microfiche version, is ordered in three sections: geographic names in a single sequence using Map Library geographic headings; a names/title sequence; and a subject sequence. Details of some 260 digital cartographic and remote sensing UK databases, located as a result of a Birkbeck College project sponsored by the Research & Development Department, are also included. Whether or not this will prove to be the last printed catalogue to be published remains uncertain. Accessions since 1988 are recorded in the Cartographic Materials File, a microfiche catalogue in the Map Room.

In April 1992 British Library embarked on an ambitious project to convert its cartographical records, not only in the Map Library but elsewhere in the Library, to machine-readable form in order to incorporate them in the OPAC to be installed at St Pancras. The UK's first online database of cartographic material, updated monthly, was launched in 1988 on BLAISE-LINE, but this only included maps, atlases, and books on cartography accessioned in British Library's collections since 1975. Consequently, the vast bulk of the Map Library's impressive historical collections was not covered and was recorded only in a number of dissimilar printed catalogues employing a variety of cataloguing practices and record layouts and even, in a few instances, in manuscript listings. Within these catalogues access to particular maps was often restricted to a single geographical heading; and information on personal names associated with older maps was frequently sparse and inconsistent. The new retroconversion project, bringing together the disparate records into a single file, will also greatly enhance and standardize the range of possible access routes.

The project is in three phases: the first, scheduled to last two years, involves the conversion of the *Catalogue of Printed Maps*, the *Ten Year Supplement*, and the *Catalogue of Manuscript Maps Charts And Plans Of The Topographic Drawings in the British Museum* (3 vols, 1844–61). When the conversion is completed in 1994 the post-1974 cartographic materials file on BLAISE-LINE will be merged with the retroconverted file to provide a single unified database. Various programmes to make the data more consistent, and to add new data, will then be run to enable the file to be published on CD-ROM, and possibly in hard copy, by Research Publications International, providing access via period, theme, cartographer/publisher, country of publication, and physical form, and on a range of scales. The second phase will concentrate on assimilating records from other catalogues, including those of various historical collections which do not appear in the main printed catalogues, such as *A Catalogue of Maps, Plans, and Views of London, Westminster, and Southwark Collected and Arranged by Frederick Crace* (1878) and *A Catalogue of Manuscript and Printed Reports, Field Books, Memoirs, Maps etc. of the Indian Surveys deposited in the Map Room of the India Office* (1878). At this point records will be added from a separate project listing individual maps in pre-1800 atlases in British Library collections.

Finally, cartographic records for material dispersed in H&SS, Western Manuscripts, SRIS and OIOC will be assembled, and the ultimate objective of this massive project – to collect some 300,000 records, representing some 2 million maps, into a single file, allowing comprehensive access to all British Library cartographic collections – will be attained. Its full story – including technical detail, its limitations, the inadequacy of present resources to collate and remedy inconsistencies in cataloguing practices which accumulated over the years and are still evident in the *Catalogue of Printed Maps*, the compromises made in order to use simplified MARC coding, and the programme of record enhancement – is recounted in Geoff Hutt's 'Maps retroconversion at the British Library',

Mapping Awareness & GIS in Europe, **6** (10), December 1991:8–9.

In the process of compiling a database index to maps in Western Manuscripts Collections, some 600 printed maps bound up in volumes of manuscripts came to light along with letters from cartographers, publishing proposals, and invoices which had previously escaped attention. Some outstanding examples are recorded in Tony Campbell's 'Laying bare the secrets of the British Library's map collections', *Map Collector*, **62**, Spring 1993:38–40, which also explains how the database listing will facilitate the location of manuscript maps throughout the Library's vast collections.

A number of duplicated A4 information sheets can be obtained in the Map Room. *Atlas Maps And How To Find Them* gives instructions on how to locate atlases in the Map Library's collections and a list of the most useful cartobibliographies and their shelfmarks; the *Select Reading List on the History of Geography* (1989, 4pp.) is in four A–Z by author sections: General, Great Britain, Ordnance Survey, and Ireland; *Map Dealers* is a single-sheet select list of dealers in old atlases and maps in England and Wales; and *Where Manuscript Maps Are Held In Britain* (1989, 5pp.) is arranged chronologically and thematically into types of maps, and where to find them, with details of relevant books and articles. Recently published book-length studies include P. D. A. Harvey's *Medieval Maps* (1990, 96pp.), which traces the development of western mapmaking from the early Middle Ages to the first printed maps of the late fifteenth century, taking into account their artistic and technical achievements and use; and A. Crispin Jewitt's *Maps for Empire: the first 2000 numbered War Office maps* (1992, 556pp.), a comprehensive listing of the maps produced by the Intelligence Department of the British War Office 1881–1905.

PHILATELIC COLLECTIONS

Now estimated to consist of over eight million items, the British Library's Philatelic Collections include postage and revenue stamps, postal stationery, artwork, essays, proofs, covers and entires, 'cinderella' material, specimen issues, official and private posts, from nearly all countries and all periods. In one respect the Collections are unique in that they have all been acquired through gifts, bequests, or deposits by the Crown Agents, who supply the Library with all sets of stamps they produce, and by the Universal Postal Union who distribute complete sets of all new postal issues from member countries. Thirty-six separate general, air mail, Great Britain, and country collections are briefly described in an illustrated 10cm x 21cm folded leaflet, *Philatelic Collections* (1993), which also gives information on philatelic displays in the King's Library exhibition gallery, the photographic services, and student facilities (all the Collections are available to students and researchers by appointment).

The most recent acquisitions include the Fletcher Collection of philatelic material, 300 volumes containing examples of virtually all the services provided by the British Post Office, from the middle of the seventeenth century to the 1960s, transferred from the London Borough of Haringey; the Landmark Trust Lundy Island Philatelic Archive, consisting of artwork, essays, proofs, and issued stamps since 1969, and 48 handstamped postmark devices dating from the introduction of the postal service on Lundy Island, in the Bristol Channel, the oldest local post of its kind still operating; the Peter Langmead Collection of Private and Post Office Telegraph Stamps of Great Britain and Ireland, 1854–1881, including issues of the 13 private companies from 1854 to nationalization in 1870, a unique £5.00 De La Rue hand drawn essay of 1876, and stamped telegraph forms from 1870 to the reign of George VI, received by the British Library in lieu of tax; and the Foreign and Commonwealth Office Collection of British Commonwealth postage and revenue stamps, and postal stationery, which dates back to 1890 when the Colonial Office issued instructions to all British territories that examples of postal and revenue stamps were to be sent to London for this official collection.

R. F. Schoolley-West's 'The Philatelic Collections', *Friends Of The British Library Newsletter*, **4**, September 1990:3–4, focuses mainly on the foundation Tapling Collection bequeathed to the British Museum in 1891; whilst D. R. Beech's 'The Philatelic Collections And The British Library As A Philatelic Research Centre', *Friends Of The British Library Newsletter*, **11**, December 1992:5–6, looks at a number of rare stamps in the Collections and gives an insight into the range of philatelic material available throughout the British Library. Schoolley-West's 'Philatelic Sources at the British Library with particular reference to Australian and New Zealand material', pp.125–9, *Australian and New Zealand Studies* (1985) also repays a close reading. Janice Anderson's *The British Library: Humanities & Social Sciences Collections* (British Library, 2nd ed., 1990) identifies some of the principal collections and various outstanding individual items. *The Care and Preservation of Philatelic Materials* by T. J. Collings and Schoolley-West (British Library, 1989) is a practical guide which explains the reasons for the deterioration of fragile philatelic items and advises on storing and exhibiting collections to preserve them in the best possible condition.

6

COLLECTIONS AND PRESERVATION

Collections And Preservation 'is responsible for storage management, including space allocation, relegation and retention policies, book delivery services to the London reading rooms, and humanities document supply services to remote users. It determines and implements the Library's preservation and conservation policies, manages the Library's bindery and conservation workshops, and is responsible for the humanities photographic and reprographic services' (*The British Library Structure and Functions*, publicity leaflet). Formulated in recognition of the need to co-operate with other national and research libraries, the priorities in British Library's preservation policies are outlined in *For scholarship, research and innovation*:

> (1) heritage material and unique or rare material including manuscripts, certain special collections, archives, rare printed material, material of bibliographic or structural importance, or material classed as artefacts; (2) material comprising the national collections of British publications; (3) material that is heavily used now and has become fragile or that may be expected to receive heavy use in the future and has already or is likely to become fragile; (4) material not available elsewhere; (5) material belonging to the research archive; and (6) low-use material which is too fragile to be consulted or copied (para. 50, p.27).

Established within British Library in 1984 to heighten the general awareness of the need for preservation, to promote good preservation practices, and to act as a collection and dissemination of information centre, the National Preservation Office (NPO) works at individual, local, and national levels. Exactly how is revealed in Patricia Chapman's 'The National Preservation Office', *Archives*, **19** (81), April 1989:26–9. For answering individual enquiries a microcomputer database is maintained with files of products and suppliers, the names and addresses of conservators, training courses for professional library and conservation staff, and a bibliographic file to references on all aspects of conservation and preservation. Local-level activities consist mainly of the publishing and dissemination of information, bookmarks and posters, a survival kit, and a collection of factsheets designed to give practical advice on various aspects of preservation. At national level NPO works in close co-operation with the National Preservation Advisory Committee, a group of senior librarians and archivists responsible for the preservation of collections of national importance, with representatives of book trade and professional organizations. Following a seminar on library security in 1988, NPO extended its role to include the alerting of libraries to the security problems they faced. It also provides an information and advisory service on disaster planning and on preservation microfilming standards.

To the benefit of many in the library and information profession, Chapman clarifies precisely what conservation is, what preservation is, and what the differences are between them:

> Simply, preservation seeks to retain the intellectual and/or physical structure of an item. Conservation, the craft of repairing and restoring items, is one option for preserving a book or manuscript. Preservation encompasses a range of activities all designed to safeguard collections and includes the introduction of substitutes, such as microfilm; the general care and maintenance of collections, by cleaning and simple repair; preparation of contingency plans to safeguard collections from fire or flood; control of the environment in storage areas by maintaining temperature and humidity at safe levels; and the conservation of items ranging from protective bindings for current journals and newspapers to the skilled conservation of valued books or manuscripts.

A corpus of literature on NPO's origins, progress, and activities is gradually building up which, although to a certain extent derivative, is also cumulative in nature. The background circumstances leading up to the establishment of NPO, its effect on the growth of preservation awareness nationally, the British Library's influence in persuading professional bodies to lend their support, and NPO's achievements in its relatively short life-span, are authoritatively portrayed in F. W. Ratcliffe's well-documented introduction to *A Reading Guide To The Preservation Of Library Collections*, compiled by NPO, edited by Geraldine Kenny (Library Association Publishing, 1991, 106pp.) whose short essays and annotated reading lists cover preservation policies, surveying collections, storage and environment, setting up a conservation workshop, conservation, substitution, disaster control planning, security, exhibitions and loans, and new technology. David W. G. Clements's 'The National Preservation Office in the British Library', *IFLA Journal*, **12** (1), 1986:25–32, also looks *inter alia* at NPO's prehistory, notably F. W. Ratcliffe's *Preservation policies and conservation in British libraries* (Research & Development Library and Information Report, 25, 1984), which underlined the national lack of preservation expertise and training facilities. Clements also examines British Library activities in support of preservation, the priorities for debate and action within NPO, and the painfully slow process of raising the general awareness of the need for preservation. Some of this ground is also covered in Chapman's 'The National Preservation Office', *Assistant Librarian*, **81** (1), January 1988:6–8. Valerie Ferris's 'The National Preservation Office: its role in the 1990s', *Aslib Information*, **21** (2), February 1993:63–4, presents an extremely useful updated summary of its functions, operations, and publications, and concludes 'much of the emphasis has been on creating an awareness of the importance of preservation in all of its many guises. This has included defining some of the problems, promoting the need for immediate action in some areas, and collecting and preparing information which puts those needs into the context of library and archive management'.

British Library's technical laboratories have always enjoyed a high reputation, partly no doubt built on the goodwill inherited from the British Museum's laboratories but also justified by the advanced technology it has employed in recent years. Nowhere is this more evident than in NPO's pioneering operations. In 1983 H&SS acquired a freeze-dryer and separate freezing and cold storage units primarily intended for experimental use but with the added advantage of possessing the capacity to hold up to 2,000 water-damaged items for emergency treatment if required. Tony Parker, who was responsible for the Library's work on freeze-drying, explains the general principles of the process and evaluates its usefulness for treating a wide range of library materials in his 'The Freeze-Drying Process', *Library Conservation News*, **23**, April 1989:4–5. Another aspect of the use of this process is revealed in Peter Lawson's 'Freezing As A Means Of Pest Control', *ibid.*, **20**, July 1988:6, which describes how pests were eradicated from a valuable nineteenth-century work. Side benefits of this process are that it uses no toxic material and is completely inflammable.

The whole question of preservation and technology was discussed at NPO's third annual seminar, held at the University of York, 20–1 July

1988, to consider the types of technology under development and their implications for library preservation programmes. Papers were read on the range of formats available for the production of information and the need for libraries and archives to define their storage problems; the growth of preservation awareness; the role of reprography and the problems it might create; the work of the Library Association's Sub-Committee on Preservation and Conservation; the theme of preservation in the context of interlibrary lending; selection and retention policies; the use of optical discs for permanent data storage; how the ADONIS document delivery system might lead to more advanced systems; and how technology could help solve the brittle paper problem. All these papers are printed in *Preservation and Technology* (NPO, 1989).

A British Library organized seminar on library book theft and mutilation in 1987, reflecting on the one hand its recent extremely thorough review of its own security procedures and on the other a general growing concern nationally, led to a unanimous call for a national centre to co-ordinate efforts to overcome what was rapidly becoming a serious problem. Inevitably, perhaps, the task fell to the NPO. Because the Library Association was already addressing the problem of personal safety and security, NPO was able to concentrate on two aspects: preventing theft – in Marie Jackson's words, 'presence is the very tenet of preservation' ('Preservation – Who Cares?', *North Western News*, **44**, June 1990:3) – and on securing collections from potential loss or damage caused by negligence. On the question of preventing theft, specific advice was offered on security equipment (what is available, newly marketed products); building security (good practices on doors, windows, and alarms); general procedures (library layout, staff training); and staff awareness.

Described as 'a handy do's and don'ts on the subject', *Security Guides*, a four-page leaflet issued in 1990, offers 'a mixture of common sense and know-how', and advises a survey of existing security arrangements. Once problem areas are identified, appropriate measures can be adopted. Nothing beyond the most basic advice was attempted but at least a list of simple precautions was consolidated and a number of libraries may have been encouraged to review and overhaul their security procedures. *Library Security: Who Cares*, a 22-minute video, provides 'a glimpse of attitudes to library crime and of ways to minimise the effects of library villains'. Four types of villains are distinguished: the businessman in a hurry, the careless non-returner of books, the petty thief, and the deliberate rare book thief. Jackson's 'Please can we have our books back?', *Library Association Record*, **92** (5), May 1990:359–60, 363, reports on NPO's campaign to persuade librarians to face up to their security problems.

Library security was the theme of NPO's 1991 conference at the University of York. Delegates included public, academic, copyright, and special librarians; archivists; police crime prevention officers; and representatives of library security systems companies. A full review of the seminar papers is given in Jackson's 'National Conference on Library Security', *Library Association Record*, **93** (6), June 1991:394, 397, whilst her 'Library Security: facts and figures', *ibid.*, 380, 382, 384, is a reprint of her paper at the Conference. She outlined NPO's function in this area in 'The national framework: the role of the National Preservation Office', chapter 12, *Security and crime prevention in libraries*, edited by Michael Chaney and Alan F. MacDougall (Aldershot: Ashgate, 1992). That the problem shows no sign of going away is confirmed in *Theft and Loss from UK Libraries: a national survey* (Home Office Policy Research Group, 1992), the report of an NPO-instigated survey, which estimates that book losses cost libraries in excess of £150 million a year. Most of the current methods libraries use in fighting crime – fines, amnesties, electronic security systems – are evaluated and the report highlights book count deficiencies. Astonishingly, fewer than 20% of libraries have a security policy. Copies of the report are available from the NPO.

After receiving a cheque for £200 completely out of the blue from a couple who had learned that it cost that much to restore one book, NPO decided in 1987 to launch the 'Adopt a Book Appeal' on the grounds that a lot of other people would be prepared to do likewise. *Adopt A Book And Save Our Literary Heritage*, a 95mm x 210mm folded leaflet, outlines the formidable costs of conservation, indicates what individual adoptions entail, and suggests various fundraising schemes. William Greaves' 'Foster a binding relationship', *The Times*, **63,818**, 22 September 1990:14, investigates why such an appeal should be necessary, and outlines the processes which a restored book undergoes before it can be returned to the Library's shelves for further use.

In addition to priced publications, bibliographies on *Disaster Control, Security, General Preservation, Preservation Policies, Audiovisual Materials on Preservation*, and *Preservation: A Survival Kit* (a set of ten information papers), NPO also issues a number of informative 'freebies'. Three A5 Preservation Guides, *It Just Came Apart In My Hands, See The Film And Save The Book*, and *Photocopying Can Damage Books*, respectively give cogent advice on how to handle books, NPO's microfilming programme, and the dangers of attempting to photocopy certain categories of books. Riley Dunn & Wilson sponsor four A5 pamphlets in the Preservation Policies series: *Boxing, Mould, Encapsulation,* and *Fasciculing.* In A4 format, *Preserving The Past For The Future. The British Library's Commitment To Preservation,* a twice-folded leaflet, 'describes some of the ways in which the British Library is not only combating the consequences of the deterioration of material but also trying to prevent such deterioration in the first place'. It also illustrates how the Library helps in the preservation of other collections. *The National Preservation Office – a national focus for preservation and security in libraries* carries notes on current preservation and security issues and on NPO's activities, whilst Susie Clark's *Photographic Conservation,* a folded leaflet sponsored by the Hulton Picture Company, provides guidelines on handling, storage and basic housekeeping techniques, and the environmental factors which affect photograph preservation: temperature, relative humidity, air purity, and light. *Library Conservation News,* a quarterly newsletter, started life in April 1983 as a current awareness bulletin including news items, book reviews, and article abstracts. A broadening of scope commenced with issue 8, July 1985, when articles taking a more reflective approach and illustrated accounts of practical conservation were introduced. Owing to rising mailing and production costs this excellent publication became available on a subscription-only basis with the January 1989 issue. What effect this had on its circulation figures is not recorded.

Comprehensive guidelines indicating practical ways in which damage to collections can be avoided – including advice on simple library-based repair techniques, together with a short bibliography, and a list of suppliers of materials for conservation, shelving and environmental monitoring and control – are printed in an unattributed feature, 'Preserve us from mould – and humans', *Library Association Record,* **95** (7), July 1993, Trade Supplement: 20–1 which is unquestionably of NPO origin.

For a long period microfilming seemed the only way to preserve books and other printed material, notably nineteenth- and twentieth-century newspapers printed on wood-pulp paper, and it still remains a powerful factor in libraries' preservation programmes. D. W. G. Clements's detailed survey, 'Preservation Microfilming and Substitution Policy in the British Library', *Microfilm Review,* **17** (1), February 1988:17–22, estimated that H&SS collections contained some 1.6 million volumes published since 1850 which were in urgent need of preservation treatment, with another 60,000 being added to that number annually. In view of the high cost of hand conservation, and the limited availability of skilled manpower – to say nothing of the immensity of the task facing British Library, legally required to maintain the UK printed archive – the preservation of the intellectual content of large quantities of material appeared to depend on a transfer to a substitute medium. Only a small proportion of those items of intrinsic and bibliographic value could be provided with hand conservation in the foreseeable future. Clements especially examined the role of preservation microfilming, which permits the exploitation of the intellectual content of items of special value without inflicting further wear and tear of the original, and outlined the progress achieved. At the moment British Library retains the originals but in the long term a change of policy may have to be imposed because of continuing deterioration precluding further preservation treatment. Agreements with two micropublishers, Research Publications and Chadwyck-Healey, augment the Library's collection of microform copies, thus extending the restricted use of rare and valuable items.

So vast is the growth of British Library's microfilming programme that the need was soon apparent for a list recording the existence of microfilm masters in order to prevent costly and unnecessary refilming of originals on request and to assist the development of co-operative microfilming projects. In the first instance the Library's Photographic Service maintained a card index recording archival negatives, some 80,000 items filmed to order, but when the Library embarked on a programme of conservation microfilming in 1983, running in parallel with the customers' orders system, it was decided that instead of maintaining two separate indexes, a single file would be more economic. Valerie Ferris's 'Don't film it if you're not recording it', *Library Conservation News*, **22**, January 1989:3, 8, provides details of the Register of Preservation Microforms (RPM), a MARC-based file accessible through BLAISE-LINE. RPM entries are brief, record both the original and its microform, and indicate whether use of the original is restricted. Funding for the stepped-up microfilming programme was partially forthcoming from the Andrew W. Mellon Foundation of New York which awarded the British Library $1.5 million, and Cambridge University Library and the Bodleian Library $500,000 each, for a five-year co-operative microfilming project. 'This five year programme means that vastly more UK scholarly material will be available to researchers. But the Mellon project aims to go beyond simple availability. It is a preservation alternative to paper strengthening, especially of rare material' ('Boost for UK microfilming', *Seventeenth Annual Report 1989–90*, p.36). Now based at

NPO, the Mellon Microfilming Project has issued two A5 leaflets. One outlines the problems faced by many scholarly collections in UK libraries because of the rapid deterioration of wood-pulp paper; the other, *Choosing a 35mm Microfilm Reading Machine* (1992), explores the factors to look for: ease of use, reliability, performance, overall design, and cost.

The Conservation and Binding Department boasts one of the world's longest traditions of craftsmanship in every aspect of bookbinding. Its techniques and skills, its expertise and workmanship, its modern resources – which range from deacidification equipment for the stabilization of paper, suction tables for the intricate and delicate treatment of fragile manuscripts, beta radiography for the examination of old bindings, a video spectral comparator for the examination of paper pigments and palimpsests, to freeze drying equipment – are now available to the general public. All styles of binding and restoration work can be carried out, including paper and parchment repairs; new binding and rebinding; design binding and presentation volumes; flapcases, slipcases and boxes; portfolios; facsimile bindings; map and document repairs; seals; refurbishing work; and the treatment of water-damaged items. Full details are printed in a 39cm x 21cm folded brochure, *Conservation & Binding Department.*

A significant step forward in the British Library's capacity for dealing with one of the core areas of preservation that had increasingly occupied its attention was reported as coming closer to a successful conclusion in Ed King's 'British Library Book Preservation Process', *Library Conservation News*, **35**, April 1992:1–2. Librarians and conservators had long grappled with the problems caused by the acidic decay of printed materials. What was required was a bulk deacidification and paper-strengthening process which could simultaneously rid paper of acid and strengthen brittle paper that was further weakened by previously used acid neutralization processes. King describes how a process using ethyl acetate and methyl methacrylate became the basis of research, how the process was refined, and how in 1986 feasibility studies began to scale up the process from a laboratory research project to a bulk treatment system. Capitalizing the project out of the British Library's own resources was out of the question but, because of its commercial potential, the Library was able to find a partner, Nordion International, a Canadian company, to develop the process as a viable business venture. A technical study concluded that a commercial market existed and that a pilot plant should be built and operated in the UK. Currently British Library is discussing a fundraising initiative with other major libraries, the Library being prepared to contribute £300,000 a year from its own resources for an initial period.

The three main preservation projects engaging Collections and Preservation staff attention at the time of writing are an investigation into the deterioration of vegetable tanned leather; the feasibility of retaining leather bindings by the use of an organo-aluminium compound; and the development of adhesive archival labels for DSC.

Early in 1990 H&SS's Photographic and Reprographic Service was redesignated British Library Reproductions. Currently situated in various small outhouses on the Bloomsbury site, with units at the Newspaper Library and OIOC, its operations range from the photocopy service for H&SS users to an express service for urgent orders from publishers and the media, a contract service for large microfilming projects, and a postal service for customers unable to consult the collections in person. Its volume of work – in 1991 20 million microfilm frames, 6,500 black and white photographs, 4,500 colour photographs, and a huge quantity of photocopies – is revealed in Tony Mason's 'Copy cats keep an eye on the cash in Bloomsbury', *Library Association Record*, **94** (3), March 1992:188–9. In addition its staff are often called upon to support the work of the Press Office and to supply transparencies and photographs for British Library publications and exhibitions. An eight-page A5 pamphlet, *British Library Reproductions. Photographic and Reprographic Services at Bloomsbury* (n.d.), describes the types of copy provided (paper, microfilm, and conventional photography); the Rapid copy, Standard and Express services; terms and conditions, and copyright restrictions. This is augmented by *British Library Reproductions*, a 12cm x 21cm folder holding eight colour-coded slips confiding the cost of its service menu along with the terms of order and delivery.

7

PUBLIC SERVICES

Public Services is responsible for exploiting the British Library as a major cultural centre and will act as the public's first point of contact in the St Pancras building. It operates the Library's publishing programme, the bookshop, the exhibition programme, a general information service for visitors, and admission facilities for new readers.

Great strides have been made in the British Library's publishing programme in recent years. In addition to scholarly works and a whole range of bibliographical publications, it now publishes books of popular interest, notably a generously illustrated Discoveries and Inventions series in which 'specialist science writers focus on areas of everyday life which have been vastly changed by discovery, research and invention'. The 1993 edition of the annual *Complete List of Priced Publications* extends to 62 pages, and encompasses art, bibliography and reference, business information, cartography, education, gifts and cards, history, library and information science, literature, medicine, microform and CD-ROM publications, music and recording, oriental studies, preservation, publishing information, religion, science and technology, serials, translated research journals, and videos. Not many mainstream publishers can offer such an extensive list. Descriptive *New Titles* catalogues are also issued. Sales distribution, formerly the responsibility of the British Library Publications Sales Unit at Boston Spa, was transferred to Turpin Distribution Services Ltd, Blackhorse Road, Letchworth, Hertfordshire SG6 1HN, with effect from 23 August 1993.

Presently situated in the centre of the Granville Library in the British Library's galleries in the British Museum building, the British Library Bookshop was officially opened on 14 December 1988 by Magnus Magnusson, the writer and broadcaster. Although British Library had been an important publishing house for many years, this was its first major showcase and retail outlet. Previously Library publications had been distributed to two British Museum bookshops on the same terms as to other shops. By opening its own shop a full range of publications could be stocked without losing trade discount. Designed as a free-standing structure of 50 square metres, the shop contains over 100 metres of bookshelf space, eight racking panels, and eight triangular showcases for the display and promotion of exhibition tie-ins. A photograph appears in the illustrated brochure, *The British Library Past Present Future* (1989). Not only British Library publications are stocked; many other titles in music, history, reference, literature, printing, book art, and popular children's books are held. Facsimile maps, posters, and other stationery and gift items are also available. Several years' retail experience will be invaluable when a permanent bookshop, six times the size of the present shop, opens at St Pancras; when the present structure is to be dismantled for probable use as a mobile exhibition bookshop.

For scholarship, research and innovation makes abundantly clear the Library's intention to attract a million visitors to St Pancras each year: 'We shall offer a lively and entertaining exhibitions programme which will make full use of the latest display technologies . . . Our exhibitions will depict the significance of printing in the development and spread of ideas and describe the primacy of the book amid the welter of new information storage techniques. They will celebrate Britain's cultural contribution to the world' (para. 26, p.19). Its education programme will be geared to 'support teachers in schools and in adult education and will extend to the general public within an imaginative programme of lectures, gallery events and other activities' (para. 27, p.20).

8

RESEARCH AND DEVELOPMENT DEPARTMENT

RESEARCH GRANTS

Research & Development (R&D) is the major funding agency for research and development work in the UK library and information science (LIS) field. Most of the projects it supports are 'individual fixed-length projects based either at academic institutions or in working libraries and information services. The work is carried out by one or more researchers under the direction of a Project Head, who will be of acknowledged standing in the field' (*Introducing The British Library Research And Development Department*, 1990, A5 illustrated brochure). R&D does not undertake research itself; its work is intended to benefit the UK library system in general and is not specifically aimed at British Library needs, although these loom large in some areas. A substantial publishing programme disseminates the results and findings of its funded projects.

With knowledge based on experience, R&D is aware that many potential researchers have little or no idea of how to prepare a research proposal that will attract either notice or support. Consequently a set of notes, *Guide to the Preparation of a Research Proposal* (1990, 8pp.), produced to assist applicants for grants, deals with the scope of R&D's principal subject interests, expenditure coverage and non-coverage, application procedures, the format of formal research projects (project definition, expected benefits, dissemination plans, methodology, time-scale and timeliness), financial estimates, and post-application procedures. Similar information is given in *Small Grants in Library and Information Science: A Brief Guide to Applicants* (1990, 8pp.), which also indicates what kind of research is appropriate in this category. *Guide to Awards* (1990, A4, 6pp., s.d.) describes the purpose and scope of the various types of awards available whilst *General Conditions of Grant* (1990, A4, 14pp., s.d.) is a detailed guide to the overall administration of research grants once they have been awarded; for example, the responsibilities of the Project Head, the employment of project staff, travel and subsistence, intellectual property, and the commercial exploitation of research results. *Making An Impact: Guidelines on the dissemination of research* (1990, 12pp.) reinforces R&D's insistence that the results of approved research should be widely disseminated on three counts: the aim of R&D funded research is to bring about beneficial changes to library and information systems; to achieve this research results must reach the intended audience; and, not least, increased awareness is a justification for the spending of public money. Advice is given on the basic issues of dissemination and monitoring the impact of research carried out.

Martin Ince's 'ESRC move to protect library work', *Times Higher Education Supplement*, **1016**, 24 May 1992:3, floated a story that the British Library was about to hive off R&D to the Economic and Social Research Council (ESRC) in order to avoid a steep decline in funded library research. In the past universities had experienced no difficulties in covering R&D-funded research projects' overheads, which were regarded as insignificant in comparison to the research grants awarded. In the straitened circumstances most universities now found themselves in it made sense, so the story ran, to transfer library research to ESRC who, unlike R&D, fully covered institutions' overheads. An R&D spokesman remarked that the Library had asked the OAL for new money to cover these costs but even if this proposal were agreed to it would take some years for the money to arrive. As for a transfer of R&D to ESRC, this was an issue for the DNH. ESRC's chairman denied it had any contact with the British Library on this matter in a letter to *Times Higher Education Supplement (THES)*, **1018**, 8 May 1992:3. If R&D's trepidation was momentarily eased, it returned in full force when the Secretary of State for National Heritage announced at the Library Association's UmbrelLA 2 conference in Manchester in July 1993 that he proposed to set up a new library commission to advise the DNH, and other government departments, on all issues affecting library and information provision. In his conference address the Secretary of State mentioned R&D as one of a number of bodies providing important co-ordinating work. What its role would be *vis à vis* the new commission, or even whether it would remain within the British Library, was by no means clear.

For many years R&D has taken on board a wide range of activities not really related to its original emphasis on awarding research grants – so much so, in fact, that a new departmental structure of five sections

(Research Grants; Development; Information Policy Research; Consultancy Services and International Office; and Support Unit) was unveiled in a four-page A4 leaflet, *R&D Reveals Its New Organisational Development Strategy* on the occasion of its Open Day, 15 November 1992. A summary appears in 'New Look For The R&D Department', *Research Bulletin*, **8**, Autumn 1992:1–2.

Research Grants' main responsibility is to provide financial support for approved research projects, to identify trends, to develop new programmes, and to influence the way information is used by disseminating research results. Its broad aims are to facilitate the improvement of libraries and information systems; to improve the transfer and use of information; to encourage the development of information handling skills; to stimulate developments in the education and training of information professionals; and to encourage the flow of information on new developments and best practice. *Priorities For Research 1989–1994*, an A4 information sheet issued in January 1989, and reproduced verbatim in *International Journal of Information and Library Research*, **1** (1), January 1989:82–3, outlined the parameters within which the new Research Grants section would presumably operate. In that document the type of research programme that would attract support was listed as:

(1) Research into the applications and implications of IT, including electronic publishing and library automation.

(2) Industrial, business and commercial information research, bearing in mind the value of information for economic development.

(3) Information policy research, including library policy and the economics of information, because of various developments which are affecting, or are likely to affect, library and information services.

(4) Basic and strategic information research which examines the underlying principles of information storage and retrieval, with a longer-term aim of developing more effective systems.

(5) Research into information handling in the humanities, particularly into ways in which new technology can be applied.

(6) Educational research concerned with the whole process of finding, using, and communicating information, especially work in the further education sector and work relating to new curricula such as the GCSE.

(7) Research into manpower, education, and training for the library and information profession, taking account of the changing nature of the work and of recommendations arising from earlier studies in this area.

(8) Library research where such issues as the management of change and constraints on funding are important.

(9) Research aimed at improving library and information services through studying the needs of users of services, including researchers and practitioners in the pure, applied and social sciences, as well as the general public.

Priority was also to be given to the dissemination of results by publications and at conferences, seminars, workshops, and so on.

Development Section, which could already claim a wealth of contacts with other funding and influential institutions, was to manage British Library's strategic corporate development projects and to administer the special funds entrusted to the Library by external organizations. In essence the Section's aims were to extend and improve public libraries through administering the Public Library Development Incentive Scheme (PLDIS); to preserve collections of national importance through administering the National Manuscripts Conservation Trust (NMCT) and other funds for preservation; to encourage the flow of information on developments and best practice within the British Library; and to manage the Library's research and development programmes for the benefit of the Library and the UK library and information service.

Information Policy Section will develop a programme to study aspects of the use, acquisition, and provision of information, including government policies and legislation in these areas. Broadly, its aims were listed as to identify and monitor areas for the development and improvement of a national/international information policy; similarly, to identify and monitor trends which affect the development of library and information services policy; to develop a wider awareness of the need for a co-ordinated approach to the emergence of information policies at the local, national, and international level; and to publish information to inform R&D's clients of relevant research and developments. Simultaneously with the circulation of R&D's Development Strategy another leaflet, *Information Policy Section* (A4, 4pp.), was distributed to define the new section's role within the context of current information policies and to outline the scope of its future programme and priorities. Its immediate priorities would be to produce a brief review of information policy issues in the UK over the previous five years; to produce a bibliography on Information Policy which would update Margaret Mann's *Information Policy: a select bibliography*; and to follow up policy issues emerging from Information UK 2000.

British Library Consultancy Services, aimed primarily at overseas library and information services, was set up in 1987 to exploit the Library's unique collections and staff expertise in providing high quality, cost recovery consultancy services. An attractive 12-page, A4 booklet, *The Consultancy Services of The British Library*, provides guidance to prospective clients on the expertise available; the sequence of events once the Library is consulted; collection building, preservation, and accommodation; science and technology information, business information services, and cultural heritage studies and exhibitions; the effective management of resources and their exploitation; library support systems, publishing, and database services; library automation, reprography and electronic storage and delivery; and British Library contact details. In Consultancy Services and International Office the aims of Consultancy Services remain largely as before: to improve library services in the UK and overseas; to make available the Library's unique staff resource; to facilitate staff development; to promote the knowledge and use of British Library collections and other services; to generate revenue for the Library (probably the sole reason for Consultancy Services' existence in these income-generating days); and to co-operate with other consultants in the LIS field. R&D has long enjoyed a high profile overseas in an era of increasing internationalism of LIS research. The International Office provides a prominent focus for British Library's international activities and its aims, although far from specific, may prove to be more and more important as the IT explosion brings the nations of the world together. They are designed to increase the value of the Library's international activities; to improve the quality of policy and decision making on international matters within the Library; to broaden knowledge and understanding within the Library and the UK LIS community about international library and information matters; to enable libraries and other organizations to take opportunities for growth and development; and to contribute to international library and information development.

Finally, the Support Unit facilitates R&D's smooth running. Its tasks encompass dealing with financial matters, including the processing of grant claims; the running of the office; maintaining mailing lists; the despatch of literature for seminars; and all the other humdrum but essential matters that invariably encumber departmental administration.

Most of the millions of pounds awarded to the British Library by the Wolfson Foundation and the Wolfson Family Charitable Trust, 1986–9, was expended in grants to libraries, record offices, museums, learned societies and institutions, either to save important heritage items or collections of national importance from loss by physical deterioration or, in a few instances, to purchase items which otherwise might have gone overseas. A second grant of £750,000 over three years, 1990–2, followed. Details of how R&D processed applications, how they were assessed, and some examples of the projects supported are outlined in 'Wolfson Gift To The British Library', *Research Bulletin*, **1**, Winter 1987:5, and in Stephanie Kenna's 'The Wolfson Grant to the British Library', *Library Conservation News*, **30**, January 1991:1 + 3.

PUBLIC LIBRARY DEVELOPMENT INCENTIVE SCHEME

Between 1986 and 1989 R&D and the DNH jointly funded a research programme leading to the preparation of a series of Library and Information Plans which provided a framework for co-operation between all library and information services in the public, private, and voluntary sectors within a specific locality in order to make the best possible use of their combined resources. Following the success of this joint venture, other R&D and DNH co-operative measures were set in motion: the Public Library Development Incentive Scheme (PLDIS); sponsorship and follow-up studies to the government's 1988 Green Paper on public library finance; management tools for public libraries, including a manual of performance indicators training package; and other general public library studies. A four-page A4 leaflet, *DNH and R&DD: Partners in Projects*, gives background information on all these joint enterprises with details of the reports and other publications they spawned.

Announced to run for a three-year period in December 1987, and continued for a further three years in September 1990, the PLDIS is funded by the DNH.

> The Scheme is intended to encourage new enterprises, which extend or improve public library services in England. Activities likely to promote cooperation between public libraries and other libraries or organisations in the public or private sector are of particular interest and the long-term viability of the project after the period of award is an important criterion when assessing applications.

Priorities for awards have remained constant since the Scheme was first launched: proposals which were either investigations of the scope for innovations in the effective use of contractors for public library functions or services; projects arising from Library and Information Plans; improving the operational efficiency of effectiveness of services through co-operation between public library authorities or with private sector organizations; collaborative training courses in marketing, management, and technology; establishing innovative revenue earning services especially through joint ventures; and participating in the European Library Plan. Applications were welcomed from English local library authorities or their co-operative agencies (such as the regional library systems) or by any public or private organization, including those in the voluntary sector, which could demonstrate that the proposed development would be innovative and contribute to the quality and cost-effectiveness of public library services.

R&D's responsibilities include administering the Scheme, the continual monitoring of the Scheme's success as a whole and of the progress of individual projects, and the preparation of annual progress reports. Two reports about the Scheme, Dean Harrison's *Public Library Development Incentive Scheme 1988–1990*, and Roy Huse's *Public Library Development Incentive Scheme 1988–1992: a strategic examination*, are among the reports of projects funded made available for loan or reference by the British Library Information Sciences Service.

EUROPEAN DRAFT PLAN OF ACTION

Draft Plan of Action for Libraries in the EC, a product and service orientated activity designed to improve the European library infrastructure, was published by the European Commission in July 1988. In conjunction with the OAL (now incorporated into the DNH) R&D became responsible for organizing meetings to keep the UK library and information community informed of developments. At Regents College on 30 November 1988, the background to the Plan, its aims and objectives, were presented to an audience of over 100 librarians and information workers. R&D allocated £50,000 of its 1989/90 budget to help UK libraries and systems suppliers prepare proposals which fitted into one of the Plan's five Action Lines: library source data projects; international linking of systems; innovative technology-based services and products; exchange of experience between member states; and the provision of targeted support for project preparation. The scope and structure of the Plan and subsequent changes following its integration into the Telematics Chapter of the European Commission Framework Programme are outlined in *Research Bulletin*, **3**, Spring 1989:10–11 and **4**, Autumn 1989:9. Further progress with details of EC information packs, funding mechanisms, and the preferred priority themes, is reported in issue no. **6**, Autumn 1991:9–10.

INFORMATION UK 2000

Operating against a background of rapid technological advance – the increasing use of CD-ROM as a publishing medium, computer applications to virtually every aspect of library and information operations, the advance of desk-top publishing systems, the tele-ordering of books, and the revolution in newspaper publishing, were cited – Information UK 2000 was the name given to a programme of linked studies examining the likely impact of these technological developments and of social, political, and economic factors, on the production, storage, and use of information in the 1990s and into the twenty-first century. In initiating and supporting the programme R&D aimed:

> to provide a better framework for policy and decision-making within the information community, at a time of substantial technical innovation; to identify those issues and technologies which, because of their impact on information handling, require a higher priority in terms of research and resources; and to raise awareness within the community at large of the opportunities offered by technical change for new and improved services over the next ten years ('Looking To The Future', *Research Bulletin*, **4**, Autumn 1989:10–11).

Because some of the more important issues were already receiving attention, and because financial and time constraints allowed only a limited number of studies, a task force approach was adopted in order that the expertise of those actively involved in the information industry could be fed into the project. Eleven task forces, consisting of librarians and archivists; information workers; book, journal, and database publishers; researchers and consultants, covered the entire information world:

1 **Social trends** – quantitative estimates of change in all areas directly or indirectly affecting the library and information world.
2 **The technological imperative** – information processing, computer systems and peripherals, basic computer and electronic research.
3 **Archives, libraries and information** – the information services provided through libraries and archives, their management and organization.
4 **Recording and reproducing** – capture, copying and recording devices for sound, vision and graphics.
5 **Communications infrastructure** – all forms of communications and services offered through networks.
6 **Publishing, new products, distribution and marketing** – effects of technology on production, distribution and marketing.

7   **Individual and domestic use of information** – changes in the individual's need for and use of information and information-related services.

8   **Organizations and their use of information** – changes in organizational needs for information, and in the provision of services to meet those needs.

9   **Manpower, education and training** – education and training needs in the library and information community, employment trends and prospects and the impact of information developments on education in general.

10 **Policy issues for information users** – issues likely to be the subject of debate in the coming decade, from the point of view of information users and intermediaries.

11 **Policy issues from the policy makers' viewpoint** – issues likely to be the subject of debate, from the point of view of policy makers.

Members of each group prepared individual papers which were then combined to provide a consolidated forecast. The programme was guided by an Advisory Committee which counted among its members representatives of the Royal Society, British Telecom, the DTI, and the Science Policy Research Unit.

Edited by John Martyn, Peter Vickers, and Mary Feeney, and published by Bowker-Saur in the British Library Research Series, *Information UK 2000* (1990, 293pp.) consists of four unequal parts. An overview provides a factual summary of the technological, communications, publishing, social and organizational, and educational environment within which the programme operated. Next came the main contents of the book, the separate Task Force reports followed in turn by the implications for the research community, the information industry, government, the training sector, and the LIS profession. A strong call is made for government intervention and a national information policy:

> What is needed is for some overall concern with the information environment to be assigned at Cabinet level. Some of the actions that might arise from such an assignment would be concerned with access to and exploitation of government – collected or government-generated information, with considerations of what the library systems are for, who should control them, and how they could be paid for, with efforts to increase awareness of information values, and with the development of mechanisms to encourage and where necessary regulate the development of the information industry.

Lastly, a paper produced by three members of the programme's Steering Group looks at the Task Force forecasts specifically in the context of the information market-place, the information business, and the impact of technology, and asks whether the library and information community is ready for the challenge.

In addition to the main report, others were published which consisted of the papers comprising the original contributions to individual task forces: *Information UK 2000: Social trends* (1991, 100pp. R&D Report 6015); *The technological imperative* (1991, 69pp. Rpt 6016); *Archives, libraries and information services* (1991, 68pp. Rpt 6017); *Recording and reproducing; communications infrastructure; telecommunications futures: 2000 and beyond* (1991, 212pp. Rpt 6018); *Publishing new products, distribution and marketing; bookselling and library supply* (1991, 111pp. Rpt 6019); *Individual and domestic use of information; organizations and their use of information* (1991, 93pp. Rpt 6020); *Manpower, education and training* (1991, 54pp. Rpt 6021); *Issues for information users; issues of policy from the policy-makers' view* (1991, 96pp. Rpt 6022); and *Additional contributions* (1991, 133pp. Rpt 6023), the contributions specially commissioned for the main report. They are all noted in *Research Bulletin*, 6, Autumn 1991:15–16.

Almost 2,000 copies of *Information UK 2000* were sold in the first 18 months of publication. Some of the forecasts it contained have already been confirmed or realized ahead of time, others have been invalidated or materially changed by new developments. Without attempting to revise the original report, or any of its conclusions, an account of some of the changes and new developments that may influence future information services is given in John Martyn's *Information UK 2000 An Update* (R&D, October 1992, A4, 12pp.). Demographic and economic changes, notably unemployment and the recession, have already had a marked effect on the information market. A gain in power and performance and a reduction in processor costs, a new generation of satellite telephone systems, rewriteable optical disc drives based either on magneto-optic or phase-change technology, and the relaunch of the 12-inch laser disc testify to hardware and software advances. In networking, the development of SuperJANET, database equivalents of a number of citation indexes, and the networking of CD-ROMs by academic libraries for their students are all visible.

A surge in consumer spending on books, video cassettes, CDs and prerecorded cassettes is evident with the growth in the book trade especially showing no signs of diminishing. Electronic publishing is showing signs of imminent take-off. A final comment adds:

> in the library and information world, although technological advances
> will continue to change and in many cases improve the ways in which
> we store, access and use information, major changes in organization
> and service operation are unlikely to take place without changes in the
> underlying infrastructure . . . development rather than simple cutback,
> tends to require public investment, and in the present economic cli-
> mate such investment is unlikely to be forthcoming.

In discussions with book trade and library organizations in January 1992
it was agreed that in order to pursue further the objectives of Information
UK 2000 a series of small-scale studies should be launched to present
and discuss the implications of new developments. Home-working and
tele-commuting, network developments, public libraries, and journal
publishing were mentioned as possible topics for early coverage. It was
also recommended that a working party should be set up to consider the
possible effects and impacts of electronic publishing on library and information services with particular attention to archiving and legal deposit
and the terms of library use of electronic publications. All in all
Information UK 2000 seems destined to become one of R&D's most
seminal, most celebrated, and most long-lasting initiatives ever. R&D
never expected its findings to meet with universal agreement but its
assumption that they would form a basis for debate and planning was
proved wholly correct.

Information UK Outlooks 1993/94 is the name given to a series of
papers designed to stimulate discussion on present trends and likely
future trends and their impact on library and information services. Edited
by John Martyn, ten papers a year will be published by the Library
Information Technology Centre (LITC), South Bank University, on a
subscription basis. Sponsored by R&D, all papers will be in a standard
format: introductory statistics will establish the context; developments in
the recent past and trends over the next few years will be described; and
the consequences, the likely impact, and the major issues involved for
library and information services will be discussed at length. The series
will include a discussion forum for readers' comments on the issues
raised.

BNB RESEARCH FUND

R&D administers the British National Bibliography Research Fund
(BNBRF) which was set up in 1975 when the assets of the Council of the

British National Bibliography Ltd were transferred to the newly established British Library. The Fund – to which the Library allocates an annual sum, currently £30,000 a year – commemorates those libraries, professional and trade associations, and other institutions which, as members of the Council, supported the *British National Bibliography (BNB)* in its early years. BNBRF supports bibliographic research in the UK which is not likely to fall within the remit of British Library's own activities and research programmes. Although prepared to receive proposals for any relevant research project, the Fund currently favours three research areas: the interaction between libraries, booksellers, and publishers; the effects of IT on the publishing chain; and publications and their use. Funding is not made available to support students on undergraduate or postgraduate courses or for the compilation of bibliographies. *The British National Bibliography Research Fund an introduction and guide to applicants* (1992, A5, 16pp.), contains information on who is eligible to apply, what is and what is not covered by awards, how to apply for an award, what sort of content is required in research proposals, and the dissemination of results. Two appendices give examples of recent projects and a list of 61 BNBRF Reports produced 1977–92. Derek Greenwood's 'The BNB Research Fund: cutting across the boundaries', *Journal of Librarianship*, **21** (4), October 1989:246–59, looks at the Fund's financial resources and the type of project it has supported since its inception.

NATIONAL MANUSCRIPTS CONSERVATION TRUST
Following a Royal Commission on Historical Manuscripts survey in 1985 which revealed the parlous state of some of Britain's archives and manuscripts holdings, the National Manuscripts Conservation Trust was jointly created as a registered charity by the Commission and British Library. The Trust was formally launched on 23 November 1989 with government funding of £100,000 a year, provided this sum could be matched by sums raised from private sources. This was soon forthcoming from the British Academy, some major charitable trusts, and from antiquarian booksellers and auction houses. Administered by R&D, awards are made for the preservation of manuscripts by their owners on the understanding that they themselves bear half the cost. Applications are accepted from record offices, libraries, colleges, historical societies, and other publicly-funded institutions not directly supported by the Exchequer.

Once established, the Trust launched a further appeal for £1 million to strengthen its permanent endowment and to maintain the amount available for its annual awards at a reasonable level. To this end it issued an A5 folded leaflet, *The nation's memory. The National Manuscripts Conservation Trust*, outlining the need for help in safeguarding the nation's record offices and libraries, which between them contain 800,000 shelves, stretching 450 miles, holding unique and irreplaceable records.

Some 4,000,000 manuscript volumes, files and documents are consulted by over 750,000 researchers a year. But about one-quarter is not fully available because they have not been adequately listed, records simply too fragile to handle fill some 35,000 shelves, and an immeasurably larger quantity needs treatment to halt the continuing deterioration caused by past neglect and present wear and tear.

The work of the Trust; historical and background notes to the awards made during the year; reports on current projects; a list of donations from charitable trusts, institutions, and corporations; and a balance sheet are printed in the Trust's *Annual Report & Accounts*.

BRITISH NATIONAL CORPUS
Along with Oxford University Press (the consortium's leader), Longmans, Chambers, Oxford University Computing Services, and Lancaster University's Unit for Computer Research on the English Language, the British Library is participating in the British National Corpus, whose goal is the creation of a machine-readable corpus of 100 million words of contemporary spoken and written British English. This three-year project, which started in January 1991, is partly funded by the Department of Trade and Industry and the Science and Engineering Research Council. In the IT world software designers will use the corpus in the development of speech recognition for computers, machine translation, computer assisted language learning and 'intelligent' word-processing software; for British Library the Corpus will be an important resource in developing an electronic archive. More detail is available in 'The British National Corpus', *Research Bulletin*, 7, Spring 1992:8.

R&D PUBLICATIONS
R&D publications are of three types:
(1) publications sold like normal trade books;
(2) deposited reports, i.e most R&D reports, some BNBRF reports, and out-of-print reports in category (1) which are available for purchase as microfiche or as photocopies from DSC; and

(3)   reports published and sold by other institutions.

The problems of the dissemination of research results, of estimating their commercial potential, and the reasons for discontinuing the Research Papers, except for a very few instances, are discussed in the Editorial in *Research Bulletin*, **6**, Autumn 1991:1–2.

In category (1) are Library And Information Research Reports, an A5 paperback series containing accounts of R&D-funded research in LIS; British Library Research Papers, reports on R&D-funded research projects and meetings reproduced in house in A4 format in the form they are received from authors; and British Library Information Guides, a series of guides, directories, and manuals in LIS. Titles of particular interest include Margaret Mann's *Complete List of Reports Published by The British Library R&D* (1988, 322pp.), a list of reports in numerical order within each series with full bibliographical details and short abstracts; and *Libraries And Information In Britain* published by The Information Partnership (1992, 88pp.), which was first published to coincide with the 1987 IFLA Conference in Brighton. British Library R&D Reports can refer to either grant-aided, commissioned, or internal British Library research. They fall into categories (2) and (3). British Library Research Lectures series comprises the text of the biennial lectures on library or information science to specially invited audiences of policy makers. They are available free of charge from R&D. BNBRF Reports fall in either category (1) or (2).

In 1988 R&D in collaboration with the LITC at the Polytechnic of Central London began publication of Library and Information Briefings whose aim was 'to offer busy professionals authoritative, but easily digested, briefings on information technology, policy issues and other technical and socio-economic developments. LIBs brings together information from various sources, assesses the issues raised in the professional press and offers practical information in a convenient readable form' (Mary Feeney, 'Library and information briefings – a new service for the information profession', *Aslib Information*, June 1988:147). The first ten Briefings, covering Open Systems Interconnection; Value-Added Network Services; CD-ROM; Desktop Publishing; Public/Private sector relationships; Library and Information Plans; Online Catalogues; Integrated Services Digital Networks; Standard Generalized Markup Language; and International Standards, were cumulated into a single volume, *Library & Information Briefings: the Book* (LITC, 1989).

Early in 1990 Bowker-Saur entered into an agreement with R&D to publish a selection of the Department's forthcoming titles in a new series of works of international significance designated British Library Research. So far the most influential title has been *Information UK 2000*.

Descriptive lists of all these series, with the exception of the LITC Briefings, are printed in an annual indexed catalogue, *R&DD Publications*. From time to time R&D issues booklet catalogues of its publications centring round specific themes and topics. *Imaging and Multi-Media Information*; *Information Skills in Education*; and *Library Research* are three examples. Up-to-date information on new research awards, the latest published reports, R&D's international activities, forthcoming conferences and seminars, is printed in *Research Bulletin* (Winter 1987–) a twice-yearly newsletter. An annual report is also published (1990–1 was subsumed in *Report 1990/92*) which covers all R&D activities during the year, its initiatives, grants, publications, exhibitions, and facts and figures on its expenditure.

An R&D publishing casualty came at the end of 1990 when *CABLIS* folded because it was not covering its costs and looked unlikely to do so in the immediate future. Redesigned and relaunched in January 1989 – it had previously been the responsibility of BLISS – its purpose was to alert readers to developments in library and information services and techniques and to publicise British Library resources. *CABLIS*'s last issue (December 1990) contained news items from the arts, libraries, museums and galleries, library and information services, the information industry, IT, education and training; news from overseas; a review of online and CD-ROM news; plus contents listings of professional periodicals and additions to the BLISS collections. To bow out with a bang, a special literature review of information policy was also included.

Paul Baxter's 'The role of British Library R&D Department in supporting library and information research in the United Kingdom', *Journal of the American Society for Information Science*, **36** (4), July 1985:275–7, reprinted in Maurice B. Line and Joyce Line's *National Libraries 2. 1977–1985* (Aslib, 1987), examines its operating philosophy, its expenditure on research and kindred activities, and the diversity of its research programmes. Paul Sturges's *Review of British Library Research and Development Department Research on Humanities Information* (BL Research Reviews, 1990, 58pp.) assesses R&D achievements in this area since it succeeded the Office for Scientific and Technical Information (OSTI) in 1975. Sturges divides his review into general information, bibliographic issues, source materials, IT, a list of consequential reports, and an additional bibliography.

9

SCIENCE REFERENCE AND INFORMATION SERVICE

Unlike British Library's other London-based reference collections, which require a reader's pass to be presented before entry is allowed, access to Science Reference and Information Service (SRIS) reading rooms is open to all. A signature in a visitor's book is all that is necessary. SRIS is currently based on three sites. The Holborn Reading Room for business information on companies, markets and products; physical sciences and technologies; engineering; British, European and Patent Cooperation Treaty patents; and trade marks. The Chancery House Reading Room, directly opposite, is for foreign patents and trademarks; and the Aldwych Reading Room is for life sciences and technologies, including biotechnology, medicine, and agriculture, mathematics, astronomy, and earth sciences. The locations of these reading rooms are mapped with 'bus route details on *information gap*?' in a folded 10cm x 21cm brochure (December 1992) for potential users, '*Come in and see how we can help you fill it*'. Needless to say, SRIS is eager to consolidate its services on one site at St Pancras and progress there is frequently reported in *SRIS Newsletter*.

What is now described as SRIS's total information package presents three levels of service: identifying the information required; getting hold of that information; and added-value services. Subject, online public access, and microfiche catalogues can be consulted to locate the material needed; staff are on hand to discuss research requirements in detail and to trace the documents required, either in SRIS or other British Library departments. Basic enquiry services are free but extended manual literature or online database searches are charged for. Alternatively, equipment can be hired for personal use if passwords are held. Most databases can be searched free of charge but if data are downloaded a floppy disk has to be purchased.

Because SRIS collections are so extensive – 33 million patents (the largest collection anywhere), 243,000 books, 67,000 journals including 25,600 current titles, 3,000 market research reports, 3,000 trade and business directories, 1,700 company house journals, 3,300 company annual reports, 30,000 company catalogues, company card services, product literature, technical indexes, abstracts, and bibliographies – it is likely that the original items required will be held in one of SRIS's reading rooms. English language books, periodicals, and patents published over the past ten years are on the open shelves; older and foreign-language material in an off-site store, but available on request with a delivery time of up to two hours. Added-value services include basic language help, the publication of key titles for libraries and other professional interests, and expert staff help on consultancy projects.

The suspension of subscriptions to 162 cover-to-cover translation journals and 38 other primary journals in the field of science and technology precipitated by the declining value of the British Library's grant-in-aid, the short-term costs of relocating staff and services to Boston Spa, and a Treasury decision that only half of the proceeds from the sale of Store Street could be used by the British Library, was a severe blow to SRIS in the late autumn of 1990. Many of the titles suspended were high cost and high use items, but only by selecting relatively expensive titles was it possible to effect rapid economies. The total effect of these cuts was graphically underscored in Alan Gomersall's 'The End Of Periodical As We Know It?', *Serials*, **4** (3), November 1991:13–18: 'our expectation remains high that the steady attrition of the national scientific/technical periodical collection could continue throughout the 1990s without any relief as periodical subscriptions increase and budgets remain fixed'. Drastic reductions had already been made in SRIS's book purchasing programme, no books published overseas had been ordered since April, whilst the binding programme was also reduced with priority being given to English-language serials and major patent series.

Books in the SRIS reading rooms are shelved according to a unique classification scheme based partly on that devised for the Patent Office Library by Wyndham Hulme. Main classes are arranged so that pure sciences are collocated with the appropriate technologies. Recent amendments and attempts to accommodate new subjects and modifications, to bring together subjects which the advance of science and technology have linked, culminating in a rolling revision programme, are outlined in 'The SRIS Classification Scheme Comes of Age', *SRIS Newsletter*, **19**, October 1992:4. *SRIS Classification of Science and Technology: the schedules and index* was published in the autumn of 1992.

What catalogues and indexes are available to locate material, and which should be used for finding specific types of material, are described in an eight-page A5 pamphlet, *Using The Catalogues*. This ends with two appendices: (1) which classmarks are in which reading room and (2) what the location mark prefixes and suffixes mean and where the items can be found. Described as the biggest single development in SRIS's public catalogue since the 1975 introduction of the computer-output microfiche system, SCICAT, an online public-access catalogue (OPAC) became available in the Holborn Reading Room in the summer of 1989. Its most distinctive feature – 'An Online Catalogue In SRIS', *SRIS Newsletter*, **9**, September 1989:1–2 claimed – is its use of the SCICAT classification. Step-by-step illustrations at the end of this article show how the OPAC catalogue can quickly identify appropriate entries. SCICAT is available on BLAISE-LINE and on microfiche issued four times a year by subscription.

An annotated list of CD-ROM technical, bibliographic, business and patent databases, including *Compendex Plus, Jane's Defence And Aerospace Information, Science Citation Index, Ulrichs Plus, Boston Spa Serials, Boston Spa Conferences, Boston Spa Books, Disclosure* (see 'New Business CD-ROMs Ready To Search AT SRIS!', *SRIS Newsletter*, **19**, October 1992:1), *Disclosure Worldscope, Predicasts F & S Index Plus Text, Access, EP'B', Espace, APS, Bulletin, Cassis*, and *PraCTIS*, is the main feature of a 10cm x 21cm folded brochure, *CD-ROM Service Holborn Reading Room*. A companion brochure, *CD-ROM Service Aldwych Reading Room*, similarly lists *MEDLINE (CSA), Excerpta Medica, Life Sciences Collection, BIOSIS, CAB, Books In Print, Ulrich's* and *Boston Spa Serials*. Also in the same format, *Welcome To The Holborn Reading Room* (1992) and *Welcome To The Aldwych Reading Room* (1992) give details of the enquiry desk's services, the catalogues, the open- and closed-access stock, the photocopy service, and specialist SRIS services. Floor plans are also shown.

For many years SRIS has produced a variety of publications for different markets which serve to draw attention to the depth and quality of its collections and to provide its users with practical guides and newsletters to keep them up to date with new material. Alan Gomersall's 'SRIS Publications Look To The Future', *SRIS Newsletter*, **13**, September 1990:1–2, points out that significant revenue is earned from publication sales. Having invested in staff and financial resources in the production of new titles, and improved the quality of their presentation, it follows that only titles likely to sell well will be slotted into SRIS's future publishing programme. Brief notices of important reference publications are included in this present work at the appropriate point. *SRIS Newsletter*, the successor to *SRIS News* and *SRL News*, first appeared in June 1989 and is now issued two or three times a year. It carries features on new services and publications, courses and seminars, and, increasingly, information on the impending move to St Pancras. SRIS's new catalogue of publications, *Working Guides For Working Professionals*, groups titles under the main headings of Science and Technology, Business, Patents, Environment, and Library Reference Guides. Kenneth R. Cooper's 'British Library Services for Science, Technology and Industry', *International Forum of Information and Documentation*, **13** (4), October 1988:22–8, is an authoritative overview of SRIS's history, services, and commercial ventures, slightly dated in that it was printed when SRIS and DSC were still incorporated within the Science, Technology and Industry Division. *Information for the Nation* (n.d.), an 18-page, large size illustrated brochure, and *SRIS. The One-Stop Information Shop* (n.d.), an eight-page A4 brochure, introduce SRIS specialist information services.

SCIENCE AND TECHNOLOGY INFORMATION SERVICE

The Science and Technology Information Service (STIS) provides a priced enquiry service for all areas of science and technology. Specializing in furnishing lists of references and other material culled from both online and printed sources, its strong areas of expertise embrace new materials, physical property data, online searching, and science policy. Some of the databases used are computerized versions of well-known abstracting and indexing journals such as *Biology Abstracts*, *Chemical Abstracts*, and *Inspec*. Topics covered include computing, electrical and mechanical engineering, chemistry, pharmaceuticals, geology, and agriculture. Information on how to request an enquiry, what information needs to be supplied, what databases are available, delivery costs, deadlines, how to pay; ample notes on the service; where to obtain the full text of documents retrieved; translations; and terminals for hire, is published annually in an updated A4 folded leaflet, *Science And Technology Information Service*.

By far the largest publicly-available collection of chemical information in the UK – covering pure chemistry, all sectors of the chemical industry (rubber, plastics, paper, textiles, pharmaceuticals, cosmetics, food, petrochemicals, colours and dies, etc.), biochemistry, and geochemistry – is held at SRIS. Details of the services available and some of the principal printed and online research sources – including access to over 400 online databases and databanks, further enhanced by a recently announced chemical structure searching service – are to be found in 'Getting The Chemistry Right' and 'A Brand New Facility At SRIS – Chemical Structure Searching', *SRIS Newsletter*, **20**, June 1993:1–3.

In September 1987 the former Computer Search Service within SRIS was renamed the Online Search Centre. With access to all the major database hosts, the Centre covers all the areas of relevance to the work of STIS. Besides information on staff specializations, request procedures, and database access, 'Online Search Centre', *SRIS Newsletter*, **3**, January 1988:2–3, provides admirably concise definitions of computerspeak for IT illiterates.

Written by SRIS's team of expert searchers, *Online Searching In Service And Technology: an introductory guide to equipment, databases and search techniques*, edited by Chris Baile (3rd ed., 1993, 96pp.), is a concise, practical, and jargon-free guide to online searching including search strategies, hardware and software, output options, and reviews of databases in the biomedical and environmental sciences, chemistry, and engineering. Edited by Karen Blakeman, *Advanced Online Searching in Science and Technology* (1993, 128pp.) advises the more experienced searcher on strategic searching and advanced techniques.

IRS–Dialtech, the UK national centre for the European Space Agency scientific and technical bibliographic information retrieval service, was transferred from the Department of Trade and Industry (DTI) to SRIS in April 1991. Originally set up in 1970 to provide scientific and technical information for the research and development needs of the European space industry, it now offers access to almost 200 databases covering most aspects of science and technology. 'Introducing IRS–Dialtech', *SRIS Newsletter*, **16**, July 1991:2, presents outline information on user support, billing, training, marketing, and promotion of this priced online service. *IRS Dialtech your access to . . . a world of information* (1993), a folded 10cm x 21cm colour brochure, introduces the service, lists its benefits and advantages, and provides details of its training and support facilities.

Science And Technology Policy. A Review Of Recent Developments (1988–), a news-review-with-abstracts journal surveying trends in technology, and supplying full bibliographical details of key documents for easy retrieval, now published bi-monthly, addresses the main questions in science policy: how government and industry allocate resources and funds to education and research in science and technology; the impact of those decisions on the size, structure, creativity, and effectiveness in transforming research into marketable products; and their impact on economic development. 'News and Views' (a commentary on topical issues based on the national press, scientific and business journals, and government publications); 'Recent Publications' (a selection of newly published reports, journal articles, and abstracts dealing with scientific policy); and, since October 1990, 'World View' (feature articles by acknowledged experts on all aspects of scientific policy in the UK and overseas) add up to a clear and accurate guide to this vital area.

Janet Gilbert's *Guide to Directories at the Science Reference and Information Service* (3rd ed., 1992, 144pp.) provides details of over 3,000 directories listing addresses, products, company profiles, names and associations worldwide, arranged by subject with title and subject indexes. Compiled by Rodney Burton, Hilda Vedic, and Vicky Tattle, *Scientific Abstracting and Indexing Periodicals: A Guide to SRIS holdings and their Use* (4th ed., 1991, 64pp.) focuses on over 400 English-language abstracting and indexing journals arranged by the corresponding headings in SRIS's classification scheme supplemented by an alphabetical list. Review articles, conference papers, and report literature are also covered whilst an introduction reviews online and CD-ROM searching and describes *Science Citation Index*, *Current Contents*, and some major abstracting journals such as *Chemical Abstracts* and *Biological Abstracts*.

BUSINESS INFORMATION SERVICE

Holding the largest public collection of business source material in the UK, SRIS's Business Information Service (BIS) 'helps users to investigate new market sectors, to gather information for business plans, track the competition, check on possible partners, obtain mailing lists, prepare important presentations or interviews, and to identify products and suppliers' (*Information for the Nation*, p.6). Its resources are vast: in addition to the thousands of business and trade journals, company reports, directories, market research reports, held on site, it provides access to a wide range of databases including CERVED, an Italian host system holding a number of company databases; DATA-STAR which contains an increasing number of European business-oriented files such as ABC Europe, ICC databases, and Hoppenstedt; DIALOG, whose 350 databases include a strong coverage of US companies and markets, D&B, Investext, Moody's, and Thomas Register; Dunsprint, Dun & Bradstreet's own system with information on 16 million companies worldwide; ECHO, the EC's own system; FIZ-Technik; GBI, a German business information host with databases covering companies, markets, and management; GENIOS, which includes the full text of key German business and marketing periodicals, German and Austrian newswires, and Eastern European coverage; Infocheck, providing credit rating information on British companies, information on mergers and acquisitions, and gateways to the Analysis Corporation and to databases of European company information; KOMPASS online, containing details of firms in 12 European countries and the US; ORBIT, offering industrial databases; FT Profile Information, which has the full text of market research reports online; Reuter TEXTLINE, the most comprehensive source for international news stories with full text or summaries of 1,500 newspapers and business journals; and Telesystemes Questel, containing European databases.

But BIS is not solely about the latest electronic communications marvels. Although it subscribes to the MITAC system of annual reports – a microfiche collection which covers approximately 3,500 UK companies, including all the publicly-quoted companies and the nationalized industries – the bulk of its trade literature collections consists of hard-copy annual reports, stockbrokers' reports, house journals, and advertising brochures, shelved together by company name to provide an overall picture of a company's activities in a single file. Collection development of this scale is only possible with the continuing co-operation of many thousands of companies which regularly donate material. Similarly, product-based information includes hard-copy collections complemented by systematically updated and indexed microform files containing the product literature of 30,000 British and foreign companies selling products or services in the UK. Information on access to the collections, on the card indexes listing the companies included, and the in-house computer file that SRIS staff can search for users, is contained in 'Trade Literature At SRIS', *SRIS Newsletter*, **6**, October 1988:4–5.

Launched in 1987 the priced Business Research Service carries out searches on business topics, exploiting not only SRIS's own in-house databases, BISMARK, BUSPER and BISHOP – respectively covering market reports, trade journals, and trade literature – but also external online services and British Library's overall resources. The data supplied include information on markets (market size, segmentation; production, exports and imports, market leaders); information on companies (company profiles, credit checks, company reports, lists of top companies, and companies in a certain field, or of a certain size, or in a geographical area); product information; and miscellaneous information on individuals, management issues, economic indicators, and so on. Staff time is charged for searching and for each company profile, news story, or whatever. If online searches produce no result only the time spent is charged for. Delivery is by fax, courier, or post – whichever is most convenient. A selection of recent client profiles and examples of enquiries and costs can be found in 'Making The Business Information Service Work For You', *SRIS Newsletter*, **16**, July 1991:3, and 'How The Priced Research Service Can Help Your Company', *ibid.*, **19**, October 1992:3.

A strong publications list includes *Business Information a brief guide to the reference resources of the British Library* (1987, 32pp., A4), designed to assist users to exploit the business stock in full, which includes notes on all types of business information sources, company information, product information, market information, journals, house journals and newspapers, statistics, stockbrokers' reports, and abstracting, indexing, and online database search services. An introductory leaflet, *Your Business Needs Our Information* (1991), outlines BIS's clients, services, and costs. *Market Research: A Guide To British Library Holdings*, compiled by Michael Leydon (7th ed., 1991, 194pp.), lists over 2,000 market research reports, industry surveys, and country profiles published since 1986, arranged under alphabetical subject headings. *Guide To Libraries In Key UK Companies*, compiled by Peter Dale (1993, 188pp.), has detailed entries for over 200 libraries in industrial companies and large companies in the service industries. Listed alphabetically by company, each entry includes full address and contact information, opening hours, services provided, and their availability to outside users. Companies are also listed in an industrial sector index. Nigel Spencer's *Instant Guide To Company Information Online – Europe* (2nd ed., 1993, 84pp.) contains a detailed table of 102 company information databases; a set of tables for 16 different European and pan-European databases, each summarized under key headings; an A–Z listing of the databases with details of coverage, language, and special features; and a country-by-country listing of company types and disclosure requirements.

Although not formally a constituent part of the British Library, the Business Information Network, 'an association of libraries and information centres committed to providing quality business information services to their user community' was launched in 1991, largely as the result of an SRIS initiative. Accommodated at SRIS's Holborn site, the Network is actively involved in:

promoting the exploitation of business information resources throughout the UK; improving the overall standard of business information provision through training courses and Quality of Service Guidelines; providing an effective focus for the development of business information products and services; developing partnerships with information providers in Europe and the rest of the world; raising awareness amongst the business community regarding the value of business information; and organising and participating in seminars/workshops for the information profession.

The libraries' joint resources and expertise are publicized as one network enabling member libraries to offer a more effective service. Overall the network aims 'to improve the performance and competitiveness of British enterprise through the better use of business information'.

Full membership is open to any library or information service providing business information to its users and having the equivalent of one member of staff working full-time on business information. A monthly *Newsletter* (August 1990–) was relaunched in September 1993 as a new-look bi-monthly. A *Directory of Members* is published containing the names and addresses of 130 participating library and information centres worldwide, and also tables of the services and resources these centres can offer.

The development of the British Library's business information provision, the aims and objectives of the Network, its membership and functions, and the way forward, are fully outlined in Alan Gomersall's 'A BIN or a BLIP: a proposed national business information initiative', *Refer*, **6** (2), Summer 1990:1–5.

PATENTS

The British Library's patent collection now numbers more than 10 million specifications, from over 40 countries, with abstracts and abridgments, official journals and gazettes, and trademarks and designs from a further 50, making it the finest of its kind in the world. Although separated from the UK Patent Office – now located in South Wales – both administratively and geographically, there has been no general groundswell of opinion hardening against this apparently illogical bifurcation. In fact there were manifest advantages to be derived from shelving the national patent collection in close proximity to SRIS's non-patent technical literature. Exchange agreements with overseas patent offices account for the acquisition of most foreign patents and gazettes. SRIS has assumed responsibility for the international exchange of such material since 1989.

SRIS points out that the law requires that all UK patent applications be published 18 months from the date of the original application, faster than either books or most technical journal articles, yet very few organizations use patents as part of their research intelligence. The Patents Information Service helps users to exploit fully the potential of SRIS's vast resource of primary technical and commercial information represented by its unparalleled patents collection.

Increasing by approximately one million specifications a year, not allowing for official journals and abstracts, the storage of patents presents severe problems. After a major reorganization in 1987 (see 'Patent Stock Move', *SRIS Newsletter*, **2**, October 1987:4), the present arrangements are that published British and European patent applications, British-granted specifications, British specifications published under the Patent Act 1949 (from December 1973 onwards), and applications published under the Patent Cooperation Treaty (signed by more than 40 countries), are all housed at Southampton Buildings either on the ground or lower ground floor. Older British specifications are shelved in the vaults there. Other recent specifications are kept at Chancery House whilst older foreign material is accommodated in the Micawber Street store. A regular van service operates through the day between there and Chancery House.

Besides its own list of patent titles, British Library also publishes a number of invaluable guides and bibliographic aids. Brenda Rimmer's *International Guide to Official Industrial Property Publications*, edited and updated by Stephen van Dulken in a third edition and published in the Key Resource series in 1992, covers over 50 patenting authorities, and includes information on legislation, international conventions, the numbering and publication procedures for specifications, contents of official gazettes, what patent indexes exist and what they cover, what published information is available for designs and trade marks, where to find reports of legal judgements, illustrations of patent specification front pages, and computer-based online and CD-ROM searching aids. New to this edition are chapters on the International Patent Classification and the international design and trade mark schemes, revised information on Germany since unification, and recent legislation and documentation changes for the countries of the former Soviet Union. This edition is sold as a complete reissue in paperback although loose-leaf updates are also issued to the second edition. Published on 284 diazo microfiches, *UK Patents for Inventions: index to names of applicants* is a 'who's who' of inventors and companies and organizations associated with inventions in British patent specifications. The fiches are available in a full set

1617–1980 or in three part sets, 1617–1899, 1900–29 and 1930–1980.

Introduction To Patents Information, edited by Stephen van Dulken (SRIS, 2nd ed., 1992, 126pp.), whose origins are rooted in SRIS seminars on patents information, is inclined towards those either totally new to patents or who have not yet fully mastered the basics of how to approach them. An introductory chapter explains what patents are, what information advantages they offer, the criteria applied in granting them, and their layout. A study of British, European, and Patent Cooperative Treaty signatories' patent publications follows, whilst the remaining chapters concentrate on aspects of exploiting patents: patent classification and information retrieval systems, online and CD searching, a bibliography of industrial property publications, and a glossary of patents' terms. Richard Garner's 'Out Of The Shadows – Patent Services From The British Library', *Interlending & Document Supply*, **20** (1), January 1992:3–7, looks at the characteristics of patents, the growth of patent literature, SRIS's patent collection, and Patent Express and other SRIS patent services. *SRIS Newsletter*, **18**, May 1992, was largely given over to patent services.

D. C. Newton's *Trade Marks: An Introductory Guide And Bibliography* (2nd ed., 1990, 202pp.) is substantially based on Brenda M. Rimmer's *Trade Marks: A Guide to the literature and directory of lists of trade names* (1976). It has a dual focus: part 1 gives information on the nature of trade marks, their history, trade mark law in the UK and overseas, international treaties and conventions, and trade mark searching; part 2 is a list of over 700 lists of trade names grouped by class.

One of the main recommendations in Trevor Roberts and Brian Holt's *Review of the Arrangements for the Dissemination of Patents Information*, the report of an efficiency scrutiny jointly established by the DTI, the OAL, and the British Library, published by the DTI in 1987, was that the SRIS patent collection should recover its full costs by operating as a business with higher charges and providing a much improved service for its mainly commercial customers. To that end the Patent Express service was innovated and soon 'dramatically transformed the standard, scope and usefulness of its services, vigorously marketing them in North America and, to a lesser extent, in Europe' (Peter J. Robson, 'Access To Special Materials – Patent Specifications', *Interlending and Document Supply Proceedings of the Second International Conference held in London, November 1990*, edited by Alison Gallico, IFLA Office for International Lending, 1991).

Launched at the WIPO International Patent Fair in Geneva in 1988,

Patent Express supplies users with preprinted forms which may be used to order as many as ten items either by fax or by post. Online searching through DIALOG or ORBIT, by telephone and telex, is also possible. Two levels of service are available: REGULAR, with completion usually within 48 hours of receipt of application, or RUSH with guaranteed completion after only three hours. Delivery may be arranged by first-class inland mail, a same-day or next-day service, by hand to all parts of the UK, by fax, airmail, or by overnight international courier. Full details are printed in *Patent Express. Document delivery from the source you can trust*, an A4 eight-page laminated brochure and wallet.

A similar brochure, *Patent Express Currentscan*, provides details of a current awareness service initiated in 1990 which monitors British, European, and world patent applications as they appear and matches them against prearranged customer profiles of companies or subjects. For a basic annual subscription, allowing a match of any subject area defined in terms of the International Patent Classification, or up to ten companies, complete specifications fitting the profiles are generally despatched on the same day as publication on an item copy charge basis. A year later Patent Express further enhanced its portfolio of services with the introduction of Patent Express Transcript, providing copies of foreign patents and a competitive estimate of the cost of translating them into English. In normal circumstances the turn-round is two weeks although a quicker service can be arranged. 'Transcript Breaks Through The Language Barrier', *SRIS Newsletter*, **18**, May 1992:1–2, carries details.

A big step forward towards the British Library's objective to become established as a centre for the capture, storage, and transmission of electronic documents came in 1993 with the creation of possibly the world's largest international patent database on CD-ROM. Over 1,000 discs, representing 1 million US, UK, European, and PCT patents are stored in 12 Incom jukeboxes. Up to 25% of Patent Express's 600,000 annual requests for copies are expected to be satisfied through this medium during the first year of operation. Remote user access to the system 24 hours a day, automatic faxing, file transfer, and billing are among future plans.

Patent Express Newsletter, published three times a year, began publication in Spring 1989 to improve communications with Patent Express users. Its objective is to report on items of interest such as changes in patent law (e.g. 'Copyright, Designs and Patents Act 1988', 2, Autumn 1989:2), conference reports and news of forthcoming conferences, and recent SRIS acquisitions.

The Patents Online Search Service accesses databases covering the activities of all the major patenting authorities. Coverage is comprehensive from the early 1970s although some earlier material can also be covered. On receipt of brief summaries of search topics and synonyms for technical terms to be covered, Online Patents can provide subject searches, state-of-the-art reviews, problem solving, chemical structure searches, status data, English language equivalents, commercial intelligence, statistical analyses, and current awareness/patent watches. A regular, updated service at considerably less cost than the original search is also available. Details of how Patents Online can help, of the information required from users, on what form the search results are produced, and an indication of costs are printed in *Patents Online*, a 10cm x 21cm folded information leaflet.

Patent databases accessed at SRIS include *CHINAPAT* (Chinese Patent Abstracts in English); *Claims/US Patents Abstracts*; *FPAT* (bibliographic, status, and administrative information, plus some abstracts on French patents); *INPADOC* (details of patent documents from fifty-six patenting authorities); *Japio* (bibliographic data and English-language abstracts on Japanese unexamined patent applications); *PATDPA* (information and abstracts on German patent documents and utility models); *USPA* (bibliographic information and text of front page and claims of US patents); and *World Patent Index* (bibliographic details and abstracts of patent documents from 33 patenting authorities). 'Trademark Searching At SRIS', *SRIS Newsletter*, **11**, March 1990:3, reports that:

> Having recently signed up with the computer host IMSMARQ, SRIS can now offer trade mark searches from even more countries. British trade marks and service marks (except device marks) can be searched for on the UK Trademarks database, produced by Pergamon Financial Data Services supplied by the Patent Office . . . searches can also be carried out for US, French, German and Italian marks, for marks registered in the Scandinavian countries and for marks registered internationally under the Madrid agreement.

A growing number of CD-ROMs containing foreign patent data are being made available for personal searching at a small charge. They fall into two categories: full text storage of patent specifications and bibliographic databases. The latest information on databases currently accessible via CD-ROM, on the available and impending workstation facilities at SRIS, and on the cost of staff searches, is printed in 'Patents Data On CD-ROM: speeding up access to information', *SRIS Newsletter*, **18**, May 1992:3.

Created in 1980 to promote patents as a source of information for industry, the Patents Information Network (PIN), which is located at 13 regional centres throughout the UK, is supported by British Library and by the UK Patent Office. Its hub and driving force is SRIS's patents collections. All Network centres maintain a patents collection and provide a free basic enquiry service. Since 1990 strenuous efforts have been made by the Library to extend the reach of the Network by inviting a wide range of libraries, information, and advice centres to join it as Patent Gateways, that is, as primary contact points, which 'will be provided with a portfolio of documentation covering the basic principles of patent information; they will receive a supply of publicity and educational material and be kept in touch with patent information activities in their area and nationally' ('Profit From Patents', *British Library News*, **158**, June/July 1990:2). 'The aim is to raise awareness of patents amongst staff and enable them to refer enquirers to Patent Information Centres, the Patent Office or the British Library' ('BL bid to boost PIN gateways', *Library Association Record*, **95** (6), June 1993:327).

In direct line of descent from *Patents Information Network Bulletin*, *Patents Information News* (Winter 1987–) describes the information content of some of the more interesting and newsworthy patents as well as reporting on topical stories resulting from recent patent specifications. Formerly published two or three times a year, it has seemingly fallen on hard times and is now an occasional publication for which sponsoring is sought. SRIS also issues *Annual Reports From The Patents Information Network* in which all PIN member libraries report on their collections, accommodation, services, staff, and promotional activities. D. R. Jamieson's 'Patents Information Network. A review after its first six years', *CIPA*, November 1986:55–9, tells how British Library became responsible in 1975 for the cost of providing patent publications to provincial libraries, prompting it to examine closely the potential of this provision as an information and document supply service to the patents community and UK industry, a scrutiny that eventually resulted in setting up the Network. Jamieson also looks at the present and future patterns of service at regional level.

JAPANESE INFORMATION SERVICE

Systematic collecting of Japanese and Japan-related material started in British Library long before the Japanese Information Service (JIS) was formed in May 1985. Official publications, white papers, gazettes, parliamentary proceedings, legal documents, and statistical digests had all been accumulated from 1951 through an exchange scheme with the

National Diet Library in Tokyo (see Yu-Ying Brown's 'Japanese Official Publications In The British Library', *IOLR/OC Newsletter*, **39**, September 1987:14–15). Even after budgetary pressures brought about a switch from blanket to selective exchange, SRIS was still allocated 50 serial titles. Japanese patents too had long been collected. The immediate impetus for JIS's formation was a marked upsurge of interest in Japanese science, technology, and industry, in the light of Japan's marked industrial and economic progress. An SRIS seminar to indicate what type of information was available, how to obtain material, and how to overcome the language barrier met with such an encouraging response that the decision was taken to set up a specialized information service. JIP's aims are to promote the use of Japanese information in science, technology and business; to co-ordinate British Library resources in this field; to make use of other existing UK resources and services; to investigate the need for published Japanese information in the UK; to identify gaps in the provision of such information and to encourage access to Japanese sources; to provide an enquiry and referral service; and to liaise with similar initiatives abroad.

When it first came into operation JIS could offer immediate access to online searching, including Japanese databases; to over 3,500 scientific, technological, and commercial journals; over eight million patents, and virtually all Japanese industrial property specifications; market and industry surveys, company, business and trade information; conference reports; and to translation journals and indexes (from 'Japanese Information Service', *SRIS Newsletter*, **5**, July 1988:1–2). In 1990 a direct link via satellite was established with NACSIS, Japan's National Center For Science Information Systems, which includes information on dissertations, conference papers in electronics and chemistry, and a database of research reports from laboratories and universities throughout Japan. Both the link and the terminals capable of handling the Japanese-language database in British Library are funded by the Japanese Ministry of Education, Science and Culture.

Early in 1991 JIS's operations had to be curtailed following the retirement of vital staff but in November it was announced that a full business, statistical, scientific, and technical service about Japan for UK users would be reintroduced in close co-operation with the BIS. Further expansion would depend on a business plan currently being developed in conjunction with the DTI. A reminder of the services available was printed on an A4 leaflet, *Japanese Information Service. The Fastest, Most Comprehensive And Expert Source Of Japanese Information*, distributed in March 1992, and in 'Japanese Community Information Ready and Waiting' and 'Everything You Ever Wanted To Know About Japanese Companies-Online!', *SRIS Newsletter*, **19**, October 1992:5. A useful aid to enquirers and researchers is *Japanese Business Publications in English: a select annotated list of recent publications held by the British Library*, edited by Shirley King (4th ed., 1990, 80pp.), a guide to the most important directories, statistics, market information, industrial surveys, trade and business journals, company reports, and abstracting journals, arranged in broad subject areas.

King's 'The British Library Japanese Service in Science, Technology and Commerce', pp.133–44, *Japanese Studies: papers presented at a colloquium at the School of Oriental and African Studies, University of London, 14–16 September 1988* (British Library, 1990), outlines SRIS holdings of relevant sources including scientific and technical periodicals, patents, conference proceedings, abstracting and indexing journals, report literature, and business information on companies, products, markets, and statistics. A number of important databases are described, among them JICST (Japan Information Center of Science and Technology); Nikkei Telecom (Mitsui's online financial and economic system); HINET, industrial and technological information from the Heiwa Information Center; and PATOLIS and JAPIO (online databases of the Japan Patent Information organization). G. J. Sassoon's 'British Library Japanese Information Service In Science, Technology & Commerce', *Infomediary*, **3** (3–4), December 1990:153–6, is also an authoritative and extremely informative study.

ENVIRONMENTAL INFORMATION SERVICE

Based at SRIS, the Environmental Information Service (EIS) was launched in November 1989 in partnership with the Confederation of British Industry (CBI). It was designed to provide companies involved in environmental issues with a comprehensive package of current awareness, research, and document supply services, coupled with a seminar and publications programme. SRIS hoped to help industry overcome its environmental problems – waste disposal, pollution, and the quality of the environment – with rapid and up-to-date information on such topics as environment legislation, waste management, clean technology, and recycling. For its part, the CBI was troubled about plummeting sales due to obsolete and environmentally unfriendly products and the hazards of falling foul of new legislation. The reasoning behind the establishment of the new service was cogently expressed in a leading article, 'SRIS Goes

Green', *SRIS Newsletter*, 11, March 1990:1–2: 'Both manufacturing and service companies must now start to face these information demands for which they are often not equipped. Advance warning of new laws and regulations concerning the environment, navigating complex official documentation, and finding and transferring clean technology from foreign sources and unexpected industries, are just some of the problem areas looming.' The EIS would act as a 'one-stop shop' for environmental data, calling not only on SRIS resources but, when necessary, on DSC and OP&SS within British Library, and on outside libraries and information centres, the Health and Safety Executive, the Ministry of Agriculture, Fisheries and Food, and the DTI.

A prime example of the information services provided by EIS is in the field of eco-toxicology – the study of the adverse effects that chemicals can have on living organisms when released into the environment. An indication of the access it enjoys to appropriate databanks, and a selective list of sources relating to the latest UK and EC legislation and regulations, is contained in 'Where To Find Up-To-Date Eco-Toxicology Information', *SRIS Newsletter*, 20, June 1993:3.

True to its proclaimed purpose, EIS embarked on an accelerated publication programme and now has an impressive string of titles to its credit: Nigel Lees' *Hazardous Materials: sources of information on their transportation* (1990, 80pp.), a literature guide covering the key aspects of transporting hazardous materials in the UK and Europe; *Green Belt, Green Fields and the Urban Fringe*, edited by Lesley Grayson (1990, 112pp.), a bibliography which includes sections on government policy, the threat to the environment, planning restraints, and land use; *Recycling – New Materials from Community Waste: sources of information* (1991, 154pp.) and *Recycling – Energy from Community Waste: sources of information* (1991, 143pp.), both edited by Grayson, focusing respectively on legal, political, technical and social aspects of recycling and on energy recovery in the UK, Europe, and USA; *Environmental Auditing: a guide to best practice in the UK and Europe*, edited by Grayson (1992, 66pp.), which identifies crucial UK and EC legislation and regulations; *Environmental Auditing: an introduction and practical guide*, edited by Helen Woolston (1993, 77pp.) and based on papers presented at a British Library seminar held in March 1992; and *Environmental Information: a guide to sources,* edited by Lees and Woolston (1992, 180pp.). This last is a directory of where to go for information and help on green issues and includes sections on technical, government, business, and patents information; UK and European legislation; environmental auditing, assessment, and policy; and sources of information on pollution, waste disposal and recycling, energy, transport, conservation, agriculture, and food.

Woolston's 'British Library Environmental Information Service' *Assistant Librarian*, **85** (11), November 1992:172–4, outlines its range of services, and its available resources, notably the internal databases staff have developed to improve the service provision. The November 1991 issue of *SRIS Newsletter* was largely given over to environmental issues with short articles on environmental auditing, key environmental sources, environmental legislation, and descriptive notes on recent and forthcoming publications.

The former Biotechnology Information Service emerged from the European Biotechnology Information Project in 1987 and continued to function until the end of 1990, when it quietly vanished from the scene. A biotechnology current awareness service still operates under the aegis of the EIS. A quarterly *Biotechnology Information News*, the successor to *EBIP News*, ran for ten issues from March 1988 before it disappeared. A number of useful publications were issued: Lesley J. Downs' *The Biotechnology Marketing Sourcebook* (1990, 148pp.), intended for marketing managers, science, technology and medical publishers, conference organizers, and information officers, furnishes information on advertisers and circulation figures for over 250 English-language periodicals, newsletters, and abstracts in the life sciences, biotechnology, and biochemistry; *Introduction To Biotechnology Information*, edited by Michael Eusden (1991, 90pp.), a practical guide to the most important information sources in biotechnology worldwide with specific chapters on scientific information, biotechnology in patents, online databases, British official publications, business information in biotechnology, and bioethics; and Rupert Lee's *How To Find Information. Life Sciences. A guide to searching in published sources* (1992, 20pp.), which describes the different types of literature available, identifies the major reference works and the key abstracting and indexing sources, explains CD-ROM and online searching, and shows how to conduct basic CD-ROM searches.

PART III
BOSTON SPA

10

Document Supply Centre

The National Lending Library for Science and Technology was officially opened by Lord Hailsham, Minister of Science, on 5 November 1962, to serve the interlibrary loan needs of UK scientists and technologists. Its coverage was extended to all subject fields when it joined with the National Central Library to form the British Library Lending Division in 1973. Renamed the Document Supply Centre (DSC) in September 1985 to more accurately reflect its current role of providing a rapid loan and photocopy service – although it still acts as the hub of the national network for book interlending – it now describes itself, with some justification, as 'the most extensive, varied, and up-to-date source of information and knowledge in the world'. Always in the forefront of the application of new technology to optimize both its services and revenue raising operations, it has expanded its services to all parts of the globe with 25% of demand now originating from over 100 countries overseas.

> From being a heavily subsidised national asset the quality and scope of the Centre's unrivalled services have allowed it to depend less on government funds. This trend is expected to continue as the Centre, taking account of customer needs and making appropriate use of new technology, marketing skills and a dedicated staff, seeks to capture an even larger slice of the expanding document delivery business ('30 years of document supply', *Document Supply News*, **36**, December 1992:1, 4).

To obtain loans and photocopies libraries and information centres need to register and purchase DSC request forms. Full details of how to make the best use of its service are contained in the *UK Customers' Handbook*, supplied at the time of registration. This provides guidance on the completion of postal request forms, the submission of automated requests, and DSC finding procedures; and notes on the transport schemes for interlibrary loans. A pocket inside the back cover houses customer update leaflets. A *Directory Of Library Codes Including Guidelines To The National Network For Interlending And Document Supply* is also issued.

DSC is situated at Boston Spa in Yorkshire, two miles east of the A1 (Great North Road) near Wetherby. Although the Reading Room (open Monday–Friday 9.15 a.m.–4.30 p.m.) is in no way intended as an alternative to DSC's normal lending service, in some circumstances a personal visit can be extremely useful. An open-access representative collection of reference books, bibliographies, and the more important abstracting journals is available, and any item in DSC's stock can be requested. There is a restriction on the number of items that can be requested: four satisfied requests per reader if submitted on the day of visit or ten advance notice requests on DSC Reading Room request forms to be received in the Reading Room at least five working days prior to the visit. A coin-operated photocopy machine is located in the Reading Room. It is not normally possible to borrow items on personal visits. The Reading Room includes the Northern Listening Service, which makes accessible by appointment a week in advance the whole range of the NSA's resources. Details of these services along with notes on the online search facilities, tours of DSC, travelling to Boston Spa, and catering and banking services, are printed in an A4 folded leaflet, *Services For Visitors*.

Two factors account for DSC's worldwide reputation: the professional approach and expertise of its staff and the comprehensive nature of its collections,which enable it to satisfy 95% of the 3 million requests flooding in by post, fax, telex, and computer every year. In November 1990 DSC issued *Acquisitions Policy At The Document Supply Centre*, a four-page A4 leaflet, revised in September 1992, to provide an overview of its acquisitions policy in the hope that customers would be able to identify the broad range of material currently purchased.

The *Collections Portfolio*, an A4 laminated wallet, protecting 12 colour-coded information sheets, each relating to a specific category of the collections – for example, serials, books, official publications, the Oriental Collections, was published in 1992. It, too, is intended to give customers some idea of the breadth and depth of the collections, to explain acquisition criteria, and to assist in exploiting the collections to the full. Each leaflet defines what is meant by a serial, book, official publication; describes DSC's holdings, and instructs on how best to trace and locate individual items. Updating sheets will be despatched as the collections develop and grow. Other information on specific collections can be gleaned from a series, 'Highlighting The Collections', which has been featured in *Document Supply News* since September 1991: US Congressional Information (September 1991); Reports (December 1991); European Community Documentation (March 1992); Translations (June 1992); Microform Research Collections (September 1992); British Official Publications (December 1992); Older Books (March 1993); and Monograph Selection (September 1993).

COLLECTIONS AND THEIR EXPLOITATION

Currently DSC subscribes to 49,000 'worthwhile' serial titles; that is, those required for higher educational, research, or industrial purposes with certain other recreational or other low-level titles if it is apparent that there is a steady and sizeable demand. Six basic criteria are brought into play in their selection:

(1) demand;
(2) cost – very expensive items are only acquired if there is evidence of current demand and continuing use;
(3) availability elsewhere;
(4) level;
(5) language and script – DSC collects material in all European languages, Russian, Chinese, Japanese, and Korean; and
(6) country of origin.

In the autumn of 1989 DSC was forced to cancel a number of subscriptions to keep within a reduced acquisitions budget. Four main areas were targeted: low-level and out-of-scope titles which would not have been selected under recent more rigorous criteria; specialized abstract journals with little or no recorded use; foreign-language titles currently taken by DSC and SRIS which showed no use since data collection began; and multiple copy subscriptions (from 'To Cut Or Not To Cut', *Document Supply News*, **24**, December 1989:3).

Published annually since 1978, *Current Serials Received* lists all serial titles held either at DSC or SRIS and is divided into three A–Z sections: all titles other than in the Cyrillic script; serials in Cyrillic script with their titles transliterated; and cover-to-cover translations from Cyrillic script. Alongside each title the DSC shelfmark is given to expedite customers' requests.

Inside Information is an electronic table of contents service providing details of all articles printed in each of DSC's 10,000 most used scholarly journals. Authors, article titles, journal, and issue details of each article are entered onto the Electronic Table Of Contents database along with the page number, DSC shelfmark, ISSN and a unique item identifier. The first output at the end of 1992 was on a weekly ASCII file on magnetic tape or as a daily file transmission to a library's own network. 'Coverage will be more relevant to researchers' needs than any comparable service, because it is based on demand data' (*Document Supply News*, **38**, June 1993:1). An added advantage stems from DSC's ability to add articles within 48 to 72 hours after receipt of the journal at Boston Spa. *Inside Information on CD-ROM* was introduced in the Spring of 1993, containing records from journal issues received since January, and is published monthly as a cumulating disc. The December disc contains approximately 1 million records. 'Amongst the many powerful search and retrieval features, which have been included in the product, are searching for all or latest additions, saving search profiles for regular use, marking records for future reference, identifying local journal holdings, alternative sorting of records, save, print and order options. Inside Information is available for trial and evaluation prior to purchase' (advertisement). *Inside Information on CD-ROM List of Titles* (1993, 78pp.) lists journal titles A–Z with their DSC shelfmark and notes that 'the database is a dynamic file and it is possible that further titles may be added and some titles removed. The list should be regarded as a guide rather than a definite statement.'

Inside Information ETOC The Electronic Table Of Contents Service is a wallet containing promotional literature and notices of two British Library partnerships. One is with EBSCO Industries, whereby the two bodies agreed jointly to market *Inside Information*; the second is with Bath Information and Data Services (BIDS), University of Bath, making *Inside Information* available to BIDS subscribers over JANET.

Keyword Index To Serial Titles (*KIST*) consists of a set of over 200 (48x) microfiches providing rapid access to information on 450,000 serial titles held not only in DSC, SRIS and H&SS, but also in Cambridge University Library and the Science Museum Library. Produced from DSC's continually updated master file, it includes in a single alphabetical list all the significant words in serial titles on specific subjects, to locate serials where the precise title is unknown, and to identify titles and shelfmarks before submitting requests. *KIST* is published quarterly and annually, suscribers receive a set of fiche with an introductory guide in January and replacement sets every quarter. *Boston Spa Serials on CD-ROM*, published twice yearly, provides details of serial titles and holdings of the same collections recorded in *KIST*. Keyword/Boolean search, browse, save, print, edit, and ordering in the ARTTel (automated request transmission by telephone) format are the options available.

Published jointly with the United Kingdom Serials Group, *Current British Journals* (6th ed., 1992), edited by Mary Toase, is an authoritative subject guide to 10,000 UK journals. Arranged in abridged UDC order, entries provide information on title; date of first issue; previous title(s); publishers/booksellers' name, address; an indication of subject content; availability of indexes; availability in other than printed form (microform, CD-ROM); ISSN; name of sponsoring organization; price; and frequency.

Journals In Translation (5th ed., 1991), published in association with the International Translations Centre, Delft, contains over 1,300 A–Z titles (150 new to this edition), covering all subject areas, which are either translated cover-to-cover or selectively, together with journals consisting of translations of articles collected from multiple sources. Entries give bibliographic data, original title, date translation began, publisher of translation, and DSC or SRIS shelfmark (if any). An original title index, a keyword-in-context subject index, and a list of publishers and distributing agents are also included.

The book collections at Boston Spa now number 2.7 million and are increasing by 46,000 volumes annually. Purchases are restricted to those books presenting a serious scholarly approach to most academic disciplines at undergraduate level or above. Juvenile literature, recreational literature (entertainment, travels, pets, cookery, health and beauty, the occult, sport), and practical manuals are invariably excluded. Price is not regarded as a criterion for purchase except for very expensive items. Books accessioned after 1980, some official publications, and conference proceedings are all recorded on MARS, DSC's online Monograph Acquisitions and Records System, available on BLAISE-LINE, and other databases. Records for pre-1980 English language and for all foreign-language books irrespective of date are held in the Union Catalogue of Books, a card catalogue containing records of DSC's holdings and locations in other UK libraries. The part played by the loan of older material is well captured in 'Successful first year for NCB' (i.e., Non-Current Books), *Document Supply News*, **23**, September 1989:2.

Books At Boston Spa, now published and cumulated annually on 48x reduction microfiche, lists in one alphabetical sequence all English and Western European language books published from 1980 onwards held by DSC. Entries contain author, title and edition details, publication information, ISBN, and DSC stock location. An introductory guide, fiche file, and pockets are included in the initial set. First released in 1992, *Boston Spa Books on CD-ROM* enables users to search by author, title, publisher, ISBN, series title, date, and place of publication.

Probably the most comprehensive and easily accessible collection of conference proceedings in the world is held at Boston Spa. On the basis that conference material is a vital source for the most current information, and as an indicator of future developments and research, DSC has always attempted to acquire all 'worthwhile' conference proceedings regardless of subject, language, or format. They are notoriously difficult to trace and many are brought to DSC's notice by customers' requests. *Index of Conference Proceedings*, published monthly, covers the proceedings of conferences, symposia, expositions, workshops, in all disciplines. In total it provides access to the papers of 314,000 conferences (the present annual intake is 14,500). *Index of Conference Proceedings 1964–1988* (K. G. Saur, 26 vols., 1989) indexes 270,000 conferences under 750,000 subject key terms taken from titles and organizing or sponsoring institutions. Only conferences for which DSC holds proceedings are included but, by virtue of DSC's comprehensive collection, the *Index* is indispensable for tracing this awkward category of material. The cumulation is also available on microfiche. The *Index* was first available on BLAISE-LINE in 1980 and in 1991 *Boston Spa Conferences on CD-ROM* was introduced. Published quarterly, this CD-ROM version provides rapid access by title, series, sponsor, venue, keywords, and date, either separately or by combining with Boolean searching. Records are displayed in up to six different formats, two of which may be customized by the searcher. Mike Curston's 'Boston Spa Conferences on CD-ROM', *Aslib Information,* **19** (6), June 1991:216–17, describes DSC's collection and the use of CD-ROM to improve awareness of what is considered to be an underused resource, whilst Joan Day's 'Boston Spa Conferences on CD-ROM', *CD-ROM Information Products: The Evaluative Guide,* **4** (1), January 1993:16–23, looks at user hardware and software requirements, configuration software (search menu, viewing and printing retrieval records, Browse, etc.) and concludes that 'it must be seen as a major advance' in locating this type of material.

A similar service to *Inside Information, Inside Conferences* was launched in October 1993 indexing the 500,000 conference papers acquired by DSC every year significantly improving access to this type of material.

Directory of Acronyms (1993), to be updated biennially, gives details of over 8,000 acronyms present in DSC's Conference Index database of 300,000 records relating to societies, organizations, conference titles, and medical and scientific terms.

Special efforts are made to acquire 'grey literature' – that not readily available through normal book-trade channels. DSC was instrumental in establishing SIGLE (System for Information on Grey Literature in Europe), operated by a consortium of national libraries in EC countries which collect, index, and provide document delivery of this type of material. The consortium produces a database of its holdings which is accessible through BLAISE-LINE. A prepaid subject service based on DSC's holdings of British grey literature from 1980 was announced in September 1993.

Report literature in all nature and life-sciences disciplines, in technology, agriculture, medicine, the humanities, and the social sciences is assiduously collected. Over 10,000 report series and over four million documents are in stock, mostly acquired from the National Technical Information Service, NASA, the American Institute of Aeronautics, the US Department of Energy, ERIC, and from the International Nuclear Information System. British reports are also heavily represented, including virtually all reports emanating from government departments, research associations, industry, and academic institutions. DSC's acquisitions of report literature are announced in its monthly current awareness bulletin, *British Reports, Translations and Theses*, which also includes market research material held by DSC and most doctoral theses accepted at British universities. Arranged in three major sub-divided sections, Humanities, Psychology and Social Sciences; Biological and Medical Sciences; and Mechanical, Industrial, Civil and Marine Engineering, it includes a monthly keyterm index, an annual index, and quarterly cumulating author, report number, and keyterm indexes on microfiche.

A portfolio of information bulletins on British research is introduced in January 1994: *Focus on British Biological and Medical Sciences Research*; *Focus on British Business and Management Sciences Research*; *Focus on British Engineering and Computer Sciences Research*; and *Focus on British Environmental Sciences Research*. *Alphanumeric Reports Publications Index* (*ARPI*), originally devised as an in-house listing to assist staff trace individual series through the thickets of primary and secondary report numbers in dispersed locations at Boston Spa, now provides easy access to over 10,000 report series. Each entry gives the DSC location, the country of origin, and either the expansion of the alphanumeric organizing body or a subject heading. *ARPI* is published as a single volume which includes a free microfiche edition.

Since 1971 DSC has collaborated with most UK universities in acquiring and making available doctoral theses which are now microfilmed on their receipt at Boston Spa. DSC does not retain the original but from its master microfilm it can supply a film, microfiche, or paper copy. The abolition from 1993 of the universities' requirement for users to sign a copyright declaration allows DSC to sell theses not only to individuals but also to libraries. All theses acquired are registered in *British Reports, Translations and Theses. The BRITS Index, An index to the British Theses Collections (1971–1987) held at the British Library Document Supply Centre and London University* was published in 1988 by IPI in association with the British Library in three author, subject, and title volumes.

The main strength of DSC's collection of official publications – those issued by central government or government-funded departments, government-sponsored organizations or intergovernmental publications – lies in the HMSO collection, which includes everything HMSO makes available on its Selected Subscription Service. DSC also subscribes to the Chadwyck-Healey microfiche collection of *British Official Publications Not Published By HMSO*. American federal government publications are acquired selectively to meet demand. The US American Statistics Index and Congressional Information Services microfiche collections are acquired, as are Canadian federal government publications. Good collections of United Nations and International Labour Office titles have been built up on demand.

Although UK local government publications are usually regarded as being intended only for local distribution and use, many have a much wider application and significance both as historical records and in disseminating information on current issues and practices. For that reason DSC initiated a special programme in 1980 designed to identify and capture this neglected, sometimes obscure, but important material. The collections now amount to 25,000 items which are being added to at a rate of approximately 500 annually. Acquisitions are noted in *British Reports, Translations and Theses* and so find their way on to the SIGLE database.

DSC has been an officially designated depository for EC documentation since 1966, which means that virtually all EC publications and unrestricted documents arrive at Boston Spa. Holdings include all sections of the *Official Journal*, which gives the texts of official legislation and official announcements, and over 1,200 other serial titles, of which over 400 are currently received. Large quantities of material dating back to 1950 and many publications produced by the UK government, independent research institutions, and commercial publishers about the EC are also held. The *European Community* sheet in *The Collections*

Portfolio clarifies EC terminology and distinguishes some important categories of EC documents in DSC's collections.

Historically DSC's collection of material in the Slavonic languages, either in Cyrillic or Roman script, is rooted in the initial brief for the establishment of the National Lending Library for Science and Technology, which required a comprehensive acquisition of serials and scientific and technical monographs from the USSR. This emphasis no longer continues – DSC abandoned purchasing scientific monographs in the Cyrillic script in 1992 – but the policy of acquiring Slavonic-language serials in all subject fields, especially in science and technology, is still actively pursued. Among DSC's holdings are thousands of reports from research establishments in the former Soviet Union and 600,000 papers released by VINITI (Vsesoiuznyi Institut Nauchoi i Tekhnicheskoi Informatsii) 1969–85, which give access to otherwise unpublished material. DSC's Slavonic-language works can be traced via *Index of Conference Proceedings, KIST, Books at Boston Spa* and *Current Serials Received.*

Serials, reports, and conference proceedings published in the Far East, and a small collection of books in oriental languages, are held at Boston Spa but it is likely that requests for oriental material will be passed on to DSC's national network of back-up libraries. Such titles as are held can be traced through DSC's series of bibliographical and indexing publications.

In some ways DSC's large collection of over 100,000 individual music scores and sets of chamber music parts is the Cinderella of Boston Spa. Of the 14,000 requests received daily only a small proportion is for music and, in recent years, the music service has suffered cuts in funding and staff resources. 'Since 1990, the service has had its bookfund cut from £44,500 to £10,000, and staffing has been reduced from 3.5 to 1.5 full-time equivalent posts' (Debby Raven, 'Music loans discord', *Library Association Record*, **95** (3), March 1993:138). Raven also reported that negotiations were taking place to transfer DSC's music lending service to Wakefield to be administered by the Yorkshire and Humberside Joint Library Service. DSC's Director is quoted as stating 'this was a suggestion from YHJLS. They have a music section which would complement the services we provide, resulting in a better national service.'

The strength of DSC's collections lies in collected editions, academic series, and facsimile reprints, but music of all types is purchased – including anthologies of popular songs which are indexed in *POPSI: the popular song index*, first published as a cumulating annual on microfiche and disk in 1990. *POPSI* gives composer, song title, alternative title, and first line details, and covers a wide variety of popular songs from music hall to top hits of the 1980s. Some practical hints on the best use of *POPSI* appear in John E. Starbuck's 'Seven ways to make your POPSI better!', *Audiovisual Librarian*, **17** (2), May 1991:105–7, which concludes: 'POPSI looks a sure bet for a relatively inexpensive but effective music information service in its present form.' Sets of orchestral parts and multiple copies of vocal scores are not acquired but DSC publishes the *British Union Catalogue Of Orchestral Sets* (*BUCOS*) (2nd ed., 1989) containing information on nearly 10,000 orchestral sets held in 66 UK libraries. Arranged A–Z by composer and title, entries also give details of each work's orchestration, its duration, the lending policies of participating libraries, and an extensive title index. Supplements to, and new editions of, *BUCOS* are already being planned.

COPYRIGHT

In 1989, publishers from 50 countries, led by the United States delegation, passed a resolution at the International Publishers Association (IPA) Congress condemning DSC for its photocopying activities and urging the British government to take steps to end DSC's illegal export of photocopied material.

> The IPA statement maintains that 'simple, efficient means are readily available' to allow the DSC to conduct its business in accordance with accepted copyright law and practice by utilising the services of the various national Reproduction Rights Organisations. It asks the British government . . . to prohibit the DSC from 'exporting photocopies to commercial entities in other countries without payment of freely negotiated compensation to copyright owners', and to require the DSC to get 'enforcable assurance' from photocopy recipients within the UK that the copies will not be exported' (Carol A. Risher, 'Publishers, Librarians, And Copyright', *Library Acquisitions: Practice & Theory*, **13** (3), 1989:213–16).

Later in the year, 'BL under international pressure over contempt for copyright', *Bookseller*, **4377**, 10 November 1989:1, reported that the STM Group at the Frankfurt Book Fair had urged the government to act against DSC's exporting activities, and that in Rome the International Federation of Reproduction Rights Organisations had asked the government to ensure that DSC respected the principles of copyright as set out in the Berne and Universal Copyright Declarations: 'The bone of con-

tention in a complex area is that the BL is systematically copying material without passing any fees onto the copyright owners, and distributing
this material overseas in contravention of other national copyright laws.'
The Copyright Licensing Agency (CLA), formed in 1982 by the
Authors' Licensing and Collecting Society and the Publishers' Licensing
Society for the purpose of licensing the reprographic copying of literary
works, also protested at DSC's contempt for the interests of copyright
owners. British Library, however, was firmly of the opinion that it was
operating within the provisions of the 1988 Copyright, Designs and
Patents Act. The publishers had no doubt that even if this were true it
was not within the spirit of the law.

In this context the law itself came under attack: 'even though recently
reviewed and updated, British copyright laws are . . . quite unjust in
allowing unrestricted photocopying of copyright material . . . publishers
have every right to protest and to press for further review and eventual
adjustment more to their favour', remarked the Director of Microinfo Ltd
in a letter to the *Bookseller*. He concluded that 'the provision of unfair
subsidized competitive services from the official sector, and services that
do not recognize the legitimate rights of copyright holders, will continue
to provide a source of conflict between on the one hand the British
Library and, on the other, publishers in the private sector information
industry' (R. B. Selwyn, 'BL and copyright', *Bookseller*, **4382**, 15
December 1989:1926).

At this point in its history the last thing the British Library wanted
was a prolonged skirmish with the publishing industry, and its uneasy
relationship with the CLA was brought to an end with a licensed copying
agreement signed at the Second International Conference on Interlending
and Document Supply, 19 November 1990, to come into effect on 1
April 1991. The agreement enabled DSC to offer a range of copyright
cleared services. Customers who chose to use these services would pay a
small fee for every DSC-supplied photocopied article. Fees would be
collected by DSC and passed to the CLA for distribution to the publishers. All DSC's royalty-free services would continue but overseas users in
particular would welcome the opportunity to choose the new copyright
cleared service, with a small payment (£1.10) for each photocopied journal article supplied to end the need for separate royalty arrangements.
The only remaining restriction is that further copying, other than that
allowed by copyright legislation, is not permitted except with the agreement of the copyright owner. 'The agreement has brought to an end the
wary relationship which previously existed between BLDSC and pub-

lishers. It heralds a new era of mutual understanding and potential cooperation which can only be of further benefit to both them and the academic, research and industrial communities which they serve' (Mick
Osborne, 'Copyright Cleared Services', *Serials*, **5** (1), March 1992:30).
Copyright cleared material is available through the Urgent Action and
LEXICON services. To clarify the new situation DSC distributed a
twice-folded A5 leaflet, *Copyright Cleared*, to answer any questions customers might have.

Following legal advice, and in the light of recent interpretations of
United States copyright law, the British Library held discussions with the
Association of American Publishers about DSC's photocopying service
to its US customers. The outcome was that the British Library withdrew
its royalty-free service and undertook in future to provide only the
Copyright Cleared Service.

BOOKNET

An independent review by Capital Planning Information of the role of
the Gift and Exchange System (GES) – whose purpose it was to assist
libraries to dispose of no-longer wanted items, either by receiving them
into DSC's own stock, to ensure that at least one copy survived for
national loan, or else by offering them to other libraries – was completed
by the autumn of 1988. The British Library decided that GES should
continue although funding constraints demanded procedural and financial changes to ensure it could become self-supporting within three years.
The aim of BookNet, the razor-sharp name under which GES was
relaunched in January 1989, was to provide an efficient cost-recovery
service which allowed 'organisations to dispose usefully of unwanted
publications; the Centre to augment its stock with worthwhile items; and
significant relocation of material to libraries where it is needed' ('Launch
of a new service', *Document Supply News*, **19**, December 1988:1–2).

BookNet is financed through a standard charge for items received
rather than by charging for regularly distributed lists of material available. GES charged £52 per annum for these lists; BookNet distributes
them *gratis* with a fee of £3.50 plus postage and VAT for each item
received. 'This means that those making most use of the service will pay
accordingly rather than paying the previous blanket charge irrespective
of the amount of material ordered. For DSC it means paying directly for
the 20,000 items that it expects to add to stock, rather than covering the
running costs of the previous scheme' ('BookNet Service', *British
Library News*, **145**, February 1988:1). Objections to the new arrange-

ments were voiced by the Trade Union Side at Boston Spa, principally to the perceived emphasis on commercial values over the national good:

> Not only will libraries be charged considerably more, but the DSC itself will also have to pay to add to its stock items that have been freely donated by other libraries. At a time of considerable pressure on the acquisitions budget, it is inevitable that something will have to give. Further cuts are bound to occur and it will be surprising if the DSC is able to add anything like the present number of donated books to its stock, and so many items will not be available on the national interlending system (Tony Reed, 'Anxiety at Boston Spa over new service', *Library Association Record*, **91** (1), January 1989:29).

A swift reply came from DSC's Director, denying that GES's replacement by BookNet reflected predominating commercial values:

> This is not the case. By charging for items rather than lists and setting the service charge to achieve cost-recovery (but *not* profit) we are aiming to spread the cost of the service fairly among all beneficiaries (including the DSC) and to keep the service going on a sound financial basis. A service for the national good does not have to be free ('BL's BookNet . . . spreading the cost more fairly', *ibid.*, **91** (3), March 1989:146).

Twice monthly BookNet sends a subject classified list of material available for redistribution and a request form for wanted items. Requests are dealt with in order of receipt and items still available are despatched within a few days. Donations in reasonable condition can be sent to DSC although prior consultation is advised for large consignments. The expectation was that costs incurred in transferring material would be counterbalanced by the facility to clear shelves quickly of unwanted items. BookNet's operations initially were confined to the UK although it was announced in September 1992 that 'in the near future it is intended to offer an on-line service which will be available worldwide' ('Spotlight on BookNet', *Document Supply News*, **35**, September 1992:2–3). By that time BookNet's UK customers numbered over 800.

MEDICAL INFORMATION SERVICE

A number of related functions from different directorates were coalesced into a restructured Medical Information Centre in 1992. British Library had been involved in medical literature provision for over 30 years, notably as the UK host of the US National Library of Medicine. In its capacity as the UK MEDLARS centre it indexed British medical journals for the MEDLINE database. The increasing significance of information on alternative medicine and allied health topics led to DSC developing its own internal database, AMED/CATS, available online through MIC-KIBIC and DATA-STAR, which includes physiotherapy, occupational therapy, rehabilitation, and complementary medicine. An *AMED/CATS Thesaurus*, A–Z hierarchical lists of its 2,500 headings, and the *AMED/CATS List of Journals Indexed* may be purchased. Besides direct access to MEDLINE, TOXLIT, and the National Library of Medicine's databases, the Medical Information Service can search a wide range of other databases including Excerpta Medica and BIOSIS (the online version of *Biological Abstracts*). Its current awareness service includes monthly and quarterly computer searches on subscribers' special topics and low-cost MEDLINE update bulletins. Photocopies of virtually every article listed in its searches or bibliographies can be supplied.

The BLAISE online information retrieval service from the biomedical files of the US National Library of Medicine began in 1977 and from 1982 to April 1992 operated by direct access through BLAISE-LINK. By December 1990 BLAISE-LINK offered access to 42 databases, all relating either to general or specific aspects of medicine, holding some 14 million records, including MEDLINE, and other National Library of Medicine files. A UK version of GRATEFUL MED, a software package, simplified MEDLINE searching by helping to formulate the search strategy before going online, automatically logging in to the BLAISE-LINK computer with the user's BLAISE-LINK code and password, entering the search and storing any references found, transferring the search results to the user's PC for offline searching, and if required printing them on the user's printer. A 10cm x 21cm folded guide, *GRATEFUL MED. Making MEDLINE easy to search*, is distributed. Having relocated to Boston Spa with the NBS in January 1991, BLAISE-LINK merged with the Medical Information Centre, which continues to run the BLAISE-LINK help desk. *BLAISE-LINK from The Medical Information Centre* (1993, 12pp.) elaborates on the services provided on its 43 databases, and those available on the TOXNET network, and provides concise instructions on how to conduct searches. *BLAISE-LINK Newsletter*, which carried technical articles, details of new databases, search hints, and announcements of alterations in fields and was intended for operational users, ceased publication with the November/December 1991 issue.

Medical Information Service monthly publications in the Current Awareness Topics series, all with cumulated annual indexes, include

Complementary Medicine Index; *Occupational Therapy Index*; *Physiotherapy Index*; *Rehabilitation Index*; and *Palliative Care Index*.

SCONUL's 'The role of the British Library for medical and health information', *Health Libraries Review*, 7 (1), March 1990:14–19, bemoans that the British Library 'is not perceived as identifying with the community of medical librarians . . . not seen as a focus for research in the use of medical information nor as leading in the re-examination of the traditional medical library role'. SCONUL recommended that the British Library should re-examine its resource allocation in order to focus on medical information activities, specifically:

(1)   to find a mechanism to consult all relevant groups in medical and health information with a view to formulating a long-range policy;

(2)   to formulate national policies for the acquisition, preservation, provision and dissemination of medical and health information;

(3)   to encourage further development of the regional medical information networks and linking of these into the European network; and

(4)   to encourage and support research and development in medical library services and medical informatics, including electronic networks, electronic publishing in medicine, the integration of information retrieval functions with other areas of medical informatics along the lines of the NLM's IAIMS project, the language of medicine and the classification of medical activity.

EXPRESS SERVICES

To ensure its customers obtain the documents they require quickly and at the least expense, DSC offers a wide range of services. Photocopies can either be ordered by post or by Automated Request Transmission (ART), the collective name given to a range of electronic ordering methods. Deliveries from Boston Spa can be despatched by post, fax, or courier. Special services are on hand for urgent requests. DSC's standard service aims to turn round requests within 48 hours. In instances where speed is crucial, the Urgent Action Service allows users to telephone or fax their requests, which are then dealt with by a dedicated team who report on progress within two hours and despatch the items requested the same day either by first-class post, by courier (delivery guaranteed the next day), or by fax.

Urgent Action Service's LEXICON – The Easy Order Service is the name given to a package of flexible services intended to satisfy particular needs with the minimum amount of paperwork to cater for users whose requirements do not fit into the standard services. A list of documents in any legible format, multiple or high quality copies, or even replacement archival copies for public sector library use, can all be supplied by this customized service. A link-up with SRIS's STIS – a comprehensive literature searching service with access to several hundred major international online databases, to provide a complete information supply service from literature searching to supplying the actual documents – was announced in December 1991. For a total UK cost of about £100, STIS supplies a list of bibliographic references and a LEXICON order form for the user to mark the required items on and return to LEXICON. Items requested are despatched by overnight courier two or three days after receipt at Boston Spa; packages containing fewer than 15 items are sent by first-class post. Full instructions on how to use the different categories of services, and details of charges, are printed in an A5 leaflet, *LEXICON The Easy Order Service Fast, Efficient And Cost Effective*. The Journal Contents Page Service, by which users receive photocopies of the latest content pages of chosen journals on a regular subscription basis, can also be expedited through Urgent Action Service, British Library's fastest growing service, expanding at the rate of 25% a year – providing an indication that the market, especially industrial users, appreciates a fast document supply service.

Primarily intended for heavy users who prefer to prepare piles of requests in advance of transmission from their own terminals directly into DSC's computer, and not designed to process requests one by one, an Automated Request by Telephone (ARTTel) service is available. *ARTTel Users' Guide* (1992) includes general information on the service, including the equipment needed, access via Global Network Services and Public Switched Telephone Network, individual requirements, and technical information. 'Automated Requests – the new generation', *Document Supply News*, **37**, March 1993:1, announced 'a totally redesigned, modern, sophisticated yet user-friendly version of ARTTel' which came into operation for UK and international customers on 19 April and 24 May respectively. The new system is reported to have a more effective procedure for logging on, a status facility which enables users to check the number of requests received, an informative help screen, and a message exchange system between DSC and its users. *ARTTel Version 2* attractively condenses information in A4 leaflet format, whilst *ARTTel – Version 2 UK User Guide* (1993) contains general information, log-on instructions, and technical information in an A5 ring-binder.

THE FUTURE OF DSC

Despite DSC's hitherto unchallenged and unrivalled position in the national library network, or perhaps even because of it, questions about its future began to be increasingly asked in the 1988/9 winter. Although 'everybody recognises the tremendous value of the Document Supply Centre to libraries throughout the world . . . the question is, however, whether the Centre has reached the peak or even passed the peak of its usefulness as a means of document supply' (F. J. Friend, 'Is the writing on the wall at Boston Spa?', *Library Association Record*, **91** (1), January 1989:29). 'The conditions under which Boston Spa flourished are now changing rapidly', he continued, 'and the solution to document supply which seemed most efficient and cost-effective in the past quarter-century may not be so in the next quarter-century'. The burden of Friend's argument was that:

> as a way of supplying copies of articles from semi-core journals to libraries which can no longer afford to purchase them, a national document supply centre may still be viable, but the cost of maintaining a very large collection of little-used journals will push up the cost per copy of those documents which are required. The British Library may have to choose between comprehensiveness and demand if it is to remain competitive on document supply.

Alternatives to DSC might be specialist companies in the American mode or modern local supply systems such as the University of London's LIBERTAS grouping.

The debate this provocative letter sparked off should have been stifled at birth by Maurice Line's 'Boston Spa and the writing on the wall', *ibid.*, **91** (2), February 1989:85, which tersely reminded the library and information world that documents have to come from somewhere (several US document supply companies obtained theirs from DSC); that competing UK libraries would have to possess the documents, many of which were uniquely held in the UK by DSC; and that they would have to supply documents heavily in demand locally, at a speed and cost comparable to DSC when staff numbers were severely constrained or reduced. Notwithstanding Line's customary hitting of the nail squarely on the head, the debate rumbled on until the recently appointed Director of DSC responded and sketched out DSC's current and future functions.

> For all types of publication the DSC is concerned that effective document supply systems should exist in the UK. To that end we maintain or encourage union catalogues, publicize interlending arrangements,

co-operate with other libraries and library organisations in the UK and
abroad . . . We try to act as leaders in document supply, helping to
ensure that systems operate well and that remote document supply is
given the emphasis it deserves, alongside reference and information
services (David Bradbury, 'Boston Spa: an uncertain future?', *ibid.*,
91 (6), June 1989:335–6).

He saw no reason to suppose that this model of service was outmoded if
only because the model was not static, especially in the field of science
and technology. In areas such as the humanities or social sciences a
change in document supply was theoretically possible if other libraries
could evolve a lending service at a lower cost. But if DSC were to bow
out of the humanities, large university libraries would soon experience
huge staffing costs and 'would almost certainly need to raise their
charges to control demand; and they would face a difficult conflict
between service to their local clientele, and service to other libraries'.
The question of costs was, of course, crucial: if the government insisted
that DSC increase its charges to a full cost (i.e., including collection
cost/overheads) then libraries might well seek documents they required
elsewhere. Demand on DSC would spiral downwards, leading to reduced
revenue, putting pressure on DSC's acquisition budget and lower satisfaction in supply, leading to further reductions in demand. Publishers
communicating with their readers might conceivably pose a greater
threat but the likelihood of this was diminishing. DSC's future was
brighter than Friend had painted.

In the same issue, Bernard Naylor's 'The future of interlending and
document supply' (pp.336–7) queried DSC's cost-effectiveness,
although conceding that supplying all interlibrary loans from the same
centre was the most efficient arrangement but the unseen factor was that
DSC subsidized the nation's library services at the taxpayers' expense.
Interlending charges only recovered the marginal costs of the service, not
the acquisitions and staff costs of collection management. 'Only in the
case of the DSC is the collection purchased solely to service inter-library
loan requests, to the extent that if there were no inter-library demand for
it, there would be no case for buying it.' Since 'the cost of acquiring and
managing the material is, as a minimum, roughly equal to the marginal
cost of running the interlending service . . . it looks as though the cost of
the loan form would have to double (as a minimum) if there was ever a
call for DSC to recover all the costs of supporting interlending'. But, in
the end, Naylor reflected, 'in so far as we do depart from the concept of
the central loan collection as a free good, we shall probably end up

regretting it, and we shall have a poorer service and only marginal savings'.

Bradbury presented a stark analysis of the financial imponderables confronting DSC in a paper at a two-day seminar on interlending and charging at the University of Lancaster, 7–8 July 1989. In DSC's operations, there were currently substantial areas of cross-subsidization 'although customer requirements, market forces or even Government pressure may lead to further changes in this area over the coming years'. Areas where changes were already evident were the demands for increased revenue earning services and international competition from central public sector-funded document supply services in a number of countries worldwide which had already eaten into DSC's high annual growth rates despite a stepped-up DSC marketing effort. On the question of full cost recovery for its services:

> we have now more or less achieved direct cost recovery for the document supply services as a whole, i.e. we earn the cost of providing the services, excluding collection costs. But we would have to more than double our UK prices to remove the need altogether for subsidy to the BLDSC as a whole from the Government grant-in-aid. How would our customers respond to this? If it happened suddenly there would of course be an outcry, and there would be massive reductions in the volume of demand on the BLDSC, leading to substantially lower use of the collections and the need for an even higher price to achieve cost recovery without drastically cutting the scale of our acquisitions.

If libraries were to decide on firm financial grounds what materials they would hold in their own collections, what they would obtain from DSC, and what from other libraries, and if government grant-in-aid were to be concentrated on the more obviously public good services at the British Library – particularly preserving the national archive, and the reading rooms at St Pancras – then in the long term it might be desirable for DSC to recover its full costs in order to guarantee its survival. But even so, that scenario, if it were to happen, would still have its down side: 'it would mean substantial increases in BLDSC prices for many years, placing strains on the budgets of our individual customers, who in turn would be unlikely to get any extra resources to cope with this. And there would be no guarantee that the BLDSC would stop increasing prices once it had achieved full cost recovery.'

And what if DSC should be fully privatized? Not all its operations would ever be profitable: the loan service of little-used older books, scientific report literature more than a few years old, music scores, official publications, and Russian scientific books, would always be loss-making services. Recent English-language scientific, technical, medical, and business journals would be a more attractive proposition to investors but the charges for lending services would still need to be increased by 200% or even 300%. Only if the government or the British Library continued to subsidize a privatized DSC would its unprofitable services for the national good be secured.

> Privatisation, then, looks an unlikely prospect for the BLDSC. More commercialism – yes, more enterprise – yes, but only as part of our role in the national library economy. We exist not to make money, not to make a profit, not even to fulfil a legal obligation. We exist as an integral part of the national library system in the UK. We exist to help other libraries do their jobs more effectively. We exist because our customers want our services.

Bradbury's was a noble peroration but reality remained:

> As things stand, there seems little prospect of the BLDSC in the next few years getting a sufficient increase in its grant-in-aid element to maintain its existing acquisition policies, even allowing for continuing efforts on our part to keep our costs down and improve our efficiency. Leaving aside privatisation, we have to choose broadly between two options . . . to continue as now, increasing our prices a little above inflation but slowly trimming down our acquisition policy. . . [or, secondly] . . . to increase our prices rather more each year until such time as we are recovering our full costs (Bradbury, 'Should the BLDSC be Privatised?', pp.24–9, *Interlend '89: Who Pays?*, edited by Robin Green, Forum for Interlending, 1990).

A year later Friend re-entered the lists, this time – on a different tack – arguing that there really was no need for the national library to be involved in interlibrary loan, and that the days of DSC were numbered, partly on the premise that access to library catalogues in the next decade would be very much easier through the development of Open Systems Interconnection. If the location of material could be easily traced, why should the national library be concerned? He also found it interesting that no comparable service to DSC had been created in any other country: 'Comprehensiveness and speed of service have a very high cost, and that is the Achilles heel of Boston Spa in this age of reducing government expenditure. The Document Supply Centre flourished in a generation which believed in government intervention and which was prepared to bear the cost of such a superb national service.' But attitudes – and technology – were changing. A scenario in which the text of journal articles could be called up, if necessary by interlibrary loan, and printed out in the user's office at a reasonable cost, based on a network of libraries and perhaps with a private sector input, was looking more and more feasible. 'The key technical factors are going to be the availability of periodical articles in machine-readable format and the availability of digital transmission over telephone lines into fax machines.' If such a service were to materialize, DSC's present cost advantages would vanish:

> under present labour-intensive methods of document delivery, the Document Supply Centre has a cost advantage over regional or local systems, because it is organised as a photocopying factory. Once online takes the place of photocopying that cost advantage disappears, as does the speed of delivery advantage . . . because, clearly, online access is just as fast if not faster to a local database than it is to a database at Boston Spa ('National library provision and relationships: inter-library lending', *Library Association Record*, **92** (8), August 1990:577–9).

Again Bradbury responded: university libraries providing interlending services would be faced with huge numbers of requests, to control demand they would probably resort to high charges; the abolition of DSC would severely damage national access to less used material, especially grey literature, 'no one is going to start collecting on DSC's scale conference proceedings, technical report literature, translations of theses, or obscure scientific serials without government financial support; and no library would assume the role of national lending repository for older material' ('Inter-library lending in the next decade – don't be too quick to knock BLDSC', *ibid.*, **92** (10), October 1990:738–9).

With consummate timing the British Library launched its Interlibrary Lending Cost Model at the Bournemouth INFO '90 conference. Coopers and Lybrand Deloitte had been commissioned to develop a computer model of interlibrary lending costs. Tested by 43 UK academic, public and special libraries, all presenting their own data, the model was designed to analyse the total staff and the associated and additional costs of interlending in a consistent way, and to provide libraries with a reliable method to estimate the cost effects of altering their interlending operations. *Modelling the economics of interlibrary lending* was also available for use on IBM-compatible PCs.

A paper by Alan MacDougall at the thirteenth annual United Kingdom Serials Group Conference considered the implications of the setting up of an East Midlands academic document supply service to replace DSC's service, the British Library's timely cost model, and the continuing debate as to DSC's future role. He invited libraries to reappraise the whole process of document supply and to plan a new strategy in the context of the existing pressures on the current interlending system, the cost-related problems of efficiency and effectiveness, and the impact of new technology. At first sight DSC's position was not threatened: it had a success rate of between 80% and 90% for requested items; the majority of items were supplied within a week; and the pricing structure continued along relatively stable lines. Nevertheless, there was increasing pressure in all library and information services to make economies, to look for further efficiency and effectiveness in cost terms, to exploit new technology, and, if necessary, to seek alternative arrangements. Could DSC escape the demands of government policy and continue to deliver the goods on time and at a price the market could bear? A recent East Midlands research project had concluded that libraries could not compete with DSC; new technology alone could not make alternative arrangements viable, whilst the potential for publishers to provide journal articles at an economic price as an alternative to complete journal subscriptions had not been realized.

> From the available information there would appear to be no sense of impending doom for libraries, or innovative alternatives for their document supply requirements. The BLDSC continues to reassess its service provision, and strives for further efficiency and effectiveness within a competitive price structure. The East Midlands Study may suggest that the continued present use of BLDSC is the most cost effective method for academic libraries but hints that in purely economic terms BLDSC is in effect subsidising their use. The real pressure will come from government requirements and market forces in a confused environment where libraries are being expected to cooperate and compete at the same time ('The Future of Document Supply: Is There an Alternative to the British Library Document Supply Centre?', *Serials*, **3** (3), November 1990:20–4).

Apart from the debate over DSC's functions and the likelihood of their continuing unscathed and enhanced into the twenty-first century, its future progress is discussed both in general and specific terms in a number of journal articles, mostly contributed by British Library staff. David

Bradbury's 'The British Library Document Supply Centre', *British Book News*, September 1989:624–5, principally a descriptive overview of its services for general consumption, also makes a modest forecast or two. The British Library is well placed to develop information services 'that help enquirers to pinpoint the document containing the answer to their query – or even provide the answer direct'. Citing the Medical Information Service, and SRIS's range of information services, Bradbury predicts that these types of services would expand, making full use of the increasing number of databases becoming available. Improvements in delivering documents to customers, made possible by new developments in facsimile transmission and the arrival of digital storage techniques, already allowed users to access a remote electronic store and have copies of documents transmitted back without human intervention. Martin Ince's 'Gilt-edged volumes help balance the books', *THES*, 1 February 1991:7 – a remarkably perceptive 'outsider's' view of DSC's scope, funding, services, workload, and earnings – also peers into the future, not only at electronic transmission of information, but also at a project looking at ways of generating 'output research' in general terms.

Malcolm Smith's 'Global marketing of managed information access', *The Electronic Library*, **9** (2), April 1991:91–4, stresses that: 'The articulation of changing customer needs through market mechanisms, the growth of competition and complex social and commercial alliances and the emergence of new technological opportunities, all demand that a library must have sufficient awareness and expertise to ensure that its assets are fully exploited; properly and easily available to those who can appreciate and benefit from their value.' In that context DSC needs to be 'very clear about [its] commitment to customer service, to providing facilities that are attuned to their changing requirements, and to provide these services with increasing efficiency'.

On 24 February 1992 Brian Lang, Chief Executive, and David Russon, Director General, The British Library, Boston Spa, addressed the Parliamentary Information Technology Committee. They presented a convincing and attractive argument that the application of IT could exploit the Library's vast collections and unparalleled experience in the electronic transmission of information to yield revenue far in excess of the £22 million a year it was already earning.

The Library's vision of the future is to make its great collections much more readily accessible to its customers around the world . . . by letting customers know what is held, making it easy for them to identify and ask for documents, and for a significant proportion of the holdings to be delivered electronically within minutes. The prices charged should be no greater, and preferably less, than current prices. The Library has a tremendous opportunity to reinforce its position as the world's foremost document supplier.

Specifically, the Library would wish:

to scan journal articles to create a database of critical mass to meet a high proportion of demand and most importantly to change customers' perceptions of the service provided. This could be done by scanning 2,000 journals, cover-to-cover, on receipt, or by scanning rather than photocopying articles as they are requested, so ensuring that an electronic copy is available for future use.

But, inevitably, there were financial restraints:

To transform the Library from an almost wholly paper-based establishment to one which is significantly electronic will require investment, something like £4 million over the next 2 to 3 years. At a time when there are so many other demands on the Library, particularly the move into the new building at St Pancras, will government recognise the investment required to retain the pre-eminent role of a great national institution? So far the need for investment in technology has not been recognised by Government. The Library believes that the consequences of lack of investment now will be grave.

There was also a need for an agreement with publishers on electrocopying; the possibility remained that they would impose royalty fees and conditions inhibiting potential developments. Government itself could do more to stimulate better information provision and access for government libraries. And there was the problem of how the nation was to acquire and maintain electronic publications for the benefit of future generations; the 1911 Copyright Act covered only the legal deposit of printed material. Lang and Russon concluded:

The British Library is, and always has been, a great national asset, which brings significant benefit to the nation's research and scholarship. It is now at a cross-roads, and the actions it takes over the next few years in coming to grips with electronic storage and delivery, and meeting the expectations of its customers across the world, will be crucial in securing its future position in serving research and enterprise. ('Unlocking the Treasure House. Information for Enterprise in the British Library', *Information Technology & Public Policy*, **10** (3), Summer 1992:171–3).

David N. Wood's 'Library Document Supply Centre', *Interlending & Document Supply*, 20 (4), October 1992:159–63, focuses on recent developments likely to have an impact on the range and quality of its services. Budgetary pressures blacken the immediate outlook since DSC has been receiving a declining proportion of the government's grant-in-aid which in any event was increasing at a slower rate than inflation. Staffing levels had fallen by 6% in the past year; the preservation budget had been sliced in half; and the acquisitions budget had been able to buy less and less – a further 6,000 journal subscriptions would have to be cancelled in the coming year. To compensate for these reductions co-operation with various European national libraries for mutual support in information provision was being explored. And, in addition to making services more attractive – Wood instanced ARTTel improvements, an automated account system, Urgent Action Service and LEXICON, and more use of electronic storage and transmission services – efforts were being made to market these services more effectively. As part of its marketing plan DSC had recently signed a global agency agreement with the British Council and it was possible that British Library would open a local office in the US to focus not only on DSC's photocopying services, but also on SRIS's Patent Express service.

DSC had already developed relationships with North American organizations: 25,000 of DSC's serial titles had been entered on the Ohio College of Librarianship's Online Union Catalogue (OCLC) with a marked increase in the number of requests; database hosts such as DATA-STAR and ESA had been cooperating with DSC to develop facilities to send requests directly to Boston Spa after searches on their own files. The potential use of JANET for document delivery was being thoroughly investigated and in due course DSC would experiment with the electronic transmission of documents over JANET direct to end-users' terminals. Quite simply *'DSC must not rest on its laurels . . . In the face of increasing competition if it cannot provide services which increasingly sophisticated customers require, at a price which allows it to depend less and less on governmental funds, then it will fail.'*

That the concept of resting on its laurels plays no part in DSC's forward planning is evident in Bradbury's 'British Library Document Supply Centre Strategy: The Next Ten Years', *Interlending & Document Supply*, 21 (3), 1993:7–11 which outlines its mission statement, purpose, objective and key strategies. Reaffirming that its purpose is 'to provide those requiring access to information for research, scholarship or innovation with documents which are not readily available locally, in order to improve the quality and effectiveness of their work', DSC's business ambition is 'to double the number of documents supplied to remote users over the decade to 2003, without reducing current levels of cost recovery.' Nine key strategies to accomplish these objectives are identified: concentrating ever more strongly on customer needs and offering good value for money and guaranteed levels of performance; making substantial investments in selected overseas markets; exploiting to the full the opportunities offered by information technology to provide faster, more efficient and more comprehensive services; ensuring that collection and access policies enable the percentage of successful requests to continue to improve; using total quality techniques to provide services as efficiently as possible; seeking to utilize and extend the skills of our staff so that everybody has the opportunity to contribute to the services provided; working with other areas of the British Library as part of the process of integrating the Library's services; developing strategic alliances to gain technological investment and expertise to improve services and access to collections; and obtaining the co-operation of publishers and agreements with them on royalties and copyright matters.'

To support these an additional six functional – and more specific – strategies are distinguished. A main thrust of the Marketing strategy is 'to increase the international demand from 25% to 50% of the total . . . giving particular emphasis to the use of intermediaries in North America and Europe.' Also highlighted is the creation of a British Library serials register and the development of a current awareness and article supply service based on the contents data of DSC serial holdings. Its Services strategy in providing efficient cost-effective services responding to customers' needs will be based on 'increasing operational efficiency, making the best use of information technology.' Customer demand will also drive DSC's Collection Strategy where 'it will be necessary to ensure that the Centre acquires sufficient material to maintain existing supply-from-stock rates. This may encompass the collection of full-text journals in electronic form and the development of strategic alliances with other libraries to provide reciprocal access to less frequently requested materials.' Because 'it is increasingly likely that users will wish to access British Library services via electronic networks' the Information Technology strategy will be geared to introducing an appropriate system which will integrate request processing, monitoring and management systems to receive and respond to requests in electronic format and to deliver retention items electronically.

It is recognized that a Financial strategy to allow the planned extension of DSC's services will have to be priced 'at levels which their markets will bear, consistent with achieving the required overall growth in demand', and so DSC 'will be actively seeking joint venture investment in information technology and marketing, particularly in overseas markets.' And 'the reorganisation of revenue-earning activities as business units, with clear lines of responsibility and accountability, should lead to much tighter control over the way finances are managed.' Besides ensuring that training and staff development are given continuous emphasis, the key Human Resources strategy is to encourage staff to play an active role in DSC's expanding operations. 'Additional resources must be injected into the priority areas of new technology, marketing and business development. The intention is to create more discrete business units within which managers will have more freedom to manage human resources, and explore the feasibility of alternative working patterns.'

DSC'S GENERAL PUBLICATIONS

Two of DSC's publications have been transferred to the private sector. Following a strategic review it was decided that *Current Research In Britain* (*CRIB*), published by DSC since 1981, 'would benefit more in an organisation which specialised in the production of research directories'. Consequently a partnership with Longman was signed during the International Online Meeting at Olympia in December 1991. Boston Spa's Director General stated at the time:

> This partnership between Longman and the British Library will bring together our expertise for the benefit of scientists and technologists along with those wanting to work with them at the frontiers of research. The agreement is part of a wider cooperation by the British Library with the private sector in order to advance knowledge in the most efficient and cost-effective way for all ('Longman Group Takes Over CRIB', *Document Supply News*, **33**, March 1992:2).

Compiled annually from information supplied from some 4,000 academic departments in over 400 institutions, *CRIB* is published in a set of six volumes: *Physical Sciences* (2v.), *Biological Sciences* (2v.), *Social Sciences and Humanities* (biennially). A CD-ROM version is available. Entries for each research project give the name(s) of researcher(s), a brief description of the topic, start and estimated end dates, sponsoring bodies (if any), proposed form of publication, and DSC stock number. *CRIB* is indexed by researcher's name, study area, and keyword.

Principally, it appears, to intensify and improve its market potential, the British Library sold its quarterly journal *Interlending & Document Supply* to MCB University Press early in 1993. The Library will continue its association with the journal by providing its editor and by representation on the editorial board. International in scope, *Interlending & Document Supply* contains current information on networking; the supply of documents between organizations in developed and developing countries; developments in new technology; acquisition, storage and photoduplication of stock; and an IFLA office for International Lending input in the form of features, articles, and bibliographies.

Document Supply News (December 1987–), distributed five times a year, covers new developments, new services, links with other organizations, staff changes, and other items likely to be of interest. A 'Spotlight' feature on a selected DSC activity, service, resource, or process, generally verging on the 'folksy', nevertheless contains hard information casting light on DSC's administrative and organizational hierarchy. Some recent examples include Customer Services (March 1991); Premium Services (June 1991); Despatch Services (September 1991); preservation (March 1992); Country Managers (June 1992); Theses (March 1993); Management Information (June 1993), and Operations (Literature Stores) December 1993. An annual *Facts & Figures* A4 information leaflet presents statistical data on requests and request methods, stock, catalogues, staff in post, information services, building and equipment, and publications.

Two publication catalogues are produced. *Document Supply Centre Publications* (horizontal A4, 8pp.), a descriptive survey of DSC's extensive programme of serials, monographs, videos, medical titles, and translated journals, with A–Z lists of titles, ISSN/ISBN, price, and availability of sample copies. *CD-ROM Catalogue* (A4, 14pp.) consists mainly of an examination of each title's search; browse; record display; save, print, edit; order facilities, and so on, and details of 30-day trial periods for each title, and an order form.

Three attractive illustrated A4 publicity brochures broadcast DSC's services to the library and information world. *The British Library Document Supply Centre. Invaluable Information Service. Important and Indispensable to the Nation* (1988, 12pp.) muses on the importance of information, outlines the range of DSC's services, proclaims that it handles a new request for information every two seconds, reminds its potential users that DSC is pre-eminent as the fastest supplier of documents and is the pace-setter in developing protocols for interlibrary lending transmission, and includes encomia from satisfied customers. *The British*

Library Document Supply Centre. A leading source of scientific, technical and medical information (n.d., 12pp.) advises how DSC can supply specific required pieces of information and how it works, and modestly assures potential customers that its resources in all fields of enquiry are of almost limitless proportions, its standards of excellence unparalleled, and its services unique. *The British Library Document Supply Centre. UK Services. The Greatest Source Of Knowledge In The World* (n.d., 8pp.) is more restrained and more factual in providing general and specific details of all its public services and in giving concise instructions on how to register as a customer.

11

NATIONAL BIBLIOGRAPHIC SERVICE

Emerging from a reorganization of the former Bibliographic Services Division, the National Bibliographic Service (NBS) has been located at Boston Spa since January 1991 although it still retains a London office. Both at national and international level its role is 'to promote, market and support the cataloguing activities of the Library to the external library and information community'. By creating bibliographic records for all books, new periodical titles, and other materials published in the UK and acquired by the British Library – either through legal deposit or by other means – it supports other libraries' book selection, acquisition, and cataloguing programmes, and assists their reference and information retrieval services.

Such is the range and rate of change of NBS's services and publications that an up-to-date comprehensive outline of its activities is not too easy to find. 'What Is The NBS?', *Select*, 1, June/July 1990:2–3, provides its administrative structure of two groups divided into six sections: Marketing & Support (Publications & Marketing, Information Services, Record Supply, and Product Development) and Planning & Standards (Management Services and Bibliographic Standards) with some indication of their principal functions. James Elliot's 'The National Bibliographic Service', *Friends Of The British Library Newsletter*, 12, April 1993:5–6, 8–9, is especially useful for its concise account of NBS's latest advances in information retrieval. Current developments are announced and discussed in *Select. National Bibliographical Service Newsletter*, issued (usually) thrice yearly, which replaced *Bibliographic Services Newsletter* in 1990, and which regularly prints profiles of NBS's units and sections. In general these are heavy on chit-chat about named members of staff, and who does what, and light on hard information on the various sections' functions and services. However, for the record, these profiles include The Administration Unit (no. 2); BLAISE Information Services (no. 3); The Product Development Section (no. 4);

The Record Supply Section (no. 5); The Marketing Planning Section (no. 6); Planning And Standards (no. 8); Customer Services (no. 9); Publications (no. 10); and The London Unit (no. 11).

Following its relocation to Boston Spa, NBS Marketing developed a market plan to improve customer services and to target more effectively its product development and marketing effort. An initial series of customer surveys was undertaken; a new customer database to provide accurate and up-to-date information on its customers was brought into operation; and a programme of regional contact days was drawn up to offer users an opportunity to meet NBS staff and to become acquainted with the latest developments in software. Full details of all these initiatives are printed in Robert Smith's 'The NBS Marketing Plan', Jean Murdoch's 'The NBS Customer Database', and Jonathan Purday's 'Keeping In Contact', *Select*, **6**, Spring/Summer 1992:1–3.

CATALOGUING-IN-PUBLICATION

CIP (Cataloguing-In-Publication) is an advance information service about forthcoming UK books which, in the view of many librarians, has lost its way. The idea was that publishers would send details of their new books three months in advance of publication to the NBS, who would incorporate them when preparing new records for the BNBMARC files. A copy of the record would be returned to the publisher for printing on the book's title page verso (the catalogue entry in the publication). Publishers were offered an opportunity to provide advance notice of their new books whilst librarians could place early orders and also were able to embark on their own internal cataloguing process when the book was received and not wait for a sometimes delayed full *BNB* entry. In theory the operation was timed so that CIP entries appeared in *BNB* two months in advance of publication.

Latterly, however, the practice has become established for publishers instead of printing the full CIP information received from NBS (now only supplied on request) simply to state that a full CIP entry is available from the British Library. The frustration of some librarians at this watered-down CIP programme was vividly expressed by a Mr Stallion, who remarked in a letter, 'Cataloguing-in-publication', *Library Association Record*, **93** (8), August 1991:515, that the British Library appeared to have forgotten the original purpose of both CIP and a national bibliography. Stallion's disillusionment was so complete that he had almost given up using *BNB* for book selection purposes. His calendar of CIP inefficiencies and unsuitabilities was severe and uncompromising:

CIP entries for books with publication dates months ahead, at times well into the next financial year, which messes up budgeting; CIP entries with no prices or with prices that are well below the actual price when the book eventually appears; CIP entries for books that never get published; post-publication entries which still lack prices; post-publication entries which are so old they are probably post-pulping; and sloppy typing and editing, resulting in wrong class-numbers, mis-spelt or missing names and titles, duplicate entries etc.

In summary:

we now have a Cataloguing-in-publication scheme where the cataloguing is not in the publication at all and a national bibliographic record which consists largely of entries for books which do not yet exist (and may never do so) and for others which did exist but were published so long ago that their inclusion is of historic interest only.

An immediate rejoinder came from Stuart Ede, Director of NBS. He argued in 'NBS answers back: Cataloguing in Publication improving all the time', *ibid.*, **93** (10), October 1991:648, that library automation has substantially reduced the need for a catalogue record in the book, most libraries now prefer to feed such records directly into their in-house automated systems from either tape, CD-ROM disc, or online. As for pricing information criticism, he referred to what the situation would be in January 1992 when CIP records would be obtained from J. Whitaker & Sons Ltd with a consequent improvement in both coverage and currency.

A contract running initially for two years was signed on 27 June 1991 whereby Whitaker's would supply advance information records for the CIP programme.

Records will be supplied in UKMARC format as detailed in the 3rd edition of the UKMARC manual. The content of records will be to at least AACR2 (2nd ed., 1988 revision) level 1, with additional fields . . . Whitaker will provide authority controlled named headings for personal names as used in the Name Authority List wherever possible. All records will contain Whitaker subject headings as subject guides which should prove useful to users on the BLAISE-LINE online information service . . . Records supplied under the new arrangement will be fully compatible with those created by the Library although . . . they will differ somewhat in form and content from those created by the Acquisitions, Processing & Cataloguing Directorate (Arthur

Cunningham, 'British Library Signs Contract With Whitaker', *Select*, **4**, Summer 1991:1–2).

Detailed information on the structure and content of the Whitaker CIP records, including record standards, the eligibility of records, and a field-by-field guide, is provided in Cynthia McKinley's 'Whitaker CIP records hit the streets', *Select*, **5**, Winter 1991:1–2:

> Significant changes to records, particularly to the price and date of publication, will be forwarded to the Library right up to the actual month of publication. This information will be used to amend and update the online file . . . these records will be upgraded by the British Library Acquisitions, Processing & Cataloguing Department once the published item has been received by the Legal Deposit Office.

More precise technical information is supplied in 'CIP Records on the BNBCMARC file', *BLAISE-LINE Newsletter*, **3**, 1992, May/June:2.

Despite all NBS's efforts and good intentions, criticism continued to flow in from irate users and publishers. In an attempt to stem the flow, and to dispel 'the most common misconceptions about CIP, cataloguing and the BNB', Neil Wilson's 'CIP Confusion In Publishing', *Select*, **5**, Winter 1991:7–9, set down (with comment) some of the 'mistakes' brought to NBS's attention in recent months. But to expect publishers to be acquainted with even the rudiments of the principles of cataloguing as laid down in AACR2, or even more to care very much, was nothing if not naïve. (Significantly, Book Industry Communication's Bibliographic Databases Working Party is preparing a manual for use by publishers when creating bibliographic data.) Surprise was expressed that, in view of the free publicity given to their forthcoming publications, publishers should sometimes expect the British Library to mark its gratitude in financial terms for their efforts and co-operation. 'Obviously it is rather worrying that any publisher may think this but it is nearly always the case that such publishers change their opinion once the true situation has been explained to them.' Observers more distant from events might suppose an adequate explanation of the true situation could profitably have been offered much earlier. Perhaps Whitaker's brochure *The British Library CIP Cataloguing-In-Action Programme*, distributed early in 1992 to inform publishers of the arrangements between itself and the British Library for the supply of CIP records, was more effective although it failed to address one of the publishers' most popular misconceptions – that a CIP statement in their books was some form of trade mark or copyright device.

Arthur Cunningham's 'Cataloguing-in-Publication: Major review of progress', *Select*, **8**, Autumn/Winter 1992:8–9, reported that NBS was on target

> to supply over 40,000 advance records to its users in 1992 and that over 8,000 amendment records relating to price, publication date and other important data elements have been processed ensuring that information supplied to users is as accurate and reliable as possible. These amendments have included deletions for titles which publishers have cancelled or postponed indefinitely allowing us to make sure that users do not have records for phantom titles on their files.

Stallion's strictures may have lost some of their force but his letter was perhaps not written and despatched in vain. A questionnaire-based survey conducted jointly by the British Library and J. Whitaker in the Spring of 1993 attempted to assess the current and future needs of CIP users. At the time of writing it was not known whether its findings would be made public.

Concurrent with the commencement of Whitaker CIP records, Cunningham's 'CIP – a gateway for publishers', *Bookseller*, 24 January 1992:192–3, explained why the British Library had looked to the private sector for the future provision of its advance record creation. Economies had been forced on the Library because of persistent underfunding and its priority in this area was now focused on creating a single core bibliographic record capable of use online throughout the Library. Consequently record creation for the CIP programme had no place in its long-term planning. 'It seemed logical for a company with the relevant expertise and competence to undertake this kind of work but on a vastly expanded scale.' Moreover, 'because of its links with the ISBN Agency, it is expected that Whitaker will be able to ensure greater coverage of new titles than was ever possible before, to the benefit of librarians, the book trade and, of course, to publishers'. Quite so, but what is needed now is a convincing explanation of why a Cataloguing-in-Publication programme does not result in catalogue entries being printed in books. The scheme no doubt has bibliographic and commercial merits of a sort but it is now obviously miscalled.

Book Industry Communications (BIC) was established and funded by the British Library and the Booksellers, Library, and Publishers Associations in March 1991 'to facilitate the provision and communication throughout the book industry, and to be responsible for the development and promotion of standards for the format and transmission of bibliographic information, commercial messages and other information designed to increase efficiency and effectiveness in trading and supply within the industry'. Its main task is to get to grips with the duplication of effort which is wasting time and money to the tune of 25% of the cost of handling business transactions, mainly because 70% of data about books is keyed into a computer not once but twice or more. Not only does this up administrative costs, it also introduces errors leading to delays and lost sales to the book industry and misleading information to the library community. Electronic Data Interchange (EDI), the paperless transmission of data between computer systems, is seen as the remedy to these ills but before this is possible the book industry has to develop new standards for use in electronic communications. Progress in this and other areas is reported in 'BIC – the story so far', *Bookseller*, **4552**, 19 March 1993:44, 46.

BNBMARC

The bedrock of NBS and the most important database on BLAISE-LINE is BNBMARC, which consists of catalogue records in the UKMARC format for books and serials published in the UK, made available in print, on magnetic tape for downloading onto libraries' own automated systems, online, and on CD-ROM. These extremely detailed records contain bibliographic information for books and serials deposited under the requirements of the 1911 Copyright Act, indexed by subject and other cataloguing data, making it an essential source for information on all British publications. Brief details of forthcoming books are also incorporated, based on information supplied by publishers participating in the Cataloguing-In-Publication programme. Basic information on the origin, subject coverage, languages, the period covered, cataloguing practice at various stages in BNB's and BNBMARC's 40 years' history, on related BLAISE-LINE files, its size (over one million records dating from 1950 with up to 5,000 added every month), and on how to access BNBMARC is contained in *BNBMARC Online. The Key to British Publishing* (NBS, 1989), together with hints for searching, print formats and sample records, search terms, and notes on BNBMARC fields. A pictorial step-by-step guide to the BNBMARC process, from the acquisition of books and serials through legal deposit to the printed *BNB* page is set out in *Fifteenth Annual Report 1987–88*, p.31.

Concern that BNBMARC records were not achieving a high hit-rate of availability *when required* in user libraries' purchasing, accessioning, and cataloguing processes, was reinforced when the Centre for Bibliographic Management (CBM) at Bath University began to monitor and quantify the success rate in 1980. A figure of 63% based on sampling confirmed librarians' worst fears; by 1987 it had improved only slightly to 65%. By no stretch of British Library's imagination could this be regarded as satisfactory and it was clear that Bibliographic Services faced a dilemma. With a likely prospect of an ever-increasing output of titles in a burgeoning publishing industry, and an equally likely reduction in its budget, the already parlous provision of up-to-date bibliographic records seemed set to deteriorate rather than to improve without a drastic change in policy.

British Library's answer was a Cataloguing Action Plan outlined in July 1987 as a four-page Consultative Paper, *Currency With Coverage. The Future Development Of The British National Bibliographic Service.* Essentially the aims now were 'to reduce current unit costs of cataloguing in the Library by 50% in order to handle current intake, to eliminate current backlogs and to anticipate the major increases in UK publisher output forecast for the 1990s' and 'to achieve compatibility of catalogue records created across the British Library in order to aid the Library's own work and to widen the coverage of the British National Bibliographic Service'. A 'minimum level' of cataloguing, based on AACR2 first level of description, supplemented with price and availability information, would be introduced for modern English fiction, children's books, science and technology, religion, and for items of 32 pages or fewer. Further economies would be secured by discontinuing the application of Library of Congress subject data to BNBMARC records. This last measure was an unwelcome blow to libraries whose catalogues were based on Library of Congress Subject Headings and it is significant that when the Standard Cataloguing project between the six copyright libraries got under way to compensate for the perceived shortcomings of the post-1987 BNB entries – both in terms of coverage and quality – the possible reinstatement of Library of Congress Subject Headings to BNBMARC was high on the agenda. A full exposition of 'the downward market vortex' in which the NBS found itself, and of the circumstances surrounding the formulation of the Catalogue Action Plan, is presented in Peter Lewis's 'Cost Savings and Service Strategies in the British National Bibliographic Service', *Alexandria*, **1** (2), August 1989:17–26. From a different perspective, Peter Fox's 'Bibliographic Record Supply: A Failure Of National Policy', *British Journal of Academic Librarianship*, **5** (1), 1990:31–41, is especially valuable for its appraisal of the costs involved in higher and lower quality records.

Jointly funded by R&D Department and by the Information Systems Committee of the Universities Funding Council, the CBM merged with the UK Office for Library Networking to form UKOLN, the Office for Library and Information Networking, in November 1992. Reports of its BNBMARC currency surveys have appeared annually in *Library Association Record* whilst Ann Chapman's 'Why MARC surveys are still a hot bibliographic currency', *Library Association Record*, **94** (4), April 1992:249, 253–4, ranges over its first ten years' operations and explains that the survey has two main objectives: to obtain an unbiased estimate of the proportion of titles with UK imprints currently being acquired by UK libraries for which a UK/BNBMARC record is available at the time it is most needed; and to establish whether this proportion is increasing or decreasing over the long term. Initially the survey sampled items as they passed from the acquisition department to cataloguing but because of the advent of automated ordering and acquisition systems a second sampling point at the stage when ordering was authorized was adopted in February 1988.

Twelve randomly selected libraries – six academic and six public library systems – are involved in the monthly surveys, each library participating for six months. Only post-1973 titles with a UK imprint within the scope of *BNB* are selected for sampling. Chapman recounts the procedures followed, and charts the improvements in the total hit-rate as the effects of the Cataloguing Action Plan take their course. Four factors that would influence the hit-rate in the future are singled out: NBS's relocation to Boston Spa; the Copyright Libraries Shared Cataloguing Project; the CIP programme and the agreement with Whitakers; and the proportion of material not deposited at the British Library (42,000 items had to be claimed by NBS in 1991/2). Whatever the reason, *British Library News* was able to trumpet 'Its A Record! Headline BNBMARC Hit-Rate Reaches 80%' (167, March 1992). The improvement was credited to the hard work of NBS staff, the streamlining of procedures, and the productivity improvements brought about by British Library's Direct Data Entry System.

Alan Reeves' 'Licence To Use British Library MARC Records', *Select*, **2**, Winter 1990:4, details the changes in the arrangements for their use and redistribution. From January 1991 onwards user licences have been issued free of charge to UK libraries who use British Library records purely for their own internal processes. The licences cover all MARC records obtained from British Library either on exchange tape, downloaded online, or obtained from *BNB* on CD-ROM. British Library records obtained from other suppliers are also covered but libraries engaged in selling or exchanging large numbers of records originating from the British Library have to obtain a Redistributor Licence which is similar in nature to arrangements in force for overseas users. Current details on who needs a licence, who doesn't, what the licence permits, and licence costs, are set down in an NBS factsheet, *Licence To Use British Library MARC Records.*

From January 1991 records created for the BNBMARC and H&SS files contain subject data from COMPASS (Computer Aided Subject System), a simplified restructuring of PRECIS which was developed in the 1970s for the production of the printed index to *BNB*. Evolved in response to the increasing number of libraries who use British Library subject data in computerized catalogues or OPACs, and to the Library's adoption of Direct Data Entry in the AP&C Department, the new system was developed very much in accordance with the Cataloguing Action Plan's aim to reduce the unit cost of cataloguing. Details of its subject authority file, which consists of terms and strings, and the new search qualifiers in the BNBMARC and H&SS files on BLAISE-LINE, are outlined in 'COMPASS – The New Subject System For The BNB And HSS Files', *BLAISE-LINE Newsletter*, **6**, 1990 November–December:3, whilst COMPASS search qualifiers are in the following issue (**1**, January–February 1991:3). Why British Library changed to COMPASS; its relationship to PRECIS; how COMPASS headings are constructed; how it treats geographical areas, historical periods, and biographies; the standards governing the use of particular terms and phrases used in COMPASS headings; and its reference structure are discussed in Neil Wilson's 'COMPASS', *Select*, **4**, Summer 1971:6–7.

In conjunction with North West Data Services (NWDS), NBS has recently introduced a retrospective conversion service, COMPCON (Complete Conversion Service). Combining British Library's MARC record database with NWDS's accurate keyboarding expertise has produced a process for a complete conversion of a manual catalogue ready to load into an automated library system. Details of procedures involving the minimum of disruption, the data quality, hit rates, and prices, are included on an NBS information sheet, *COMPCON. The Complete Conversion Service.*

Sponsored by NBS and MARC Users Group (later renamed Users of Book Industry Standards), a survey of UKMARC use was conducted by Russell Sweeney in 1991 under the aegis of CBM. The intention was that the survey's results would assist the British Library in determining how the format should be developed to make it more responsive to users' needs. Plans for formal and continuing arrangements for user consultation were outlined in Ross Bourne's 'The UKMARC Format: Proposals for future management & maintenance', *Select*, 5, Winter 1991:3–4. A preliminary consultative meeting, attended by representatives of professional and other bodies, acknowledged British Library's historical responsibilities for the format and intellectual content of UKMARC and agreed that this should continue, but decided that a designated UKMARC Office should be established to act as the focus for development, to encourage user participation, to consult appropriate centres of excellence, and to take note of users' needs. Amendment proposals would in future be accepted from all sources and the Library would consult other interested organizations before publishing them in a standard format. A 'MARC Format News' feature, to include notifications of proposed changes or amendments, would appear regularly in *Select*.

The way forward for UKMARC is considered at length in Ross Bourne's 'UKMARC – A Format for the Twenty-first Century?', *New Library World*, **93** (1101), 1992:4–8, which not only anticipates how UKMARC is likely to extend coverage to new types of material but also asks whether it is still relevant as a bibliographic format, what kind of format might be more appropriate, and how its replacement (if replaced it is) should be planned at a time when so many institutions have heavily invested in UKMARC. Bourne perceives the main arguments against UKMARC, as presently constituted, to be its tape-based nature when bibliographic exchange is increasingly either online or by CD-ROM, with records being downloaded electronically into local files. Not only does it perpetuate detailed content material when this is under constant scrutiny on value and cost grounds, it is also biased towards sequential arrangement – either alphabetically or numerically – when so many catalogues are available on random access in OPACs. This apparently crushing indictment is alleviated only by the formidable counter-argument that before tampering or jettisoning UKMARC in favour of an alternative medium for transmission, it would be as well to acknowledge that new media might advance at such a rapid rate that whatever was chosen to replace it could well be outdated before it was installed. In other words, if it's not broken, don't mend it.

Fortunately, the transformation of the MARC Users Group into Users of Book Industry Standards, the merger of the CBM with the UKOLN, and the formation of BIC have in effect created what Bourne regards as very much a sea change: British Library is no longer going it alone in prescribing the content and standards of bibliographic services but is instead manifestly working in co-operation with the whole information world in determining a suitable bibliographical format in harmony with its processing technology.

Designed for use by cataloguers involved in record creation and for computer staff working with bibliographic or information systems, the *UKMARC Manual* (3rd ed., 1990) includes five sections on MARC principles, magnetic exchange tape specification, the format of exchange records, content designators, and a guide to general fields. A long series of appendices deal with country of publication, language, geographical area, and physical description codes; a key to AACR2 rules; changes to content designators from the second edition; punctuation; American records reformatted to UKMARC; examples of exchange records; valid fields, indicators, subfields, levels, repeats; exchange tape character set; a glossary; cartographic materials codes; and recommended standards exchanged in the UK national network. Thumb-indexed for easy reference, the *Manual* is published in a spring binder to allow page substitutions (issued with *Select*) for amendments, changes, and additions.

Readers who share the author's confusion as to the precise difference between UKMARC and BNBMARC (a confusion he sought to dispel by consulting in vain three information workers he regarded as experts in the field) should get their hands on *Setting the Record Straight. Understanding the MARC format.* This 16-page A5 booklet issued *gratis* by the NBS in 1993 not only includes an invaluable glossary but sections headed 'What is MARC?'; 'The UKMARC format'; 'Anatomy of a BNBMARC record'; 'Putting UKMARC to work'; 'UKMARC and the book industry'; and, for good measure, 'Into the future with UNI-MARC'.

BLAISE-LINE

Twenty databases, many of them updated on a weekly or monthly basis, are now available on BLAISE-LINE, the online bibliographic service launched in 1977, which offers libraries, information workers, and the book trade two major facilities: an online information retrieval service whereby users can interrogate its databases for specific titles to produce booklists, bibliographies, or current awareness material covering all subject areas; and the ability to identify and retrieve high quality bibliographic records. British Library categorizes its BLAISE-LINE databases into five groups: Flagship Databases (BNBMARC, LCMARC, and Whitaker); British Library Catalogues (BLC, BLISS, CONF, DSCM,

H&SS, Maps, Music, and SRIS); Specialist Databases (HMSO, NSDC, SIGLE, UOL); Antiquarian Material (ESTC, ISTC, RPM); and Audio-Visual Material (AVMARC, HELPIS).

Updated monthly, *Whitaker* is the book trade's database containing records of UK books and English-language books published overseas but available from a UK distributor. It includes current information on prices and availability and also has details of forthcoming titles. Also updated monthly, *Library of Congress* (LCMARC) contains bibliographic records for all books accessioned by the US Library of Congress since 1968, including not only US publications but also many British books, foreign language material, and fiction. Its records are converted into UKMARC format, catalogued to AACR2, with Dewey and Library of Congress subject information.

Exactly why *British Library Catalogue* (BLC) database is not ranked among the Flagship Databases is a mystery fathomed only by British Library. Containing some 3.8 million records, it is created from the 360 volumes of the former British Museum Library Department of Printed Books' catalogue, 'a unique resource offering access to books published all over the world in a variety of languages and scripts' which 'includes material from the very beginning of printing to 1975'. It is featured in 'The British Library Catalogue', *BLAISE-LINE Newsletter*, 1, 1993, January–February:5.

BLISS includes acquisitions of the British Library Information Sciences Service from 1976 and a substantial proportion of older material. *Conference Proceedings* (CONF) is devoted to records of the published proceedings of conferences, symposia, seminars, workshops, and the like added to stock at the DSC since 1964, whilst *Document Supply Centre Monographs* (DSCM) lists DSC's books in Western European languages published since 1980. *Humanities & Social Sciences* (H&SS), updated weekly, is the current catalogue of the H&SS collections of books added since 1976 together with OIOC books accessioned since 1980. *Maps* includes bibliographic records for all terrestrial and celestial maps, atlases, charts, plans, globes, and other cartographic material acquired by the British Library since 1974 either in the Map Library or elsewhere. Music contains records of UK popular and classical printed sheet music published since 1981 and of overseas publications acquired by the Music Library. Subject searching is possible either via PRECIS or by Dewey or Coates classification.

Science Reference & Information Science (SRIS) database contains British and foreign books, citation records for conferences, and a complete listing of SRIS' periodical holdings. *Her Majesty's Stationery Office* (HMSO) database of government and official publications listed in its printed daily list since 1976 covers parliamentary items such as Acts, Bills, White Papers, non-parliamentary items published on behalf of government departments, and titles issued by various British and international organizations for which HMSO acts as a sales agent.

National Serials Data Centre (NSDC) database contains bibliographic records of all types and levels of serials first published in the UK since 1974 to which NSDC has assigned an ISSN. The NSDC is housed at the British Library's Boston Spa site. Established in 1980, and produced by the European Association for Grey Literature, *System For Information On Grey Literature In Europe* (SIGLE) database provides access to material not normally obtainable through the usual book trade outlets and therefore difficult to identify. *University of London* (UOL) database records the acquisitions of 11 University of London colleges from 1978 to October 1988 and is particularly useful for government publications and foreign language material.

Eighteenth Century Short Title Catalogue (ESTC) file holds bibliographic records for all types of printed material – books, lists, advertisements, songs and so on – printed worldwide during the eighteenth century. Supplemented by records created for the holdings of the British Library and other UK and Commonwealth libraries, it indicates library locations of each item. Updated as a co-operative project between the six copyright libraries, *Register of Preservation Microforms* (RPM) database holds records created by the NPO when a book or serial is in danger of deterioration. Its records provide a brief description of the original, the location of other copies, and locations for the microform. *AVMARC* contains bibliographic records for non-book materials issued 1960–88, updated in 1989 to include records from the former ILEA library, whilst *Higher Education Learning Programmes Information Service* (HELPIS) includes records for audiovisual materials designed for use in higher education institutions.

Notes on all these databases, along with details of access to BLAISE-LINE, subscription costs, and charges for training schedules appear in a 12-page glossy A4 brochure, *National Bibliographic Service BLAISE-LINE*, which is distributed annually. This replaces *BLAISE-LINE Advancing Knowledge* (1990?), an A4 folder protecting loose information sheets which included users' comments on services offered by individual databases selected from previously employed advertising material. 'Serials On BLAISE-LINE', *BLAISE-LINE Newsletter*, **2**,

1992, March–April:5, is a reminder that besides bibliographic records of monographs, official reports, and publications, BLAISE-LINE also holds over 200,000 records for periodicals in its databases.

A direct link between British Library and the University of London Computing Centre, one of the switching centres for JANET, allows JANET users access to BLAISE-LINE without incurring British Telecom PSS or DIALPLUS connect charges. Connection procedures are spelled out in an NBS Factsheet, *Accessing BLAISE-LINE via JANET*. BLAISE-LINE subscribers can take advantage of ORDER, an express service which enables users to check bibliographic references to loan copies of books, photocopies of journal articles, and microforms and order them from DSC, all in one operation. The BLAISE-LINE Search Service offers three types of computer search on a number of bibliographic databases: a quick search using up to ten search terms to satisfy an enquiry and printing out up to 25 references: a standard search using all the terms necessary to ensure full coverage; and current awareness searches in particular areas. The amount of information supplied in each reference can be varied to users' individual needs. How to access BLAISE-LINE, and details of the equipment and software required, are outlined in NBS's factsheet, *Connecting to BLAISE-LINE*. A similar factsheet, *International Links to BLAISE-LINE*, is produced for overseas users. New UK subscribers are offered a free password to DIALPLUS, British Telecom's Global Network Service. Connection instructions and a list of Access Points are included in another factsheet, *DIALPLUS Access to BLAISE-LINE*.

BLAISE-LINE was a main participant in a Satellite Online Searching Training Interactive Conferencing Experiment (SOLSTICE), a British Library R&D Department-funded project to investigate and assess the suitability of satellite transmission for training in online searching. A series of programmes on BLAISE use was broadcast in four weekly transmissions to a number of library sites in 1991. 'SOLSTICE', *BLAISE-LINE Newsletter*, **4**, July–August:3–4, and 'The SOLSTICE Experiment', *ibid.*, **6**, November–December:5, print full details.

The constantly updated *BLAISE-LINE User Manual*, issued in two substantial ring-binders to allow for the ready insertion of updating fascicules, includes early sections on the retrieval facilities available, followed by sections on each of BLAISE-LINE's databases. *BLAISE-LINE Mini Manual* (5th ed., 1990) provides a summary of the BLAISE-LINE system and is intended as a reference guide for searchers with a working knowledge of the system who need to remind themselves of a particular procedure or of the details of particular files. Part 1 consists of a series of units each demonstrating a single aspect of the BLAISE-LINE system; part 2 describes all the databases currently available through the system. *BLAISE-LINE Quick Reference Guide* is a folded card (9.5cm x 15cm) for use at the terminal. It has brief notes on logging on and logging off, searching, combining search terms, stringsearching, changing files, and printing records offline and online.

A separate bi-monthly *BLAISE-LINE Newsletter* began publication in 1990. It carries articles on system facilities, features on specific files, price revisions, details of training courses and BLAISE-LINE workshops, personnel changes, user profiles, the BLAISE-LINE search services, and any other relevant item judged to be of wide interest. Issued free to BLAISE-LINE subscribers as a communications document, it is intended to be kept near the machine used for online searching. The editors see no future for it as a bound periodical.

BLAISE RECORDS

Based on the BLAISE databases, backed up if necessary by the giant North American OCLC international library information network, BLAISE RECORDS, introduced in 1987, is British Library's online service supplying machine-readable records for use in automated cataloguing, acquisitions, circulation, and other stock control systems. In all over 30 million bibliographic records are available. Records are either selected online for direct downloading or despatch to magnetic tape. The most efficient method of searching is by ISBN, ISSN, *BNB* or Library of Congress card number but, should these features be lacking, an acronym search key facility made up from parts of the author's name, title, or author and title, according to a specific formula, has been devised.

The easy-to-use BLAISE RECORDER software package, specially designed to meet the needs of online BLAISE RECORDS users, includes a timesaving autologon feature which allows the storage of response sequences required to connect to the online service, thus minimizing online connect time. An Offline Record Selection Service is a cost-effective way of retrospectively converting library catalogues by submitting records on a magnetic tape containing the control numbers for which records are required. This tape is run against BNBMARC or LCMARC (Library of Congress MARC) files to produce an output tape of matched records which is supplied along with a list of 'misses'. OCLC's development of a packet-switched telecommunications network means that BLAISE RECORDS users now have access to PRISM, an improved and more versatile cataloguing service. What this implies for users in terms of access routes, equipment, and search procedures is fully explained in Robert Hill's 'The Path to PRISM', *Select*, **5**, Winter 1991:11, and *BLAISE RECORDS News*, **6**, Spring 1992:5.

National Bibliographic Services BLAISE RECORDS, an annual A4 glossy brochure, carries details of its services, databases, necessary equipment, subscriptions, and licensing arrangements. *BLAISE RECORDS Newsletter* (1989, two issues a year) provides news on the latest developments, training and demonstration facilities, changes in licensing arrangements, and price changes.

To meet the needs of smaller libraries seeking to automate their systems, but deterred by the prospective cost of converting card catalogues into computer records, NBS in conjunction with Softlink Europe, producers of Alice, the Australian developed library automation package, launched *Rapid Retrospective* in 1993. This new product is reputed to deliver high quality catalogue records automatically from the *BNB* database, to convert catalogues in days rather than years, to dramatically reduce conversion costs, and to remove the need for extra staff or outside agency help.

BRITISH NATIONAL BIBLIOGRAPHY

Now produced from NBS's BNBMARC files, the printed *British National Bibliography* (*BNB*) consists of a classified subject listing with author/title indexes of almost all new UK publications, including new serial titles received at the British Library's Legal Deposit Office under the terms of the 1911 Copyright Act. A long list of exceptions is included in Neil Wilson's 'The exclusion zone. British National Bibliography: Exclusions Policies 1993', *Select*, **9**, Spring 1993:4–5. General printed material not entered in *BNB* includes books and serials without a British or Republic of Ireland imprint; straight reprints where there is no change in text, imprint and binding from the previous edition; serial continuations; works published in Great Britain but not made available to the home market; and non-humanities research report series (these are picked up by the BLAISE-LINE, SRIS and SIGLE databases). Some official publications which may be accessed through the catalogues of the British Library's OP&SS are also excluded, as are certain classes of local material (local government administrative publications, voters' lists, telephone directories, official town guides, and non-research-level local publications). Printed music is listed in the *British Catalogue of Music* (*BCM*); sheet maps are catalogued by the Map Library and are included in BLAISE-LINE's maps file. Non-book materials, toy books, toys and games, books of camera-ready illustrations, large-print books, diaries and calendars, knitting patterns, postcards, and posters are not entered. Promotional material such as trade literature, publicity material, and prospectuses or syllabuses for educational courses are not considered eligible, nor is purely ephemeral material such as timetables, examination papers (with certain exceptions), religious or political tracts, blank stationery, and so on. Patents are catalogued by SRIS's Patents Information Service and are therefore omitted. Wilson emphasizes that exclusion from *BNB* does not exempt publishers from their legal obligations.

Catalogued and indexed by professional librarians, *BNB* is arranged according to the 20th edition of the *Dewey Decimal Classification* (*DDC*) with each catalogue entry conforming to AACR2. The last weekly issue of each month contains a subject index and a cumulated author/title index for the month. Four-monthly and annual cumulations are published. *BNB* is by far the most comprehensive single listing of UK current titles and is an indispensable bibliographic tool for stock selection, reference work, and cataloguing. It also contains details of forthcoming books under the CIP programme which, for a time, appeared in a separate classified sequence. This move naturally attracted criticism: R. J. Duckett's letter, 'Life made harder', *Library Association Record*, **93** (5), May 1992:286, asked whether there was user demand for this change and complained that two sequences would have to be checked every week rather than one.

BNB's 2,000th weekly issue was published on 17 August 1988, an occasion marked by 'BNB 2000', *Bibliographic Services Newsletter*, **46**, June 1988:4–5. Andy Stephens and Atula Gor's 'BNB 2000: The Development of the British National Bibliographic Service', *British Book News*, November 1988:824–5, is an expanded version which gives more attention to the introduction of a new generation of bibliographic service based on CD-ROM technology. A technical review of the production technologies which influenced the development of the NBS is provided in Stephens's 'Technology and the British National Bibliographic Service', *Journal of Librarianship*, **20** (3), July 1988:194–204, which chronicles the development of MARC-based services, the consequent leap forward to a model service pattern in book selection and acquisition, reference searching, and information retrieval; catalogue records for local systems; the outlook for further developments, dependent on the emergence of appropriate new technologies; and the user community's ability and willingness to adapt to new technologies and carrier media. Stephens's 'The Establishment of the British National Bibliography', pp.8–26, *Eating The Menus Essays In Honour Of Peter Lewis*, edited by Ross Bourne (British Library, 1989, 116pp.), gives equal attention to its bibliographic and cataloguing aspects. The contributions of those influential in its birth, and of those who pioneered its compilation and production, are also prominently featured.

Circulated with the September 1990 monthly index issue was a blue A4 leaflet, *A New Look For The British National Bibliography*, announcing that the British Library was to introduce a number of processing changes altering *BNB*'s format in 1991. Perhaps the most significant change for non-cataloguers was that records selected for *BNB* would gain in currency because AP&C staff would be using Direct Data Entry on to the online system without sending data forms to a keyboarding bureau first. Subscribers were also alerted to the replacement of PRECIS by COMPASS and the technical effects this would have on the subject index, and also to the Copyright Libraries Shared Cataloguing Project, by which all six copyright libraries would co-operate in cataloguing the UK publishing output but 'these records will not appear in BNB until the British Library has received its own legal deposit copy and has enhanced the records. The effect of the programme will be to increase the number of authoritative records thereby improving currency and reducing backlogs.' Just how or why this would occur was not vouchsafed. However, shared cataloguing is cited as one of the factors influencing a sharp rise in records included in the BNBMARC Current File for the 1992 production year (the others were more effective claiming procedures for material not submitted to the Legal Deposit Office and the general increase in the number of books published in the UK), which necessitated a change in the format of *BNB* numbers. In taking this drastic step the British Library adopted three criteria: any change should take account of the approaching new century, *BNB* numbers should be of consistent length throughout the BNBMARC database, and the new format should require customers to undertake the least possible amount of costly reprogramming. What emerged is detailed in 'Change in format of BNB numbers', *BLAISE RECORDS News*, 5, Summer 1991:3. Records containing the new format number began to appear on BNBMARC files in November 1991.

Annual volumes of *BNB* from 1981 onwards, and two cumulations, are available on microfiche: *BNB Author/Title Cumulation 1950–1984*, which combines 35 annual listings into a single sequence on 430 fiche; and *British National Bibliography 1981–1992*, comprising full bibliographic records for over a half million titles arranged in classified subject order, supported by an exhaustive author/title index, on 400 fiche in a flip-lid box complete with guide cards.

BNB ON CD-ROM

Although a number of information transfer technologies have been introduced since *BNB* first appeared in 1950, its extension to CD-ROM format is likely to prove the most significant in the long term for a wide range of library applications. Bibliographic checking, the compilation of bibliographies and reading lists, current cataloguing, and retrospective conversion projects are all feasible on *BNB on CD-ROM*, whose sheer speed and flexibility allows powerful online databases to be searched within seconds on desk-top PCs and permits almost any word to be used as a search term. Searches can be made by author, title (including series title), keywords, control numbers, publisher, place of issue, date of publication, name as subject, subject headings, Dewey classification number, author/title acronyms. Records retrieved either by searching or browsing can be displayed in a variety of formats, as a brief citation, in full or customized MARC format, or as a catalogue entry. They can be put on screen, sent to a printer, or written to a PC file, and are compatible with most automated library systems.

Building on pioneering projects carried out in 1985 in conjunction with J. Whitaker & Sons, when CD-ROMs containing bibliographic data were produced and demonstrated at exhibitions and conferences, work started in earnest on CD-ROM products and services with a review of British Library developments in 1987 which confirmed that there were already three significant areas of activity. A Bibliographic Services team had been established to design and produce a range of CD-ROM products for record supply and information retrieval purposes; DSC was investigating the possibilities of a disc containing a number of stock-list files; and H&SS were considering CD-ROM as a suitable medium for specialist scholarly databases. It was clear that 'the British Library's own databases, and particularly the *BNB* file, constitute a core resource for the UK library and information community, and a properly managed publication programme would be likely to provide the necessary critical mass for the wide acceptance of the new medium'. This was not all, for 'as a national library, we are exceptionally well placed to promote the adoption of standards in CD-ROM bibliographic publishing – by ourselves developing a compatible and coordinated product line through all the operating divisions, and also by working with other national libraries to achieve a level of international compatibility' (Tony McSean, 'Developments In Bibliographic CD-ROMS In The British Library', *Library And Information Research News*, **11** (42), Summer 1988:14–17).

Following this internal review Bibliographic Services was given the task of co-ordinating British Library's CD-ROM development so that a common operating environment for all bibliographic CD-ROM products could be focused, to plan the introduction of a major CD-ROM product within 18 months, and to play a crucial role in the selection and adoption of an internationally agreed standard for the distribution of national bibliographic databases on CD-ROM. Under the aegis of the International MARC Advisory Committee – a working group consisting of representatives from the Bibliothèque Nationale, the Deutsche Bibliothek, the Library of Congress, and the National Library of Canada, with British Library as co-ordinator – began to tackle the daunting political, technical, and commercial problems that needed to be resolved before an international agreement could be reached. Working with commendable speed, the group agreed by August 1987 that a CD-ROM compatibility standard for national bibliographies was feasible and that British Library should draft an operational requirement.

Meanwhile a parallel but separate route was marked out by a meeting in Lisbon of the heads of a number of European national libraries who quickly identified CD-ROM publishing as a profitable exercise in co-operative development. A further meeting in London in December 1987 decided that British Library and the Bibliothèque Nationale would jointly fund a pilot CD-ROM disc containing 30,000 records selected from BNBMARC files, representing books on European history published 1950–88, and a comparable file on UNIMARC taken from the French national bibliographic database. It was reported at the time that:

> as well as testing the feasibility of using the same 'front-end' to search different sets of data supplied in two different MARC formats, the CD-ROM will also be a useful evaluation tool for other national agencies considering CD-ROM development. The disc will further enable the British Library and Bibliothèque Nationale to gain valuable experience which can then be brought to bear on their planning for commercial CD-ROM products ('Compact Discs For National Bibliography: Britain And France Join Forces', *Bibliographic Services Newsletter*, **46**, June 1988:1–3, also issued as an offprint).

The project was completed within a five-year period with the production of *The Explorers*, a pilot CD-ROM which combines subsets from the national bibliographies of Denmark, Italy, Portugal and The Netherlands. A complete assessment of the project, including its key objectives, its ten preparatory sub-projects, its European funding, and its results, appears in Robert Smith's 'National Libraries Project on CD-ROM', *Select*, **11**, Winter 1993:7–9.

The introduction of *BNB on CD-ROM* attracted wide attention and comment. In addition to the two articles already cited, other authoritative ventures into print included Tony McSean's 'The British Library's Commitment to CD-ROM', *CD-ROM Librarian*, **2** (6), November–December 1987:8–12; David Grinyer and others' 'The path to the Anglo-French pilot disc: a British Library view of CD-ROM developments to date', *International Cataloguing & Bibliographic Control*, **17** (3), July/September 1988:47–8; Robert Smith's 'British Library Plans For CD-ROM', *Laserdisk Professional*, **2** (2), March 1989:58–62; and Robert Smith and Tony McSean's 'Planning and producing the British National Bibliography on CD-ROM', *Program*, **23** (4), October 1989:395–413. They all cover very much the same ground and cumulatively they fully explain the development of *BNB on CD-ROM* as a viable commercial project.

Heralded as 'the most significant development in the history of the national bibliographic service since the opening of BLAISE', *BNB on CD-ROM* was launched as a quarterly operation in the summer of 1989. Progress since the British/French pilot disc is monitored in 'BNB on CD-ROM. The British Library's first CD-ROM publication is now available', *Bibliographic Services Newsletter*, **49**, June 1989:1–3. The pilot disc was distributed to over 700 libraries worldwide for evaluation and comment prior to commercial production. At the same time an EC consultant also evaluated the whole project, surveying 60 European libraries for their experience with the British/French disc, with further studies at 20 of these libraries in greater detail, including their experience of a Deutsche Bibliothek pilot disc produced earlier in the year. Following this co-operative analysis a consortium of national libraries was established to pursue the joint CD-ROM programme for national bibliographies with the principal aim of furthering the compatibility and exchange of bibliographic records in Europe. The British Library took satisfaction from the fact that the software chosen for the British/French pilot disc was fast becoming a *de facto* standard for these initiatives.

After discussion with Online Computer Systems Inc., of Maryland, whose tender came closest to meeting British Library's operational requirements, it became apparent that *BNB on CD-ROM* would need to be produced as two distinct products: a backfile of two CDs containing *BNB* entries 1950–1976, and 1977–85, each indexed separately; and a current file on a single disc containing entries from 1986 onwards to incorporate all new records entered since the previous issue. In January 1993 this cumulated current file began to appear monthly (at no extra cost), thus attaining a higher level of currency.

NBS is now contemplating a one disc version of *BNB on CD-ROM*. Designed as a reference tool for checking bibliographic details, *BNB Reference* would contain all the catalogue records which appear on the three-disc set but would have fewer indexes and no facility for displaying or downloading MARC records. In view of the heavy expense involved in developing a new disc a three-page A4 questionnaire was circulated in May 1993 to ascertain whether *BNB Reference* would be a viable commercial proposition. Modified software was introduced in 1991 to take into account the changes to the MARC record and the arrival of COM-PASS. A further development enables light pens with a BNB on CD-ROM facility to read the barcodes of books and to translate information into ISBNs which can then be used to call up bibliographic records for immediate downloading into libraries' own automated systems. This is featured in 'New Search Software For BNB on CD-ROM', *BLAISE Records News*, **6**, Spring 1992:1–2, and 'From The CD-ROM Help Desk', *ibid.*, **7**, Autumn/Winter 1992:3. The features and applications of *BNB on CD-ROM* – together with full explanatory notes on use, searching, displaying records, and details of the hardware required – are presented in a twice-folded glossy A4 brochure, *BNB on CD-ROM*. Its potential as a cataloguing tool, and developments in its software, are treated in Christopher Easingwood's 'CD-ROM for record supply: the BNB experience so far', *Library Micromation News*, **31**, March 1991:2–4.

The overall aim of the European National Libraries Project on CD-ROM was to 'improve the interchange of bibliographic records between national bibliographic agencies; and, specifically, to develop shared strategies, applications and formats for bibliographic data on CD-ROM'. Following pilot projects in Paris and Frankfurt and by NBS in England, it was concluded that CD-ROM would achieve these objectives more widely and successfully than MARC exchange tapes. The project was divided into separate sub-projects, each being run by one library with others being involved. British Library took responsibility for the following: Overview of the project, A Menu Interface for the National Libraries' CD-ROM, Linking CD-ROM to Local Library Systems, and

Online Links from CD-ROM; and participated in distribution mechanisms and marketing agreements for CD-ROM products, Multilingual Interface, Definition of a basic European character set, and Conversion between different formats for bibliographic records.

A set of ten factsheets – giving a time-scale (December 1989–November 1992), a definition, background, progress, availability of preliminary and final reports, and the libraries involved, for each project – is enclosed in a laminated wallet, *National Libraries Project on CD-ROM.*

OTHER NBS PUBLICATIONS

Listing autobiographies, biographies, memoirs, letters, diaries, reminiscences, collective biographies, and biographical dictionaries, *Bibliography of Biography* – formerly on microfiche for the period 1970–84, and in printed softbound annual update volumes, compiled from the BNBMARC, H&SS, LCMARC and UOL databases – is now on a single CD-ROM disc with annual cumulations and a *Users Manual.* There are 14 search indexes covering personal authors, personal and corporate names as subjects, titles, keywords, control numbers, languages, publication type, and publishers, together with country of issue and year of publication. It is also possible to browse through a further nine indexes. A glossy A4 brochure on the familiar NBS pattern provides full details of contents, coverage, uses, searching, hardware requirements, networking, and availability.

Derived from British Library's major databases, *Fiction on Fiche* is a detailed listing of all the novels and short story collections published worldwide in English, Gaelic, Welsh, and Irish since 1950 for which the Library holds catalogue records. Over a quarter of a million books are listed A–Z by author on more than 35 microfiche. Authoritative information on pseudonyms is also included. A second edition appeared in September 1993; subsequently publication will be quarterly with each cumulative issue replacing previous issues. *Children's Fiction on Fiche* (1993) is a similar work, listing 90,000 children's fiction titles published quarterly. Details given include publisher, year of publication, pagination, series, notes, and ISBN.

Also on fiche, *Books in English* is the major world bibliography of books published in the English language, containing records for material held in British Library and in the Library of Congress. Each year 100,000 new titles are recorded on fiche issued cumulatively every two months culminating in an annual listing. *Books in English 1981–1992* (1993) contains over 1.25 million records in a single alphabetical sequence on over 500 microfiche stored in a sturdy box. It follows an earlier cumulation, *Books in English 1971–1980*.

Serials In The British Library is a record of all new serial acquisitions of the British Library's London-based reference collections, including titles received under the legal deposit regulations. Some 4,000 titles are catalogued annually and all subject areas are covered. Entries are arranged alphabetically by catalogue heading according to the BLAISE filing rules with a comprehensive subject listing derived from keywords in each title. Published in three quarterly issues, *Serials In The British Library* cumulates into a softbound annual volume which includes entries for the fourth quarter. *Serials In The British Library 1976–1986* lists over 57,000 titles and is published on 57 1.48 microfiche in a ring-binder.

12

ACQUISITIONS PROCESSING AND CATALOGUING AND COMPUTING AND TELECOMMUNICATIONS

To Acquisitions Processing and Cataloguing (AP&C) (which includes the Legal Deposit Office) falls the task of receiving all English books and serials acquired either through legal deposit or by purchase. Before this material is despatched to its appropriate destination in the Library's collections, either in London or at Boston Spa, AP&C creates a catalogue entry for each new title which NBS transforms into a bibliographic record for BNB's hardcopy, online, magnetic tape, or CD-ROM format. Speeding up the record creation process was enormously improved when Direct Data Entry was introduced into AP&C's operations in November 1990. Direct Data Entry enhances the quality of catalogue entries and, by removing the necessity for secondary keyboarding, eliminates its potential for delay and error. Not least among the benefits of automated cataloguing systems is their ability to use records created elsewhere as source data. In turn this makes co-operative cataloguing schemes such as the Copyright Libraries Shared Cataloguing project feasible. 'Full advantage is being taken of the system to monitor the flow of material and records through the bibliographic processing system, and to produce management information at each stage. This is particularly important with the need to deal effectively with an increasing publishing output' ('Benefits Of Automated Cataloguing', p.41, *Eighteenth Annual Report*).

Continuing contact with the other copyright libraries 'to pool resources in claiming and possibly to pool responsibilities for archiving and indexing' was one of the Enright Committee's recommendations. One of the first manifestations of co-operation was a pilot Shared Cataloguing Project, November 1990–March 1992, investigating the feasibility of sharing responsibility for the cataloguing of British and Irish legal deposit printed books. *Shared Cataloguing: Report to the Principals of the Six Copyright Libraries of the Copyright Libraries Shared Cataloguing Project Steering Group* (NBS, 1993), identified the issues: the allocation of responsibility for publishing output, the creation of name authority headings, and the possible reinstatement of Library of Congress Subject Headings to BNBMARC records. A formal agreement to ensure the Project's continuation on a permanent basis was recommended.

In the event the project effectively continued to operate, contributing up to 25% of the records on the BNBMARC files, and a new Memorandum of Agreement to cover a further period of 12 months provided the basis for a permanent Shared Programme to be managed by NBS. An announcement came in the summer of 1993 that the British Library would reintroduce Library of Congress Subject Headings to improve the BNBMARC record by January 1995. Progress on the project can be reviewed in 'Copyright Libraries Shared Cataloguing Programme', *Bibliographic Services Newsletter*, **49**, June 1989:5–6; in *Select* (*passim*); and in Ross Bourne's 'Shared Cataloguing: The Way Forward', *New Library World*, **94** (1107), 1993:25–6, which sums up the lessons to be drawn from the project: 'that while national bibliographic responsibility would appear now to be too great for any one institution, even for the national library, it can be shared, and shared effectively'. No doubt this was sweet music to the British Library's ears.

COMPUTING AND TELECOMMUNICATIONS

Computing and Telecommunications, formerly a function within NBS, develops systems throughout the British Library and for use in the St Pancras building, 'to improve the coherence and effectiveness of Library-wide initiatives'. It encompasses reading room catalogues, BLAISE-LINE retrieval services, cataloguing, personnel, and finance. AP&C and Computers and Telecommunications share the ultra-modern Hookway Building, officially opened in July 1992, when an attractive, four-page colour brochure, *The Hookway Building*, was printed to mark the occasion. Details of the staffing, responsibilities, and activities of the two directorates are included.

BIBLIOGRAPHICAL AND HISTORICAL ENVOI

Thus far this present study has concentrated on current progress towards a once in a millenium Library bristling with OPACs, 'moths-eye' optical discs, access to worldwide databases, digitization, and conceptual frameworks. But, of course, British Library's reputation as a major international research library does not rest entirely on its leadership at the sharp edge of IT or in the electronic capture, storage, and transmission of documents to remote users. The wealth of its holdings, assembled originally from foundation collections, stretching back 400 years, and built up with meticulous care in the nineteenth and twentieth centuries, explains the commanding position the Library enjoys today among the great national libraries of the world and why it stands, in Lord Quinton's words, as the 'emblem of the nation's special cultural excellence'.

A spate of scholarly books on historical aspects of the Library, its collections and administration, in admirably lucid prose has recently graced its publishing programme. Elaine M. Paintin's *The King's Library* (1989, 32pp.), narrates the story of King George III's library, presented to the nation by his son, George IV, in 1823, and of the British Museum gallery completed in 1827 to accommodate it. As stipulated in the bequest, the 60,000 books which eventually arrived from Kensington Palace are kept 'entire, and separate from the rest of the Library, in a repository to be appropriated exclusively for that purpose'. At St Pancras they will be housed in an imposing six-storeyed, glass-walled 'tower of knowledge' rising from the entrance hall. Mobile shelving, internal lifts, and a stairwell will ensure that all parts of this luxurious and commodious stack will be immediately accessible to staff fetching books required in the reading rooms.

Lavishly produced, with 140 colour and 190 black and white illustrations of illuminated manuscripts, papyri, oriental and Western maps, music, prints and drawings, postage stamps, and printed books, *Treas-*

ures Of The British Library (1988, 272pp.), compiled by Nicolas Barker and the Curatorial Staff of the British Library, traces the march of events in the Library's history. It begins with Sir Hans Sloane and the foundation of the British Museum, the Old Royal Library, and the Cottonian and Harleian libraries, and proceeds down the years to Montague House and the early years of the National Library; the East India Company Records and Library; the King's Library; Antonio Panizzi and the Department of Printed Books in the nineteenth century; the development of Oriental Collections; Maps and Music; the Printed and Manuscript Collections; the India Office Library and Records; Bookbindings, Newspapers, Stamps; Printed Books and Manuscripts in the twentieth century; and America and the Spread of English Overseas. Its frontispiece, a magnificent double-page colour view of a deserted Reading Room, will doubtless induce a flood of nostalgia and regret at leaving it among its habitués, when British Library finally takes its leave of the British Museum building in the mid-1990s. If a criticism can be levelled at *Treasures of the British Library*, it is that the scholarship in evidence is perhaps a little too intense and pronounced for its 'coffee-table' format and presumed readership.

First published by Andre Deutsch in 1967, Edward Miller's *The Life and Times of Antonio Panizzi of The British Museum* was reissued by the British Library in 1988. Miller, himself on the British Museum Library staff for 40 years, was ideally placed to write the biography of this complex and remarkable man, enjoying unrivalled access to much previously unpublished source material, notably Panizzi's correspondence and the British Museum Board of Trustee's Committee Minutes. Consequently his nine 'library' chapters exude an enviable and unparalleled authority. But this is no ponderous, monumental life and times work on the Victorian pattern: the dramatic highlights of Panizzi's life – not just the British Museum years – are skilfully and consummately woven into a fast-flowing narrative. Of course, no biographer could wish for a more amenable subject, constantly embroiled in well-documented, controversial affairs at the highest level as he was.

Panizzi's career in the British Museum Library can only be described as improbable. He arrived in England penniless in May 1823, a few months before he was sentenced to death *in absentia* in the Duchy of Modena for subversive political activities. After a spell teaching Italian in Liverpool, and some occasional writing, he was appointed to the chair of Italian Language and Literature in the University of London. Then, largely due to the influence of Thomas Grenville, he was appointed as

Extra Assistant Librarian in the British Museum Library in April 1831. He reached the summit of British librarianship as Keeper of Printed Books, 1837–56, and Principal Librarian, 1856–66. Thirty years at the top, constantly enmeshed in the complicated affairs of an eighteenth-century institution he was desperately endeavouring to establish as the world's undisputed leading research library, a heavy task not lightened by the implacable hostility of some of his senior colleagues: 'They breathed, for the most part, the air of an earlier and more leisured day. Into this narrow, comfortable, amateurish little world strode Antonio Panizzi, the turbulent revolutionary and devoted professional . . . a wind that would sweep away for ever the quiet, placid life of the old Museum.'

The manuscript versus printed catalogue controversy, Panizzi's celebrated 92 cataloguing rules, his enforcement of the Copyright Act, the Parliamentary Select Committee on the British Museum, the Royal Commission to enquire into its constitution and government, the designing and building of the Round Reading Room, are all discussed at length in captivating detail.

The Library Of The British Museum. Retrospective Essays On The Department Of Printed Books (1991, 305pp.), edited by P. R. Harris, records some internal practices and workings of the British Museum Library before it was incorporated in British Library in 1973. Some of the procedures and episodes in the Library's history represented here bear a striking resemblance to its contemporary problems. F. J. Hill's 'The Shelving and Classification of Printed Books' explains how from the earliest days successive generations of staff have coped with the task of making the vast collections accessible to readers. Among the detail registered is a table of the new pressmarking system earmarked for St Pancras which has been in operation since 1986. Harris's account of the previous move from Montagu House to the newly constructed North Wing of the British Museum, planned and executed in the years 1838–42, is also of more than passing interest to present-day staff and readers. His narrative encompasses the construction of the North Wing, the allocation of workrooms and storerooms, estimating the total mileage of shelves required, the various modifications to the plans(!), the massive complications caused by the need for new pressmarks, and the inevitable snags, hitches, and delays. Who can possibly deny that history repeats itself?

Ilse Sternberg's 'The Acquisition Policies and Funding of the Department of Printed Books 1837–1959' outlines what resources were available to implement the ambitious plans drawn up by Panizzi and his successors; K. A. Manley's 'The Book Wolf Bites a Bohn: Panizzi,

Henry Bohn, and Legal Deposit 1850–53' is a study of Panizzi's no-holds-barred confrontation with outraged publishers when he attempted to apply the full force of the copyright laws. In 'The Traditional Maintenance of the General Catalogue of Printed Books', Alec Hyatt King draws upon his own experience in the Cataloguing Room in the 1930s to clarify 'the intellectual and physical methods by which the General Catalogue . . . was kept up to date with accessions and regularly corrected whenever required'. King's 'Quodlibet: Some Memoirs of the British Museum and Its Music Room 1934–76' includes his personal rec-ollections of the effect of the war years on the British Museum, his involvement in trade union affairs, and his spells as residential duty offi-cer responsible for the safety of all the Museum's collections through the night and at the weekends. The remaining essay, Paul James Cross' 'The Private Case: A History', tells the obscure story of the Library's porno-graphic material which was separated from the general collections and withheld from readers in 1841.

Appointed to the post of planning, starting the National Lending Library for Science and Technology (NLL) in November 1956, later becoming its first Director, Donald Urquhart trenchantly describes step by step the origins and development of the NLL up to the time it became part of the British Library in his *Mr Boston Spa* (Bardsley, Wood Garth, 1990, 234pp.) After the establishment of NLL, of all the services he ren-dered to British librarianship in general and to the British Library in par-ticular certainly the most far-sighted was his selection of Boston Spa for its location. 'Most important of all the NLL secured with the buildings one of the largest, if not the largest, library site in the world. Whatever happened the development of the NLL would not be held up, as that of so many libraries have been held up, by site limitations' (p.92). What happened, of course, was that because of Urquhart's foresight in 1958 British Library was able in the early 1990s to transfer some of its costly London-based activities to the 65-acre Boston Spa site.

Of all institutions British Library might have been expected to keep its archives in exemplary order yet, according to Andrew Griffin's 'Preserving an Archive of the British Library', *Library History*, **9** (1 + 2), 1991:52–8:

> the sorry truth is that . . . since its birth in 1973, it has failed to provide either for the archives it took with it from its parent, the British Museum, or for the accumulating record of its more recent past. Like so many new institutions, the BL has focused its energies on growth and new initiatives, on planning for the future.

At the moment its not inconsiderable archives are stored at Micawber Street, in the basements of the British Museum, and the Woolwich outhouse, in local stores in Western Manuscripts, OIOC, and DSC, and even in various working areas. In 1990 Griffin, who has subsequently taken up a post elsewhere, was appointed by the Library to institute a corporate archives programme and to introduce a more effective system of records management. He estimates that up to 95% of the British Library's paper output should ultimately be pulped, a disposal rate roughly in line with the Public Record Office's (PRO) expectations of most government departments. Regarding even the 5% which should be retained, 'the decision-makers in the Library [would] need strong and clear-cut arguments to be convinced that the cost of selecting, storing, conserving, cataloguing and staffing the old records of the Library is justified at a time of reducing resources'.

Griffin distinguishes four categories of obligation the decision-makers should heed when considering what to preserve. First, like other public bodies, British Library is required under the 1958 Public Records Act to select its records which should be preserved. At that point it could in theory simply parcel them off to the PRO, where they would be made available for public inspection after 30 years. He conjectures that the PRO would be satisfied with the papers of the British Library Board, its Management Committee, and with selected Directors' and Directors-General files. But the present position is a little more complicated in that British Library has been approved as an archive depository itself and can therefore select and keep its own records. In practice, fearing the outcry from the library and information profession if it were to send its archives elsewhere, British Library will allocate adequate resources for their preservation. Added to this legal obligation was a moral argument that 'the creation of the British Library itself and the move to the St Pancras building are, or will be, significant events in the nation's cultural history. The Library should take upon itself the duty of preserving records which document its past and, perhaps even more importantly, keep any unique evidence pertinent to the acquisition and safekeeping of its collections.'

On business efficiency grounds it makes good sense for the Library to manage its day-to-day records systematically: it needs to be able to locate records swiftly as a vital information source; savings can be made if inactive records can be transferred to cheaper storage and unwanted records are expeditiously destroyed; and if those essential to conduct the Library's business can be quickly identified and retained. And, lastly, described as 'a strong argument in favour of providing for a substantial

British Library archive on the Library's premises', there is the obligation to preserve 'the intellectual integrity' of the collections, and the items they encompass, in the national printed archive, by recording their provenance and location, and so on. As for the type of record which should be retained, Griffin enumerates no fewer than 28 classes of papers which should be preserved, ranging from original papers relating to the Library and its constituent parts, to its organization, functions, procedures, and staffing, through to selected unpriced British Library publications, leaflets, seminar programmes, and publicity materials.

As this book goes to press Andy Stephens' *The British National Bibliography 1950–1973: a catalogue of achievement*, described as 'a celebration of the BNB's unrivalled place in the history of bibliographic information', is published. A detailed history of the early years has long been needed.

INDEX

ALISSE 29
AMED/CATS 194
AMED/CATS List of Journals Indexed
    194
AMED/CATS Thesaurus 194
ARTTel 184, 196, 205
ARTTel Users Guide 196
ARTTel Version 2 196
ARTTel Version 2 Users Guide 196
AVMARC 222
Aalto, A. 27
'Abuse of Shaw's literary legacy'
    123
'Access To Special Materials – Patent
    Specifications' 170
Accessing BLAISE-LINE via JANET
    223
*Acquisition and Collection
    Development for Libraries* 74
'Acquisition of German material in
    the mid-nineteenth century' 72
'Acquisition Policies and Funding of
    the Department of Printed
    Books' 238
'Acquisitions policy and practice: cur-
    rently published material Federal
    Republic of Germany' 72
*Acquisitions Policy at the Document
    Supply Centre* 56, 182
Acquisitions Processing and
    Cataloguing 68, 212, 234–5
Adamson, D. 46
administrative changes 66–7
Administrative Structure 66–8
Adopt a Book Appeal 138

*Adopt a Book and Save Our Library
    Heritage* 138
*Advanced Online Searching in
    Science and Technology* 164
Advancing with Knowledge 40,
    42–4, 57
African Studies 73, 90, 117, 120
'Agreement between The British
    Library Board and The Library
    Association' 109
Aldwych Reading Room 162
*Alexandria. The Journal of National
    and International Library and
    Information Issues* 55, 216
*Alphanumeric Reports Publication
    Index* 187
Alston, R. 22, 83
American Antiquarian Society 84
American Studies Library Newsletter
    31, 113
American Trust for the British Library
    74, 112–13
'And so, dear reader, the fairytale
    ends' 19
Anderson, J. 89, 97, 119, 120, 129,
    133
Annual Report 28, 127
    Second 3
    Fifteenth 215
    Seventeenth 122, 140
    Eighteenth 29, 66, 234
    Nineteenth 12
'Another chapter' 22
Architects Journal 8, 25
Archives 134

Arrangement of Books in the British Museum Library 1843–1973 83
Artefacts Collection 92
Aslib Biosciences Group 29
Aslib Information 32, 36, 136, 158, 186
Aslib Proceedings 29
Assistant Librarian 136, 177
Atlas Maps And How To Find Them 132
Audiovisual Librarian 99, 190
Audiovisual Materials on Preservation 138
Australian and New Zealand Studies 119, 130, 133
'Australiana in the British Library' 74
Authors Licensing and Collecting Society 191
Automated Book Retrieval System 33
Automated Cataloguing: A Manual 121
Automated Request Transmission 195
Automated Request by Telephone *see* ARTTel
Automation Library Committee 40
Automation Planning Committee 40
Automation Strategy 40–1

BBC Gramophone Library
    BBC Natural History Unit (Bristol) 90
    BBC Transcription Services 90
'BIC – the story so far' 215
'BIN or a BLIP: a proposed national business information initiative' 168
'BL and copyright' 191
'BL bid to boost PIN gateways' 173
'BL under international pressure over contempt for copyright' 190
'BL's BookNet . . . spreading the cost more fairly' 193
BLAISE-LINE 68, 80, 109, 129, 140, 162, 184, 186–7, 194, 215, 220–25, 235

databases 220, 226
BLAISE-LINE Mini Manual 223
BLAISE-LINE Newsletter 80, 213, 218, 221, 222–3
BLAISE-LINE Quick Reference Guide 224
BLAISE-LINE User Manual 223
BLAISE-LINK 194
BLAISE-LINK From the Medical Information Centre 194
BLAISE-LINK Newsletter 194
BLAISE RECORDER 224
BLAISE RECORDS 224–5
BLAISE RECORDS News 38, 227, 231
BLC on CD-ROM 80–2
BLISS 108–11
    database 221
    mission statement 109–11
BNBMARC 215–20, 224, 227, 234
BNBMARC Online. The Key to British Publishing 215
BNB on CD-ROM 228–32
BNB Reference 231
BNB Research Fund 155–6
'BNB Research Fund: cutting across the boundaries' 156
'BNB 2000. The development of the British National Bibliographic Service' 226
BRITS Index 188
'Background to the British Library Catalogue conversion' 80
'Bad case of overbooking' 45
Baile, C. 164
Bailey, M. 53
Baker, F. 17
Barber, P. 130
Baring Foundation 125
Barker, N. 237
Bath Information and Data Services 184
Baxter, I. A. 119
Baxter, P. 159
Beaumont, A. 22
Beech, D. R. 133
'Benefits of automated cataloguing' 234

Bermant, C.   104
bibliographic equivalent of the M25   6
'Bibliographic Record Supply: A Failure Of National Policy   216
Bibliographic Services Division   210
Bibliographic Services Newsletter   79, 210, 226, 230, 235
'Bibliographical Sources On Armenian Periodicals'   115
Bibliography and the study of 15th-century Civilisation   87
Bibliography of Biography   232
Bibliography of British Newspapers   107
Bibliothèque Nationale   229
Bingle, R.   116
Binney, M.   26–7
Biotechnology Information News   177
Biotechnology Information Service   177
Biotechnology Marketing Sourcebook   177
Birrell, I.   12
Bishop Sound Company   92
Blake, D. M.   115–16
Blakeman, K.   164
Bloomsbury And St Pancras. A Future for the British Library   18
Bohn, H.   239
Boke of Hydrographie   128
Book Industry Communication   211–12
Book Move Control System   32
'Book Wolf Bites a Bohn'   238
'booking for a new millenium'   26
BookNet   192–3
'BookNet Service'   192
Books at Boston Spa   185, 189
Books in English   232
Bookseller   8, 20, 41, 190–1, 213–14, 226
Booksellers' Association   214
'Boston Spa: an uncertain future'   198
'Boston Spa and the writing on the wall'   197
Boston Spa Books On CD-ROM   185

Boston Spa Conferences on CD-ROM   186
Boston Spa Serials on CD-ROM   184
Bourne, R.   218, 227, 235
Bowden, R.   110
Boxing   139
Bradbury, D.   198–203
'Brand New Facility at SRIS – Chemical Structure Searching'   164
Brio   126
British Academy   156
British Bird Songs & Calls   96
British Bird Songs on CD   96
British Book News   36, 107, 203, 226
British Catalogue of Music   125–7
British Institute of Management   30
British Institute of Recorded Sound   89
British Journal of Academic Librarianship   216
'British Library: A Response to a Set of Questions'   76
British Library Act 1972   66
'British Library African resources'   73, 91, 117, 120
British Library archives   238–40
British Library at St Pancras   28
British Library Board   66, 109
'British Library Book Preservation Process'   141
British Library bookshop   143–4
British Library CIP Cataloguing-in-Action Programme   213
'British Library called to account'   8
'British Library Catalogue Conversion'   79
British Library Catalogue database   221
British Library Catalogue of Printed Maps, Charts and Plans Ten Year Supplement   130
'British Library complete At Last'   25
British Library Consultancy Services   148–9
'British Library, DDC and the new building'   35

British Library Document Supply Centre. A leading source of scientific, technical and medical information 207

British Library Document Supply Centre. Invaluable Information Service, Important and Indispensable to the Nation 208

'British Library Document Supply Centre Strategy:The Next Ten Years' 205

British Library Document Supply Centre. UK Services. The Greatest Source of Knowledge In The World 208–9

'British Library Environmental Information Service' 177

British Library General Catalogue of Printed Books 78–9, 82 (CD-ROM) 81–2

British Library: Guide to the catalogues and indexes of the Department of Manuscripts 120

British Library Humanities & Social Sciences Collections 89, 97, 119–20, 129, 133

British Library in the 1990s 21

British Library Information Guides 158

British Library Information Sciences Service *see* BLISS

British Library: a guide to its structure, publications, collections and services ix

'British Library Japanese Information Service in Science, Technology & Commerce' 175

British Library Journal 74, 115

British Library Lending Division 181

British Library National Conspectus Office 75

British Library News 33, 88, 97, 112, 122, 173, 193, 217

British Library Newspaper Library Newsletter 100–5, 107

British Library of Wildlife Sounds 91

British Library Past Present Future 22, 144

'British Library plans for CD-ROM' 230

British Library R&D Reports 158

'British Library Reborn' 20

British Library Reference Division 71

British Library Reproductions 142

British Library Reproductions. Photographic and Reprographic Services at Bloomsbury 142

British Library Research Papers 158

'British Library second rate' 10

'British Library Signs Contract With Whitaker' 213

British Library Statement Of Purpose 58

'British Library to cut back book stock' 53

'British Library 2000' 41

'British Library will survive' 64

'British Library's commitment to CD-ROM' 230

'British Library's map collections and the national topographic memory' 129

British Library's Photographic Service 140

'British Library's Policies on Legal Deposit' 55

British Museum Catalogue of Printed Maps, Charts and Plans 130

British Museum Department of Prints and Drawings 128

British Museum Department of Western Antiquities 128

British Museum Library 71

'The British Museum Library And Colonial Copyright Deposit' 74

'British Museum Library and The India Office' 115

British Museum's Shaw Fund 122–3

British National Bibliography 68, 225–8

British National Bibliography 1950–1973 241

British National Bibliography

Research Fund: an introduction and guide to applicants 156
British National Corpus 157
British Official Publications Not Published by HMSO 188
British Phonograph Industry 89, 92
British Reports, Translations and Theses 187–8
British Telecom 153
British Union Catalogue of Orchestral Sets (BUCOS) 190
Brockhurst, C. 29
Brome, V. 18
'Brought to book, library saga is classic tale of woe' 10
Brown, S. 120, 126
Brown, Y-Y. 117, 175
Bruynzeel shelving 11–12
Building 10, 25
'Building a time bomb' 25
'Building cutback to split British Library' 5
Building design 22
'Building of library runs badly for 12 years' 8
Building the New British Library 27–8
Bulletin du Bibliophile 87
Bulletin of the Society for Renaissance Studies 86
Burchell, R. 113
Burden, C. 73
Burnett, T. 121
Burton, R. 165
Business Information: a brief guide to the reference resources of the British Library 167
Business Information Network 167–8
  Directory of Members 168
  Newsletter 168
Business Information Service 165–8
  databases 165–8
Business Research Service 166–7
Byford, J. 35

CABLIS 111, 159
CD-ROM Catalogue (DSC) 208

'CD-ROM for record supply' 231
CD-ROM Information Products – The Evaluative Guide 84, 186
CD-ROM Librarian 230
CD with an IQ 98
CIP 211–15
'CIP – a gateway for publishers' 213
'CIP Confusion In Publishing' 213
'CIP records on the BNBMARC file' 213
COMPASS 218, 227
'COMPASS – The New Subject System For The BNB and HSS Files' 218
COMPCON 218
COMPCON The Complete Conversion Service 218
CPM Plus. Catalogue of Printed Music in the British Library to 1990 on CD-ROM 125
Cable & Wireless Global Digital Highway 95
Calendar of Charters and Rolls in the Manuscript Collections of the British Library 121
Campbell, T. 129, 132
Cambridge Sound Publications 94–5
Cambridge University Library 184
Campaign to Save the Reading Room 4, 14
Canadian Studies 73, 119, 129
'Canadiana deposited in the British Museum Library between 1895 and 1924' 73
'Card Catalogues in The British Library' 126
Carr, J. 36
Care And Preservation of Philatelic Materials 133
Cartographic Journal 129
'Cartographic material relating to Germany' 130
Cartographic Materials File 130
'Cash probe into super library' 4
'Cash squeeze brings new British Library delay' 13
Casson, H. 19
Catalogue & Index 35

catalogue conversion 79–81
Catalogue of Cartographic Materials in The British Library 130
Catalogue of Manuscript and Printed Reports . . . deposited in the Map Room of the India Office 131
Catalogue of Manuscript Maps Charts And Plans Of The Topographic Drawings in the British Museum 131
Catalogue of Maps, Plans and Views of London 131
Catalogue of Printed Music in the British Library 124
catalogue record creation 47
'Catalogues At St Pancras' 33
Catalogues of Additions to the Manuscripts 121
Cataloguing Action Plan 216, 218
Cataloguing-in-Publication *see* CIP
'Cataloguing-in-Publication: Major review of progress' 214
Censorship 111, 239
Center for Bibliographical Studies and Research 84
Centre for Bibliographic Management 216–17
Centre for the Book 36–7, 66, 110
Centre for the Study of the Press 103
Chambers (publishers) 157
Chancery House Reading Room 170
Chaney, M. 138
Chapman, A. 217
Chapman, M. 126
Chapman, P. 134, 136
Chesterton archive 123
Children's Fiction on Fiche 232
Chinese Academy. Institute of Social Sciences 116
'Chinese materials in the India Office Library' 117
Chinese Studies 117
Choosing A 35mm Microfilm Reading Machine 141
'Cladding' 24–5
Clark, C. 90, 96
'Classification of St Pancras open

access material' 35
Clements, D. W. G. 136, 139
Cobbe, H. 126
Code of Practice for Access for the Disabled (BS 5810) 34
Codex Sinaiticus 119
Coles, J. 13
'Colindale Newspaper Conservation Bindery' 101
Collection Development 47
'Collection development in the British Library' 49–50, 75
collection management 58
Collection Management 76
Collections and Preservation Directorate 134–42
policies 134–5
Collections Portfolio 57, 182
Collings, T. J. 133
Coman, R. 30–1
Committee of Public Accounts Eighteenth Report A New Building For The British Library 9–10
'Compact Discs For National Bibliography: Britain And France Joint Forces' 230
Complementary Medicine Index 195
Complete Conversion Service *see* COMPCON
Complete List of Priced Publications 143
Complete List of Reports Published by The British Library R&D 158
Computer Aided Subject System *see* COMPASS
Computer Enhanced Digital Audio Restoration (CEDAR) 95
Computer Search Service 164
Computing and Telecommunications 40, 234–5
Confederation of British Industry 175
Connecting to BLAISE-LINE 223
Conservation and Binding Department 141
Consortium of Scottish Libraries 75
Conspectus 49, 75–6

'Conspectus. A means to library co-operation' 76
'Conspectus: A reappraisal' 76
Construction 24
Consultancy Services and International Office 148
Cooper, K. R. 10, 163
Coopers and Lybrand Deloitte 201
Copeland, P. 93, 96
'Copy cats keep an eye on the cash in Bloomsbury' 142
Copyright Act 1911 215
Copyright Cleared 192
Copyright, Designs and Patents Act 1988 191
Copyright in the UK 111
Copyright Libraries Shared Cataloguing Project 227, 234
Copyright Libraries Working Group on Legal Deposit 56
Copyright Licensing Agency 191
copyright receipt accessions 52–3, 56
Copyright Receipt Office *see also* Legal Deposit Office 51–3, 100
Cornish, G. P. 74
Corporate Plan 1993/4–1997/8 64
Corporate Planning 64–5
'Cost Savings and Service Strategies in the British National Bibliographic Service' 216
Cottonian Library 237
Cowley, R. 105
Crace, F. 131
Cranfield, G. 104
Cross, P. J. 239
Crump, M. 36–7, 85
Cunningham, A. 213–14
'Curiosities of the British Library's Chinese Collections' 117
Currency With Coverage 216
Current British Journals 184
Current Music Catalogue 125
Current Research In Britain 207–8
Current Serials Received 183, 189
Curston, M. 186
Czechoslovak Collections in the British Library 72

'DNH and R&DD: Partners in Projects' 150
Daily Telegraph 29, 54, 101
Dale, P. 167
'Dancing in the British Library' 78
Daniels, M. 73
Darnell, B. 30
DATA-STAR 165, 195, 205
David and Mary Eccles Centre for American Studies 113
Davies, M. C. 86
Davis Langdon and Everest 22
Davison, J. 5
Day, J. 186
Day, T. 96
Declaration of Purpose 42–3
Department of National Heritage 146, 150
Department of Oriental Manuscripts 114
'Department of Oriental Manuscripts and Printed Books' 116–17
Department of Printed Books 71–2, 238
Department of Trade and Industry 153, 157, 164
'Designing a National Monument' 24
Desmond, R. 116
Deutsche Bibliothek 229
'Developments In Bibliographic CD-ROMs In The British Library' 229
Developments In Recorded Sound. A Catalogue of Oral History Interviews 96
'Developments in the Conservation of Islamic Manuscripts at IOLR' 118
Dewey Decimal Classification 35–6, 226
DIALPLUS 223
DIALPLUS Access to BLAISE-LINE 223
'Digging Deep' 24
Digital Equipment Company 33
'Digital story of a nation' 83

Direct Data Entry System 217, 227, 234
Directory of Acronyms 186
Directory of European Library and Information Associations 111
Directory Of Library Codes (DSC) 182
Directory of Rare Books and Special Collections 121
Directory of Recorded Sound Resources in the United Kingdom 95
Disaster Control 138
Discography of Tudor Church Music 97
Document Supply Centre 181–209
  collections 183–90
  copyright 190–2
  future 197–205
  history 239
  medical information service 193–6
  publications 205–9
Document Supply Centre Monographs database 221
Document Supply News 181, 183–5, 192–3, 196, 207
'Don't Film It if you're not recording it' 140
Dormer, P. 27
Downs, L. J. 177
Draft Plan of Action for Libraries in the EC 151
Down Survey of Ireland 122
'Drainage' 24
Draper, F. 46
Duckett, R. J. 226
'Dunhuang Manuscripts Project' 116
Duran, L. 90
'Dutch resources' 73
Dyas, E. 73, 103–4

EBIP News 177
EBSCO Industries 184
'ESRC move to protect library work' 146
'ESTC News' 85
Eagle, S. 105

'Early Development of The Newspaper Library' 103
Easingwood, C. 231
Eating The Menus 227
Ede, S. 75, 212
Eden, R. 73
Egles, J. D. 74
Eighteenth Century Short Title Catalogue (ESTC) 83–5
  database 222
Eighteenth Century Short Title Catalogue 1990 microfiche edition 84
Eighteenth Century Short Title Catalogue. Catalogue of The British Library Collections 84
Eighteenth Century Short Title Catalogue on CD-ROM 84
Eighteenth Century Short Title Catalogue: the cataloguing rules 85
Eleanor Farjeon papers 122
Electronic Data Interchange 215
Electronic Library 203
Elliot, J. 39, 210
Encapsulation 139
'End Of Periodical As We Know It?' 161
'English Language Branch and women's studies' 73
English Short Title Catalogue 85
English Today 37
Enright, B. 47–8
Environmental Auditing: a guide to best practice 176
Environmental Auditing: an introduction and practical guide 176
Environmental Information: a guide to sources 176
Environmental Information Service 175–7
'Epic volumes' 25
Era of Change. Contemporary UK-US-West European Relations. A Bibliography of Materials held at the British Library 113
Ernst & Young 32
Eros Data Centre 128

Esdaile, A. 71
'Establishment of the British National
    Bibliography' 227
European Biotechnology Information
    Project 177
European Community 188
European Draft Plan Of Action 151
European National Libraries Project
    231
European Space Agency 164
Eusden, M. 177
'Evaluation of Newspapers on CD-
    ROM' 101
Evelyn Waugh archive 122
Evening Standard 19
'Everything You Ever Wanted To
    Know About Japanese
    Companies – Online' 175
'The exclusion zone. BNB:
    Exclusions Policy 1993' 225
Exeter University 91, 96
Explorers, The 229–30

Factotum 85
Facts and Figures 71, 208
Families and Social Mobility 90
Family Life and Work Before 1918
    91
Farrington, A. 117
Fasciculing 139
Feeney, M. 153, 158
Ferris, D. 109
Ferris, V. 136, 140
Fiction on Fiche 232
financial cuts 10–11
Finding Electoral Registers In The
    British Library 88
'Fire Protection' 24
Fisher, M. 4
Fisher, P. 83
Fletcher collection of philatelic mater-
    ial 133
Focus on British Biological and
    Medical Sciences Research . . .
    British Business and Manage
    ment Sciences Research . . .
    British Engineering and Com-
    puter Sciences Research . . .

British Environmental Sciences
    Research 187
'Fond farewell to the Reading Room'
    20
Fontes Artis Musicae 90, 96, 125–6
For scholarship, research and innova-
    tion. Strategic objectives for the
    year 2000 57–65, 121, 134, 144
Ford, G. 55
Foreign Devils On The Silk Road
    116
Foster, Sir N. 27
'Foster a binding relationship' 138
Fox, P. 216
free access 45–6
'Freeze-Drying Of Tapes' 93
'Freeze-Drying Process' 136
'Freezing As A Means Of Pest
    Control' 136
French Quebec: imprints in French
    from Quebec 1774–1990 in The
    British Library 74
'French resources for women's stud-
    ies' 73
Friend, F. J. 197, 200
Friends of The British Library
    111–12
Friends of The British Library
    Newsletter 112, 133, 210
'From the CD-ROM Help Desk' 231
'Future of Bliss' 109
'Future of Document Supply: Is There
    an Alternative to BLDSC?' 202
'Future of interlending and document
    supply' 198
'Future of the British Library' 16, 57
'Future of the Round Reading Room'
    15

Gallico, A. 170
Garfield, S. 19
Garner, R. 170
Gateway To Knowledge 5, 36, 41–6,
    51, 57, 103
Gaur, A. 73, 116–17
Geddes, T. 72–3
General Catalogue. A quick guide 82
General conditions of grant 145

General guide to the India Office Records 119
General Information About The British Library Catalogue Of Printed Books to 1975 On CD-ROM 82
General Preservation 138
Geoffrey Leigh Room 112
George Frow Collection 92
German Studies 72, 104, 130
'German studies in the context of the Reference Division's collection development policies' 72
'Getting the Chemistry Right' 164
Getty Grant Program 117
Gift and Exchange System 192
Gilbert, J. 73, 165
'Gilt-edged volumes help balance the books' 203
'Global marketing of managed information' 203
Goff, F. R. 86
Goff, M. 78
Goldfinch, J. 86–7
Gomersall, A. 161–2, 168
Goodacre, H. J. 117
Gor, A. 226
Gordon, R. 105
Gorman, G. 74
grant-in-aid 44
Granville Library 143
GRATEFUL MED. Making MED-LINE easy to search 194
Grayson, L. 176
Greaves, W. 138
Green, R. 200
Green Belt, Green Fields and the Urban Fringe 176
Greenwood, D. 32, 156
Greig, G. 11
Granville, T. 237
Griffin, A. 239
Grinyer, D. 230
Guardian, The 13–14, 19, 25, 83
Guide to Americana: the American collections in the British Library 74
Guide to Awards 145

Guide to Catalogues. An Introduction to the British Library's catalogues and how to use them 82
Guide to Directories at the Science Reference and Information Service 165
Guide to Libraries in Key UK Companies 167
Guide to source materials in the India Office Library . . . for the history of Tibet, Sikkim and Bhutan 118
Guide to the Preparation of a Research Proposal 145
Gutenberg-Jarhrbuch 1991 55

HMSO database 87, 222
Haines, B. 73
Hamilton, G. 99, 107
Handbook of Library Cooperation 75
Handlist of unpublished finding aids to the London Collections of The British Library 83
Hanger, S. 49, 75
Harleian Library 237
Harris, F. 120
Harris, P. R. 72, 81, 238
Harrison, D. 151
Harvey, P. D. A. 132
Hazardous Materials: sources of information on their transportation 176
Health Studies Review 195
Hebrew Studies 80
Hellinga, L. 49, 55, 72, 86–7
Herbert, S. 29
Hewison, R. 4–6, 45
'Hidden Collections At The Newspaper Library' 104
'Highly important paper chase' 124
Hill, F. J. 238
Hill, R. 225
Himalayan Triangle 118
'History stored in column inches' 107
Holborn Reading room 162
Holden, C. 73
'Holdings on women studies in Italy' 73

Holman, M. 25
Holroyd, M. 123–4
Holt, B. 72, 170
Home Office Policy Research Group 138
Hong Kong Colonial Copyright 52
Hookway Building 235
Hopkirk, P. 116
House of Commons Committee of Public Accounts 9–10
House of Lords Select Committee on Science and Technology (Remote Sensing and Digital Mapping) 128
'How not to do it' 62
'How The Priced Research Service Can Help Your Company' 167
How To Find Information. Life Sciences 177
How To Find Manuscript Maps In The British Library 129
Howard, P. 21
Hughes, D. 4
Hull, D. D. 94
Hulton Picture Co. 139
Humanities and Social Sciences 67, 71–113
  catalogues 78–83
  collections 71–8
Huse, R. 151
Hutt, G. 131

IFLA Journal 80
IOLR/OC Newsletter 115, 119, 174
IRS-Dialtech 165
ISTC 85–7
  database 222
'ISTC: Reading the Renaissance' 87
'Ignorance of BLISS?' 109
'In the cause of books' 36
Ince, M. 146, 203
'Incompetence at the British Library?' 17
Incunabula in American Libraries 86
Incunabula: the Printing Revolution in Europe 86

Incunable Short Title Catalogue *see* ISTC
Independent, The 8, 10, 12, 16, 19, 27, 46, 54, 95
Index of Conference Proceedings 186, 189
Index of Conference Proceedings 1964–1988 186
Index of Manuscripts In The British Library 120
Index to Factotum numbers 1–30 85
India Office Library & Records 114
India Office Library and Records: a Brief Guide to Biographical Sources 118
India Office Library and Records Newsletter 119
India Office Records. Ecclesiastical Returns 117–18
Indian Mutiny 1857–58: a guide to source materials in the India Office Library 118
Industro-Mechanical Sound/Artefacts 92
Industro-Mechanical Sound Collection 91
Info '90 Conference 201
Infomediary 175
Information for the Nation 163, 165
Information gap? 160
Information Policy: a select bibliography 148
Information Technology & Public Policy 204
Information UK Outlooks 155
Information UK 2000 148, 152–5
Information UK 2000 153–4
  An Update 154
Information UK 2000: Social trends 154
Inside Conferences 186
Inside Information 183, 186
Inside Information. ETOC 184
Inside Information on CD-ROM 184
Inside Information on CD-ROM List Of Titles 184
Instant Guide To Company Information Online 167

Interlend 89: Who Pays? 200
Interlending & Document Supply 99,
170, 208
*Interlending and Document Supply.
Proceedings of the Second
International Conference . . .
1990* 170
Interlibrary Lending Cost Model 201
'Inter-library lending in the next
decade – don't be too quick to
knock BLDSC' 201
*International Cataloguing &
Bibliographic Control* 230
International Federation of
Reproduction Rights
Organisations 190
*International Forum of Information
and Documentation* 163
*International Guide to Official
Industrial Property Publications*
169
*International Journal of Information
and Library Research* 147
International Links to BLAISE-LINE
223
International Publishers Association
190
*Into The 1990s: Staff Development
and Training in the British
Library* 47
International Translations Centre 185
'Introducing IRS-Dialtech' 164
*Introducing The British Library
Research And Development
Department* 145
*Introducing The National Sound
Archive* 97
*Introduction to Biotechnology
Information* 177
Introduction to Patents Information
170
investment 61–2
Is The British Library Falling Down?
16
'Is the writing on the wall at Boston
Spa?' 197
Issues In Focus 76
It Just Came Apart In My Hands 138

'It's A Record! BNBMARC Hit-Rate
Reaches 80%' 217

JANET 80, 111, 205, 223 *see also*
Super JANET
Jackson, M. 137–8
Jacob, D. 118
'Jam tomorrow: the present and future
state of the British Library's
automated music catalogue'
126
James, B. 73
James, E. 72, 122
Jamieson, D. R. 173
*Japanese Business Publications in
English* 175
'Japanese Community Information
Ready And Waiting' 175
Japanese Information Service 173–5
*Japanese Information Service. The
Fastest, Most Comprehensive
And Expert Source Of Japanese
Information* 174
*Japanese Language Collections In
The British Library* 117
'Japanese Official Publications In The
British Library' 174
Japanese Studies 175
Jarndyce Antiquarian Booksellers 15
Jazz Collections 90
'Jazz Oral History at the British
Library National Sound Archive'
90
Jenner, M. 20
Jewish Chronicle 104
Jewitt, A. C. 76, 93, 132
'Jinxed library calls in the Dutch to
open shelves' 11
Johansson, E. 107
Jones, B. 105
Journal of Librarianship 50, 75, 156,
226
*Journal of the American Society for
Information Science* 159
Journal of the Society of Archivists
121, 124
Journals In Translation 185
'Just a little overdue' 14

KIST 184–9
'Katharine Manfield's letters . . . ' 120
Kenna, S. 150
Kenny, A. 64
Kenny, G. 135
Kettle, R. 96
Keyword Index To Serial Titles see KIST
King, A. H. 81, 235
King, E. 141
King, S. 175
King George III Topographical and Maritime Collections 129
King's Library, The 236
Koch, L. 91
Kulturstiftung der Länder 72

LCMARC 224
L.I.S.T. Library & Information Statistics Tables For The United Kingdom 157
Laing Management Contractors 22
Lake, B. 15, 57
Lancaster University Unit for Computer Research 157
Landmark Trust Lundy Island Philatelic Archive 133
Landset data 128
Lang, B. 11, 203
Language and Dialect Collection 91
Larby, P. M. 73
Lasdun, Sir D. 27
Laserdisk Professional 230
'Last orders, please' 19
'Laying bare the secrets of the British Library's map collections' 132
Le Corbusier, C. E. J. 27
Lealand, C. 81
Lee, R. 177
Lees, C. 12
Lees, N. 176
legal deposit 63, 78, 126–7, 239
    electronic documents 63
Legal Deposit of Audiovisual Material 111
Legal Deposit Office *see also* Copyright Receipt Office 51, 213, 224, 227, 234

Leigh, B. 49
Lenin at The British Library 72
Lennon, A. 85
Lewis, P. 216
LEXICON – The Easy Order Service 195–6, 205
Leydon, M. 167
LIBER Bulletin 39
Libraries And Information Cooperation Council 106
Libraries And Information In Britain 158
'Library accused of cultural vandalism' 16
Library Acquisitions: Practice & Theory 190
Library & Information Briefings 158
Library & Information Briefings: the Book 158
Library and Information Plans 150
Library And Information Research News 229
Library and Information Research Reports 158
Library & Information Statistics Unit 157
Library Association 108–9, 110, 137, 214
    Library UmbrelLA 2 Conference 146
    Preservation and Conservation Sub-Committee 137
    Rare Books Group 120
Library Association Record 4, 29, 109, 111, 137–9, 142, 173, 189, 193, 197–8, 201, 209–10, 217, 226
Library Confirms Leaving Round Reading Room 15
Library Conservation News 76, 92–3, 107, 118, 136, 139–41, 150
'Library Document Supply Centre' 205
Library History 239
Library Information Technology Centre 155
Library Micromation News 231

Library of Congress 229
  Subject headings 216, 235
Library Of The British Museum.
  Retrospective Essays On The
  Department Of Printed Books
  81, 238
'Library Security: facts and figures'
  138
Library Security: Who Cares? 137
'Library to lead the world' 4
'Library's unfinished chapters' 4
Licence To Use British Library
  MARC Records 217
Life and Times of Antonio Panizzi
  237
'Life of Asian women as depicted in
  oriental manuscript illustrations'
  117
Life Stories and Ageing 91
Lindisfarne Gospels 119
Line, J. L. 159
Line, M. B. 159, 197
Linehan, A. 96
Lister, D. 10, 12, 16, 46
Lloyd, M. 116
Location Register Of Twentieth-
  Century English Literary
  Manuscripts And Letters 123
'Location Register of English Literary
  Manuscripts: a second project'
  123–4
'Logistics of Moving A Map Library
  Collection' 39
London History Workshop Centre 91
London Services – Bloomsbury
  Newsletter 33, 37, 57, 78, 83
London Services Research Register
  74
Longman Group 157
'Longman Group Takes Over CRIB'
  207
Lost Voice of Queen Victoria 95
Luce, R. 4
Lymbery, E. 19

MacDougall, A. F. 75, 138, 202
McIntosh, R. P. 128
Mackenzie, A. 105

McKillop, B. 116
McKinley, C. 213
McLaren-Turner, P. 73, 120
Macmillan Archive 123
McSean, T. 229–30
McTernan, D. J. 74
MARC Users Group 218–19
MARC Users Group Newsletter 94
MARS 185
MCB University Press 208
MEDLARS 194
MEDLINE 162, 194
'MPs to scrutinise British Library' 8
Magnusson, M. 143
Making An Impact: Guidelines on the
  dissemination of research 146
'Making The Business Information
  Service Work For You' 167
Manley, K. A. 238
Mann, M. 148, 158
Map Collections in The India Office
  Records 117
Map Collections of The British
  Library 128
Map Collector 129, 132
Map Dealers 132
Map Library 127–32
  catalogues 129–31
  move of sheet map collections 39
Mapping Awareness & GIs In Europe
  132
Maps for Empire 132
'Maps retroconvention at the British
  Library' 131
Mark Longman Library 109
Market Research: A Guide To British
  Library Holdings 167
Martyn, J. 153–5
Mason, T. 142
'Materials bearing on Australian and
  New Zealand studies' 119
Matter of FAX 111
Means of Access for Disabled People
  (BS 5588) 34
Mechanical-Copyright Protection
  Society 97
Mechanised Book Handling System
  34

Medical Information Centre   193
Medical Information Service   203
Medieval Maps   132
Mellon microfilming project   140–1
Memorandum of Understanding   108, 111
Mercers Company   125
Methodist Sound Archive   91
Micawber Street Store   39, 51, 169
Microform Collections Government Publications And The Social Sciences   89
Microform Review   139
'Miles of aisles for bibliophiles'   21
Miller, E.   237
Mr Boston Spa   239
Modelling the economics of interlibrary lending   201
Moir, M.   116, 119
Monograph Accessions and Record System *see* MARS
Montagu House   83
More British Bird Songs   96
Mould   139
'Move Into Orbit House Completed'   39
'Moving London's eastern treasures'   114
'Moving the British Library'   31
Moving The British Library   38
Moving The British Library. Catalogues and Book Delivery at St Pancras   34
'Moving the British Library – the Book Control System'   32
'Multi-media plan for BL's spare land'   29
Murdoch, J.   211
Museum of Mankind   128
Music Library   124–6, 239
'Music loans discord'   189
Music Reading Area   124
'Mysterious case of Luce's shrinking library'   5

NACSIS   174
'NBS answers back: Cataloguing in Publication improving all the time'   212
'NBS Customer Database'   211
NBS Marketing   211
'NBS Marketing Plan'   211
'NBS Profile. The London Unit'   210
ND News   98–9
National Acquisitions Group   56
National Archives of India   116
National Audit Office   6–8
National Bibliographic Service   68, 126, 210–33
   administrative structure   210
   publications   232–3
National Bibliographic Service BLAISE-LINE   222
National Bibliographic Service BLAISE RECORDS   225
National Central Library   181
National Committee for Regional Library Cooperation   106
'National Conference on Library Security'   138
National Conspectus Office   75
National Diet Library   174
National Discography   94, 97–99
National Discography. The Sound Recordings Information Bureau   98
National Documentation Centre (Pakistan)   116
National Heritage Memorial Fund   72, 122, 124
'National Libraries Project on CD-ROM'   230
National Libraries Project on CD-ROM   232
National Libraries 2   159
National Lending Library for Science and Technology   181
National Library of Canada   229
National Library of Medicine (US)   193
'National library provision and relationships: inter-library lending'   201
National Life Story Collection   91
National Manuscripts Conservation

Trust 148, 156–7
National Preservation Office 134–41
*National Preservation Office – a
    national focus for preservation
    and security in libraries* 139
National Preservation Office Advisory
    Committee 135
'National Preservation Office in the
    British Library' 136
'National Preservation Office: its role
    in the 1990s' 136
national printed archive 67
National Register for Collections of
    Recorded Sound 95
National Serials Data Centre 222
National Sound Archive 89–99
    centralised online discography 97
'National Sound Archive And Its
    Relation To The National
    Discography' 94
National Theatre 90
*Nation's Memory. The National Man-
    uscripts Conservation Trust* 157
Naylor, B. 198
Nercessian, V. 115
'New British Library hit by blunders
    over wiring' 29
'New British Library hit by delay in
    opening' 12
New Building for the British Library
    6–7, 23
'New Business CD-ROMs Ready To
    Search At SRIS' 162
'New chapter delays in sad saga of
    British Library' 12
'New exhibition facilities for British
    Library' 36
New Library World 219, 235
*New Look For The British National
    Bibliography* 227
'New Look For The R&D
    Department' 147
'New Reading Room Furniture &
    Fittings' 34
'New Search Software For BNB on
    CD-ROM' 231
New Titles 143
News from ISTC 86

'Newspaper Legal Deposit Office'
    100
Newspaper Library 99–108
    Admissions and Regulations 99
    bindery 101
    microfilming 103–3
    *Notes for Readers Using the
        Newspaper Library* 99
    objectives 99–100
    reader survey 100
'Newspaper Library At War' 104
'Newspaper preservation and access:
    developments and possibilities'
    99
'Newspapers as source material for
    women's studies' 73
NEWSPLAN 104–7
Newton, D. C. 170
Nickson, M. A. E. 120
'Nineteenth-century black American
    women's writing' 73
'No catalogue at the NSA?' 94
'Non-current German collections of
    the Department of Printed
    Books' 72
Nordion International 141
North Library 81
North West Data Services 218
North Western News 137
Northern Listening Service 182
'Norwegian women writers' 73
*Notes for Visitors. Using the British
    Library Information Sciences
    Service* 109
Novello and Co. 125
Novello House 39

OCLC 205, 224–5
'OIOC Acquires Important Armenian
    Collection' 115
'OIOC Conservation Studio' 118
OIOC Newsletter 39, 103, 115–16,
    118–19
OPAC 92, 93
Oakes, T. 90
'Objectives of the Newspaper
    Library' 100
Observer, The 5, 53, 104

Occupation Project Plan   29–31
Occupational Therapy Index   195
Oddy, P.   79–80
Official Journal (of European
   Community)   188
Office for Scientific and Technical
   Information   149
Office of Arts and Libraries   6–8
Official Publications and Social
   Sciences Service   87–9
'Official Publications Library'   88
Ohio College of Librarianship's
   Online Catalogue *see* OCLC
Old Royal Library   237
'On the radio at the nsa'   90
O'Neill, P. B.   73
'Online Catalogue In SRIS'   162
'Online Catalogue Up To The
   Opening Of St Pancras'   83
Online Public Access Catalogue   33,
   82–3
Online Search Centre (SRIS)   164
*Online Searching In Service And
   Technology*   164
Open Systems Interconnection   200
Optical Info '89   81
'Oral archives at the India Office
   Library'   116
Oral History   91
*Oral History: An Annotated
   Bibliography*   96
Oral history of British jazz   90
Orbit House   38, 114
ORDER   223
Ordnance Survey   127
Oriental Collections   38, 114
   move to IOLC   38, 114–15
Oriental and India Office Collections
   114–19
   conservation studio   118
   photographic collections   117
   reading room   115
'Oriental Collections To Join The
   India Office Library'   115
*Original Manuscript Maps of the
   First Ordnance Survey of
   England and Wales*   127
O'Toole, J.   105

Osborne, M.   192
'Out Of The Shadows – Patent
   Services From The British
   Library'   170
Ove Arup   22
Oxford University Computing
   Services   157
Oxford University Press   157

POPSI: the popular song index
   189–90
PRECIS   218, 227
PRISM   224–5
Paintin, E.   236
Paisey, D.   72
Palliative Care Index   195
Palmer, G.   74
Panizzi, A.   76, 115, 237–8
Parker, T.   136
Parkes, A.   105
Parliamentary Information
   Technology Committee   203
*Parliamentary Papers. British
   Parliamentary Publications And
   Procedural Records Of
   Parliament in The Official
   Publications And Social Services
   Reading Room*   88
Parry, D.   105
Parsons, R. B.   77
Patent Cooperation Treaty   169
Patent Express   170–1, 205
Patent Express Currentscan   171
*Patent Express Document delivery
   from the source you can trust*
   171
Patent Express Newsletter   171
Patent Express Transcript   171
'Patent Services From The British
   Library'   170
'Patent Stock Move'   169
Patents Collection   168–9
'Patents Data On CD-ROM'   172
Patents Information Network   173
   Bulletin   173
'Patents Information Network. A
   review after its first six years'
   173

Patents Information News 173
Patents Online 172
Patents Online Search Service 172
'Path to PRISM' 225
'Path to the Anglo-French pilot disc'
    230
pattern of services 44
Pawley, M. 25
Pearman, H. 26
Pepinster, C. 5
Peter Langmead Collection of Private
    and Post Office Telegraph
    Stamps 133
Pew Memorial Trust 112
Pew bibliographies 112
Philatelic Collections 133
'Philatelic Collections And The
    British Library As A Philatelic
    Research Centre' 133
'Philatelic sources at the British
    Library with particular reference
    to Australian and New Zealand
    material' 133
Photocopying Can Damage Books
    138
Photographic Conservation 139
Physiotherapy Index 195
'Planning and producing the BNB on
    CD-ROM' 230
'Plans for an information future' 109
*Playback: The Bulletin Of The
    National Sound Archive* 90, 94,
    97
'Please can we have our books back?'
    137
*Polish Collections In The British
    Library* 71
*Political and Secret Department
    Registers And Indexes* 118
Pollard, A. W. 85
Pop Music Collections 90
Popular Music Periodicals Index
    (POMPI) 95–6
Preservation: A Survival Kit 138
Preservation and Technology 137
'Preservation Microfilming and
    Substitution Policy in the British
    Library' 139

Preservation Policies 136
'Preservation – Who Cares?' 137
'Preserve us from mould – and from
    humans' 139
'Preserving an Archive of the British
    Library' 239
'Preserving Sound Recordings At The
    British Library National Sound
    Archive' 92
Preserving The Past For The Future
    139
'The Printed Book Catalogues – the
    future, the interim and some
    mysteries explained' (OIOC)
    118
Printed Music before 1800 127
Priorities For Research 147
'Private Case: A History' 239
'Private papers in the India Office
    Library' 116
'Problems of Retrospective
    Conversion in National and
    Research Libraries' 80
'Production Of The CD-ROM
    Version Of The British Library
    Catalogue' 81
'Production spending' 13
'Profit From Patents' 173
Program 230
'Project Management' 24
Property Services Agency 6–9, 22
'Provision For People With
    Disabilities At St Pancras' 35
Prytherch, R. J. 75
Public Library Development Incentive
    Scheme 148–51
Public Records Office 240
Public Services 143–4
'Publications proscribed by the
    Government of India' 116
Publishers Association 62, 214
'Publishers, Librarians and Copyright'
    190
Publishers' Licensing Society 191
Publishing History 123
Purdey, J. 211

'Question Of Bookkeeping' 55

'Quodlibet: Some Memoirs of the British Museum and its Music Room' 239

'RARP: an overview' 56
R&D Reveals Its New Organisational Development Strategy 147
Ranft, R. 96
Rapid Retrospective 225
Rare Books Newsletter 16, 36, 72, 124
Ratcliffe, F. W. 135–6
Rattigan archive 122
Raven, D. 189
Reader Admission System 33
Reader Admission Office 71
Reading Guide To The Preservation Of Library Collections 135
'Records Supply In The Broad Acres' 38
'Recorded drama and literature' 90
Recycling – Energy from Community Waste 176
Recycling – New Materials from Community Waste 176
Redgrave, F. R. 85
Reed, T. 193
Reeve, A. 217
Refer 169
Register of Preservation Microforms 140
database 222
Regular Readers Group 15–19
Rehabilitation Index 195
Relocation North 38
'Remote Sensing Resources at the British Library' 128
Report Of The Study On Library Provision For The Culture Of Science Technology And Medicine 76
Research and Development Department 111, 129, 145–59
consultancy services 148–9
Development Section 148
grants 145–6
Information Policy Section 148
publications 157–9

research grants 147–8
Support Unit 149
Research Bulletin 147, 150–2, 154, 157–9
'Resources for advanced research in Canadian Studies' 119
maps 129
'Resources for Australian and New Zealand Studies . . . Maps' 130
'Resources for the study of the women's movement in Germany' 73
'Results of Newspaper Library Survey' 101
'Retention of United Kingdom Newspapers After Microfilming' 102
Review of Acquisition and Retention Policies 48–53
Review of British Library Research and Development Research on Humanities Information 159
Review of the Arrangements for the Dissemination of Patents Information 170
'Revolutionary inventions put 78s back on the turntable' 95
Revolutions In Sound: A Celebration of 100 Years Of The Gramophone 92
'Rich and poor widows' 120
Richards, H. 107
Riley Dunn & Wilson 139
Rimmer, B. 169–70
Risher, C. A. 190
Rix, T. 37
Roberts, T. 170
Robinson, E. 126
Robson, P. J. 170
Rodgers, B. 118
'Role of British Library in cooperation' 75
'Role of British Library R&D Department in supporting library and information research' 159
'Role of the British Library for medical and health information' 195
Rotz, J. 128

Round Reading Room   18–20, 82, 238
Rowan, I.   54
Royal Commission on Historical Manuscripts   156
Royal Court Theatre   90
Royal Fine Art Commission   28
Royal United Services Institution   120
   sheet map collection   129
Royal Philharmonic Society   125
Royal Shakespeare Company   90
Royal Society   153
'Running The Library Effectively'   66
Russell, R. A.   101
Russon, D.   203

SCICAT   162
SCONUL Advisory Committee on Manuscripts   123
SIGLE   187
   database   222, 225
SOLSTICE   223
SRIS Classification of Science and Technology   161
'SRIS Classification Scheme Comes Of Age'   161
'SRIS Goes Green'   176
SRIS News   163
SRIS Newsletter   160–4, 167–9, 169–72, 174–7
'SRIS. The One-Stop Information Shop'   163
'SRIS Publications Look To the Future'   162
SRL News   164
St Pancras   3–39
   construction   22–9
   delay   11–13, 23–4, 29
   disabled readers   34
   exhibition galleries   35–6
   facilities   29–38
   furniture   34
   move   11–12
   need for   3
   objectors   14–19
   occupation project   29, 68
   rationale   21

   remarks by Prince of Wales   25
   shelf arrangement   35
'St Pancras: A focus for change at the British Library'   29
St Pancras Planning (Operations and Services)   67
Sassoon, G. J.   175
Satellite Online Searching Training Interactive Conferencing Experiment *see* SOLSTICE
'Savage Attack On British Library'   8
Save the Round Reading Room for BL readers before it is too late   16
Saxton, C.   128
Saztec Europe Ltd.   79–80
'Scandinavian publications since the mid-1970s'   73
'Scholar visits China'   116
Schoolley-West, R. F.   133
Science and Engineering Research Council   157
Science and Technology Information Service   163–5
Science and Technology Policy   164
Science Museum Library   184
Science Policy Research Unit   153
Science Reference and Information Service   160–77
   catalogues and indexes   162
   classification   161
   collections   162–3
   databases   162, 221, 226
   publications   162–3
Science, Technology and Industry   163
Science Technology Information Service   163–5
Scientific Abstracting and Indexing Periodicals   164
Searching ESTC on BLAISE: a brief guide   85
Searching ISTC   86
'Searching the ISTC on BLAISE-LINE'   86
Second International Conference on Interlending and Document Supply   191
Security   138

Security and Crime Prevention in Libraries 138
Security Guides 137
See The Film And Save The Book 138
Select 87, 208–9, 213–14, 217–18, 225
Select Reading List on the History of Geography 132
Selection For Survival: A Review of Acquisition and Retention Policies 48–53, 60
Selwyn, R. B. 191
Serials 192, 202
Serials In The British Library 233
'Serials on BLAISE-LINE' 222
Seton, R. 118
Setting the Record Straight. Understanding the MARC format 220
'Seven ways to make your POPSI better' 190
Shared Cataloguing 234
'Shared Cataloguing: The Way Forward' 235
Shawyer, J. 32
'Shelving And Classification of Printed Books' 238
Sheraton House 39
Short-Title Catalogue of Books printed in England, Scotland and Ireland 1475–1640 85
Short-title Catalogue of Books printed in England, Scotland, Ireland, Wales and British America 1641–1700 85
'Should the BLDSC be Privatised?' 200
Silver, J. 92
'Simple form of Book Support' 118
Sims, J. 115, 118
Singh, A. K. J. 118
'Slimming down the volume of work' 54
Small Grants In Library and Information Science: A Brief Guide to Applicants 145
Smethurst, J. M. 21, 56, 76, 115
Smith, G. 101

Smith, M. 203
Smith, R. 210, 230
'Snarl-up at the library' 54
Social Science Research Council 146
Softlink Europe 225
Sound Recordings 96
'Sound Recordings on Optical Discs' 93
'South Asian maps in the British Library Reference Division' 130
'South Asian material in the Department of Oriental Manuscripts' 116
'South Asian material in the India Office Library' 116
South Asian Studies 116, 130
Special Collections 114–133
Spencer, N. 167
Spoken Word Collections 90
'Spotlight on BookNet' 193
Spring, M. 25
staff development 47–8, 61
Stallion, Mr. 211, 214
Stansfield, K. 24
Starbuck, J. E. 190
State Librarian 109
Steensen Varming Mulcahy Partnership 22
Stein Collection 115
Stephens, A. 75, 226, 241
Sternberg, I. 31, 73–4, 115, 238
Stickells, L. 92
Stoker, D. 84
'Storehouse of Knowledge' 24
Strachey Trust 123
Structure & functions 68, 134
Sturgess, P. 159
'Subject Bibliographies for the American Trust for the British Library' 113
Sudjic, D. 14
'Suffragettes and saris' 117
Summary Catalogues of Manuscripts 120
Sunday Correspondent 8
Sunday Times 5–6, 11–12, 26, 45
Super JANET 154

Survey of English Dialects 91
Survival of the fittest? Collection management implications of the British Library Review of acquisition and retention policies 56
Sutherland, J. 62
Sutton, D. 124
Sweeney, R. 35, 218
System for Information on Grey Literature in Europe *see* SIGLE

Tait, S. 11
Tapling Collection 133
Tarmac Construction Ltd 22
Tattle, V. 165
'Tauchnitz Editions at the British Library' 72
'Technology and the British National Bibliographic Service' 226
'Ten years of the Incuncabula Short-Title Catalogue' 87
'Thanks A Million Digital' 33
Theft and Loss from UK Libraries 138
'Theory and practice in Archive Classification' 121
Tibber, M. 99
'Ticket To History' 107
Times, The 11, 13, 26, 54, 93, 101, 114, 123, 138
Times Higher Education Supplement 20, 107, 124, 146, 203
Times Literary Supplement 14–15, 17–18
Times Saturday Review 21
Toase, M. 185
Todd-Bowden collection 72
'Trade Literature At SRIS' 166
Trade Marks: A Guide To The Literature And Directory of Lists of Trade Names 170
Trade Marks: An Introductory Guide And Bibliography 170
Trade Unions 46, 193
'Trademark Searching At SRIS' 172
'Traditional African music' 91
'Traditional Maintenance Of The

General Catalogue of Printed Books' 81, 239
'Transcript Breaks Through The Language Barrier' 171
Treasures Of The British Library 71, 129, 237
Tritton, P. 95
Trumbull Papers 122
Turner, M. 125–6
Turpin Distribution Services Ltd 143
Tuson, P. 73, 117
'20-year story with a happy ending?' 26

UK Customers Handbook (DSC) 181
UK Patents for Inventions 170
UK Office for Library Networking 217
UKMARC 80, 212, 215, 219–20
'UKMARC – A format for the Twenty-first Century?' 219
'UKMARC Format: Proposals for future management & maintenance' 219
UKMARC Manual 220
UKOLN: The Office for Library and Information Networking 217
UNIMARC 229
United Kingdom Serials Group 185, 202
United States Government Publications 89
Universal Copyright Declaration 190
Universal Postal Union 132
'Unlocking the Treasure House: Information for Enterprise in the British Library' 204
Urgent Action Service 195–6, 205
Urquhart, D. 239
Users of Book Industry Standards 218
Using Electoral Registers in The British Library 88
Using The Catalogues (SRIS) 162
Using The Music Reading Area 124
Using The Official Publications And

Social Sciences Reading Room 88

VINITI 189
Van de Vate, K. 113
Van Dulken, S. 169–70
Vedic, H. 165
'Verelst Collection' 115
Vickers, J. 90
Vickers, P. 153

Wade, A. E. 76
Waley, D. P. 119
Walker, D. 89
Wallis, H. 129
Wanley, H. 83
Watkins, T. J. 105
'Waving or drowning? – the growth of the music catalogues in the British Library' 125
Weerasinghe, L. 95
Wells, R. 104
Western Manuscripts 119–24, 128, 131
Westmancoat, J. 104
'What is the NBS?' 210
Where Manuscript Maps Are Held in Britain 132
'Where To Find Up-To-Date Eco-Toxicology Information' 176
'Whitaker CIP records hit the streets' 213
'Why MARC surveys are still a hot bibliographic currency' 217
William Petty papers 122
Williams, M. I. 121
Williams, S. 4
Wilson, C. 22
Wilson, N. 213, 225
Wilson, P. 96
Windsor, J. 95
Wolfson Foundation 149
'Wolfson Grant To The British Library' 150
'Women in the Soviet Union' 73
Women's Studies 73, 117, 120
'Women's studies in West and East Germany' 73
Wood, A. 90
Wood, D. N. 205
Wood, F. 116–17
Woolston, H. 176–7
'Work begins on National Discography' 97
Working Guides for Working Professionals 163
Worshipful Company of Musicians 125

Yorkshire and Humberside Joint Library Service 189
Your Business Needs Our Information 167

Zmroczek, J. 73